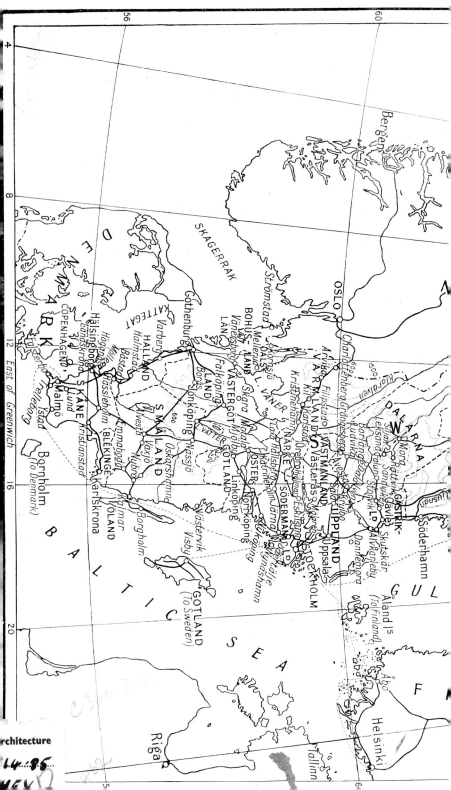

SWEDEN

Frontier
Provincial Boundaries
Main Railways
Shipping Routes
Contours in feet

6000
3000
1500
600

0 ____ 100 ____ 200 Km.
0 ____ 60 ____ 120 Miles

ATLANTIC

OCEAN

NORWAY

LAPPLAND

Trondheim
Storlien
Sylarna 5780
Åre
Storsjön
Indalsälven
Brācke
Östersund
JÄMTLAND
Långsele
ÅNGERMANLAND
Örnsköldsvik
Vannäs
Umeå
VÄSTER
BOTTEN
Boliden
Skellefteå
Skellefteälv
Arvidsjaur
Byske
Piteå
Öre älv
Lule älv
Boden
Luleå
Haparanda
Torneå
BOTHNIA

FINLAND

Marsfjället 5213
Vilhelmina
Sorsele
Tärna
Storfjället 5787
Norra
Vindel älven
Ume
Bastuträsk
Umeälven
Ångermanälven

Saltoluokta
Kvikkjokk
Sarek 6856
Jokkmokk
Kåitum älv
Porjus
Harsprånget
NORR
Torne älv
Arctic Circle

Narvik
Torne träsk
Abisko
Kebnekaise 6965
Kiruna
Malmberget
Gällivare
Karesuando

GULF OF BOTHNIA

BACKGROUND TO SWEDEN

Spring in Upsala

TERENCE HEYWOOD

BACKGROUND TO
SWEDEN

CONSTABLE *Publishers* LONDON

LONDON

PUBLISHED BY

Constable and Company Ltd

10-12 ORANGE STREET, W.C.2

*

INDIA

Orient Longmans Ltd

BOMBAY CALCUTTA MADRAS

*

CANADA

Longmans, Green and Company

TORONTO

*

SOUTH AND EAST AFRICA

Longmans, Green and Company Ltd

CAPE TOWN   NAIROBI

PRINTED IN GREAT BRITAIN BY
CHISWICK PRESS, NEW SOUTHGATE, N.11

94939

ACKNOWLEDGEMENTS

I am grateful to the editors of the following for permission to reproduce certain essays and photographs:

The American-Scandinavian Review, *The Anglo-Swedish Review*, *Årets Bilder* (*Pictures of the Year*, Stockholm), *Bulletin of the American Swedish Institute*, *ISS Review Illustrated*, *New Shetlander*, *The Norseman*, *The Oxford Magazine*, *The Scandinavian Review*, *Sunbathing Review*, *View* (U.S.A.) and publications of the Swedish Touring Club (STF); and to the editors of these for permission to reprint poems: *The American-Scandinavian Review*, *Arena* (New Zealand), *Botteghe Oscure* (Rome), *Bulletin of the American Swedish Institute*, *Canadian Ski Book*, *Chapbook* (New Zealand), *The Christian Science Monitor*, *Compass* (U.S.A.), *The Crucible* (Toronto), *Cycling*, *Cyclotouring* (Belgium), *Denver Post*, *Ergo* (Upsala), *Facet* (U.S.A.), *Fantasy* (U.S.A.), *Gale* (U.S.A.), *Graal* (Italy; translated), *John O'London's Weekly*, *The Jongleur*, *Kaleidograph* (U.S.A.), *Kingdom Come*, *Life and Letters*, *The Lyric* (U.S.A.), *Marches de France* (Belgium), *Momenti* (Italy; translated), *The New English Weekly*, *The New York Herald-Tribune*, *Nord Bygden* (Sweden; translated), *The Norseman*, *The Northman* (Belfast), *Periples* (Tunis; translated into French), *Poetry* (Chicago), *Poetry World* (U.S.A.), *Schuss* (Australia), *Ski* (Switzerland), *Skisport* (Denmark), *La Strada* (Italy; translated), *Sun and Health* (Denmark); as well as the editors of these anthologies: *The British Annual of Literature* (British Authors' Press), *Rejected Poems* edited by Keeling-Scott (Brighton), *Poetry Awards*, 1950 (University of Pennsylvania Press), *Poets' Library* (Stockwell) and *Wartime Harvest* edited by S. Schimanski and Henry Treece (Staples). One poem has also been broadcasted in America.

CONTENTS

ILLUSTRATIONS

I: ON THE WEST COAST

1 : *A Cruise in Bohuslän*

IT WAS THE freshness, the vigour that first roused my attention. I can well remember that bright July morning when, still in my 'teens, I stepped from the gang-plank at Gothenburg to find the friend who had come to meet me in his white student cap ready to hustle me through the Customs and into a car. Driving to what was apparently the sailors' quarter of the town, we picked up a jib at the sailmaker's. I was then fitted nearby for oilskins and a sou'wester—a rather unnecessary outfit I thought in my ignorance as we passed down between the warehouses in heat that was almost tropical. Then for the coast of Bohuslän, where I was to learn how to sail. As, leaving the town behind us, the high-powered Volvo (a Swedish car made by the famous ball-bearing concern of S.K.F.) switchbacked among monstrous hummocks of muscular granite, I learned all about the two-berthed cabin that had just been built into the yacht and of the cruise we would undertake as soon as I had picked up the rudiments of sailing. And when eventually we breasted the last ridge I saw below in a brilliant turquoise inlet the motor-boat which was waiting to take us out to the island.

Bohuslän is the coastal province which extends from just north of Gothenburg up to the southern border of Norway. Being exposed to the full brunt of the North Sea swept in by the prevailing wind through Skagerrak, it is much fjorded and fissured, and only in slits and gullies of the bare humps of gneiss or granite is there any soil deep enough for perceptible vegetation. But skirting the promontories is the great *Skärgård* or archipelago behind which even in the foulest weather fishing-boats and freighters can struggle from haven to haven in comparative safety. In winter, thrashed by perpetual storms, Bohuslän is damp and surly. Only in the late spring, when the herring-fleet are ready to put out for the Hebrides and Iceland, do the clouds lift, and the dull tones give way to the fresh blues of sea and sky, and the vivid green of fields reaching between the variegated pink of the rock-masses.

From June onwards it is a perfect place for sailing. There are neither tides nor beaches. Harbours are frequent and of great variety. Exquisite islands exist in tens of thousands, from Orust and Tjörn with their numerous villages and a hundred miles of roads, to the tiny outer skerries bathed in a continual shower of surf. On all but the smallest there are sheltered creaks where at a minute's notice yachts of moderate draught can be moored to a boulder and left with their sails up while one takes a meal or a bathe. And the fjords, unlike those of Western Norway, are not steep enough to force the wind into dangerous vertical currents.

This, then, is the maritime province of Bohuslän, for thousands of years the home of hardy sailors, some of whose chieftains lie beneath dolmens in the boat-shaped graves still discoverable on the hill-tops. This is the ancient Ranrike, the Alfheimer of the Sagas, into whose rocky creeks many a Viking longship was launched with jubilation. And this is a part of Scandinavia which in later times has witnessed probably as many naval skirmishes as any other. Several times has it changed hands, and not till the seventeenth century was it finally incorporated in the Swedish Kingdom. In dialect and outlook it is the closest of all the provinces to Norway, while many of its places and place-names are intimately connected with Norwegian history.

There are, for instance, the ruin of Bohus, which has given its name to the province and was for centuries one of the finest fortresses in Norway; and the nearby Kungälv, formerly the important city of Konghelle—both on the Göta River. Of a special interest is the island-town of Marstrand, founded by Haakon Haakonsson, the great Norwegian king of the thirteenth century. As the key to the herring fisheries and a place of much strategic significance, Marstrand was always considered worth

fighting about. As recently as 1719 it was cleverly captured
by the Danes and Norwegians. The long severe fortress, erected
by the Swedes thirty years beforehand, is still the most conspicuous sea-mark thereabouts. Below it lies the little town
whose harbour in summer teems with the yachts of holiday-
makers; and from its windy parapets you look over the innumerable islands which end westwards in the Paternoster
Skerries, so named by the sailors of old, who, caught in terrific
storms, would be put in mind of their prayers.

It was on one of these islands near Marstrand that I was
destined to be initiated into the breezy life of Bohuslän. . . .
Picture a 30-foot racing cutter running before the wind on
a fine morning in early July. Hand on tiller, I am receiving
my first lesson in sailing. "Always keep one eye on the sail and
one eye ahead! We'll aim at that kummel over there."
Kummel? Evidently that white sea-mark. Looks like a whitewashed cairn to me. Cairn? It's not likely he would know the
word. I suppose I shall have to learn the Swedish terms. But
those impossible vowels: he'll never understand me. And I
can't teach the English, for I don't know a killick from a
marline-spike. No, it will have to be a compromise: a little
English, a dash of Swedish, the rest invented words or nick-
names.

And so it came about. A fender became a "bumper", a
boom-crutch "scissors". The crudity of such home-made
nautical language would surely have scandalized a gaff-sail.
If, that is, we had had one. Actually the yacht was Bermuda
rigged. A very fine one she was too, with her tall mast and
deep draught—as fast a one, for her size, as ever sailed in the
Skärgård.

She was called *Lasse-Maja* after a notorious pirate of the last
century who stole from the rich to give to the poor but eventually suffered imprisonment and refined tortures in the fortress
at Marstrand. The coast, it is said, has always been troubled
by pirates. Although there are none to-day, smuggling of
spirits, which according to the present laws can be bought only
in towns and in limited quantities, is by no means uncommon.

3

Background to Sweden

Otherwise the people are as honest and law-abiding as any in the world.

After ten days' instruction in sailing and navigation I was thought to be sufficiently experienced for our projected cruise towards Norway. So on June 27th we stowed away our gear and provisions, and sailed out of the quiet baylet of Koön, turning for a last wave to members of the household aligned on the jetty.

I noticed, as we threaded our way among the islands, that all but the smallest were inhabited. On some could be seen the large chimneys of herring canneries, now for the most part deserted. For in regard to herring the coast has been over-fished, and the population have been made increasingly dependent for their livelihood on haddocks, whiting, and other flatfish, or have had to turn more and more to the remoter fishing-grounds off the west of the Orkneys.

It appears that in summer about half the craft in Bohuslän are engaged in business, half in pleasure. The pleasure-craft, apart from a sprinkling of motor-launches and the dinghies which generally carry auxiliary motors, are entirely dependent on sail. All the fishing-boats and freighters, however, now have motors; masts and rigging have been drastically reduced, and the sail when used at all is a tiny drab appendage solely for steadying purposes. Easily recognized from the homely-sounding *chunk-chunk-chunk-chunk-chunk* of their engines and from their wheelhouses rising from the afterdeck like sentry-boxes, these freighters are a very typical part of the West Coast.

Our first landfall was at Käringö, an island on the outer fringe of the Skärgård, where we moored between two immensely wide fishing-boats whose clumsy hulls threatened to squeeze into pulp our narrow stripling of a yacht. Since there was a small old-fashioned hotel we decided to dine there, after which we retired to our sleeping-bags in the comfortable double-berthed cabin.

In the morning, as we fried our bacon and eggs over the primus, youths and fishwives on the wharf alongside were busy chopping and slicing haddock on long tables, now and then throwing the waste remains into the water, whereupon the

4

gulls, ever watchful, would plop down from all directions screaming and squabbling in their greediness. All this fish, from which there was no perceptible stench, would soon be taken to dry in the sun and wind on the numerous wooden frames that covered the surrounding rocks.

We took a stroll through the village, a cluster of white, green and red houses with pink tiled roofs, all very neat and fresh, grouped round the harbour without any suggestion of streets or symmetry but with an air of rightness and inevitability. There was not a tree on the island and scarcely a blade of grass. Every cottage, however, had a tiny strip of soil for nasturtiums, calendulas and other flowers, which stood out strikingly against the light-painted clapboarding.

Just as the coastal steamer was about to make its daily call we joined a small crowd on the main jetty. The centre of interest, we found, was a schoolboy who had been spending some of his holiday on the island. They had festooned him with flowers and straw and were all pressing round for a last goodbye. As the steamer cast cable they all waved wildly and broke into songs and cheers. It was a pretty scene: youth is fêted to be happy.

Sailing at noon with a favourable breeze, we continued northwards on a course for the most part densely islanded to Smögen, one of the larger and most westerly fishing-villages though only just off the mainland. I was amazed at the number of *sjöbodar* to be found there, the red long-eaved fishing-huts built on piles over the water. Following a series of narrow galleries and platforms leading off from the main harbour, I twisted in and out between windowless wooden walls, confronted now with a brilliant panel of sail-slashed sea, now with a dim passage open only to a slit of sky, till eventually I found myself in the middle of the baylet around which all these quaint improbable little huts are huddled (Plates 2 and 3). Everything was utterly quiet at that season and time of the day, the water through the accuracy of its reflections allaying any suspicion of liquidity, and a solitary fisherman mending

5

his nets on a stool only serving to emphasize the stillness. Not then as in spring and autumn were there any scenes of activity to remind one that Smögen is among the main pivots of the fishing industry; even the local catches by those too old or too young to go out with the trawling fleet had been landed and sold in the early morning, while between then and the second outing at sunset lay many long hours of idleness.

Finding a sunny creek in another part of the island, we plunged in for an evening bathe and revelled in the warm water. But stop, unwary youth, what was that soft touch on the chest, that suspicious tingling from tummy to toe? Better swim back and lie in the sun. So with studied nonchalance, never hinting at the word jelly-fish, I sunbathed on the rocks till it was time to go up to a hotel for dinner. With admirable restraint (for the stings have now produced violent irritation all over), I choose my favourite dishes from the *smörgåsbord* table as if nothing had happened. But the food seems uninteresting; scratching furtively in as many places as possible, I begin to hate everything and everybody. Driven at last to distraction I start promenading the restaurant, remembering how someone once told me that a sting from a jelly-fish puts you in a bad mood for the rest of the day. The secret is now out: returning to the table I find my friend, looking as serious as possible, ready to issue such useful information as, "You should never sunbathe after you've been stung". He calls the waiter, who, summoning up about seventy-five per cent of his English vocabulary, repeats with great consternation, "Very terrible! Very terrible!" There is a conference; it is decided that sour milk is the only possible palliative. I go down and wait outside. Presently the waiter emerges and presents me with a huge basin of sour milk. Holding it before me like a sacred relic, I step down among the rocks till I come to a hidden nook. Discarding my clothes in the chilly evening mist, I smear the reeking liquid time and again over my shivering twitching limbs. An hour later, having eaten our dinner, we walk a mile or two to an open-air dancing-place. "You'll soon feel all right now!" But do I? Does the maddening itch leave off? Do the brisk tunes of the accordion, the wandering eyes of the

Northern girls, the laughingly circulating couples, banish the poisonous irritation? No! Sullen and angry, I eventually refuse even to dance; prowl about like a kill-joy, or lean sourly on the railings of the dancing platform. And most of the night I writhe in the sleeping-bag.

The morning was perfect. Talking to a couple of Stockholm medical students whose yacht was moored alongside, we prepared our breakfast in the best of humours. Washing up never takes long at sea, and soon we were off, hugging the coastline fairly close and presently passing on the lea of Tryggö, where a Norwegian King was buried a thousand years ago, the father of Olaf Tryggvason, the famous warrior who introduced Christianity into Norway. In the channels hereabouts there appeared to be specially large numbers of those curious little lighthouses which look like white refuse-bins. All along this part of Bohuslän huge chunks have been eaten out of the beautiful pink rock, and the fine natural contours destroyed. Thousands of masons hammer all day beneath the swivelling cranes preparing small cubic paving-sets and long cleverly shaped curb-stones, which are hoisted into capacious fishing-boats to be carried off to the cities of Western Europe and South America. Coinciding roughly with the decline in herring fishing some fifty years ago, the rise of the granite industry was steady and rapid: Swedes were literally selling their land to the foreigner. And the industry is still of much importance, despite the setback induced by the foreign import restrictions of recent years.

It was not many hours before we entered the small rather open Bottnafjord and put in at the village of Bovallstrand, lying in the shadow of monstrous rock-masses on the southern shore of the mainland (Plate 2). After tidying ourselves and having a shave at the barber's, we went up to call on some relations of my friend's whose house is towards the top of the village overlooking the salmon-coloured tile roofs of its neighbours and having an extensive view of the Fjord from the island at its mouth to the large sweep of greensward at its inner end against which the white church of Bottna stands out con-

B   7

spicuous and alone. Everything was delightful from the company and the situation to the bilberries and cream which completed our *middag*; and I can remember how we climbed the highest rock-pinnacle in the late evening to witness an astonishing pageant of colours which I afterwards tried to record in words but regretted I was not a painter:

> *Wild wand of twilight!*
> *How imperceptibly, yet with what fire,*
> *You turn with your shy light*
> *Even the tiniest islets of the skerries*
> *Into blooms, breaks, bubbles of beauty,*
> *Pouting from the fresh flesh-pink surfaces*
> *Of the water, rapturous-haloed with cherries*
> *Limned lingeringly and with lemons mingling!*
> *Bright light and white light have vanished: the evening's*
> *Embalming the aspect of the sun that it buries.*

In the morning the two girls of the party and an acquaintance came down to the yacht to try some of our coffee. As the harbour had long been astir and we were still in pyjamas and dressing-gowns, the scene is said to have excited such interest that the village gossips occasionally speak of it even today.

All that day we continued northwards, sailing among the innumerable islands. In one of the sounds we encountered two rowing boats full of black-clad people crossing from a hamlet where all the flags were at half-mast to a neat white church against which some of the mourners were already silhouetted. In the circumstances it was impossible to wave or exchange the customary greetings; we had perforce to sneak past guiltily, extremely self-conscious with our large expanse of dazzling sail. Presently the church-bells began to clang out dolorously, and the whole brilliant day was suffocated with a bandage of reproachful black. Only death was alive or real.

Our fourth day's sail took us through a further maze of islands to the tiny town of Grebbestad on the mainland. This district, having been inhabited continuously from the early Stone Age (and by the same race) and containing important remains from almost every period during the last seven thousand years, is of special interest to the archæologist. The Bronze Age rock-tracings near Tanum, which I have since seen, are remarkable for the vitality with which men, animals and especially ships have been depicted. But I implore any sensitive person to avoid the hotel nearby which is decorated with a series of vulgar travesties. More accessible, being just outside the town, is a large fourth-century cemetery, consisting of a number of *bautastenar* or flattened rectangular monoliths about nine foot high, forerunners of the rune-stones, scattered over a heath in various degrees of erectness or prostration, and quite impressive in their dumb primitive manner.

Although we were now within a short day's sail of the Norwegian border we decided to turn about. So the following day we put out to sea, having on our starboard only the lonely Väderöarna or Weather Islands between us and the prevailing wind. Hour after hour we skirted the outer skerries, now and then taking our bearings from the granite churches built in the largest villages during the last century, hideous structures at close quarters, but from a distance excellent sea-marks, as I am told they were intended to be. At one time we were in sight of an immense black structure in the shape of a man, an extremely forbidding sea-mark even in fine weather and how much more so in foul! This was by far the best day's sailing we had accomplished, for we had traversed nearly a third of Bohuslän though without seeing very much.

In the evening we entered a large fjord and joined a number of mixed craft which from various quarters were converging on a village surmounted by a conspicuous windmill. With difficulty, for the haven was very full, we found a mooring-buoy and hailed a fisherman to row us ashore. Having bribed a barber to give us a shave after closing-time, we proceeded in our best white flannels where everyone in Fiskebäckskil goes on a summer evening—to the incongruously large restaurant with its extensive dancing-floors that juts out like a pier into the water. "Fiskebäck", well-known throughout Scandinavia, is reputed to be the gayest resort in Bohuslän, and it would

9

certainly be hard to discover a larger assemblage of young people of all classes disporting themselves in happier surroundings. Here if anywhere was a pretty representative cross-section of Swedish youth-types, as we could have discovered from our dancing-partners alone who ranged from a Stockholm bank-manager's daughter to local village lassies and shop-girls (not a few of them divorced) from Malmö and Gothenburg. It was probably here that I realized for the first time how infinitely more interesting are Scandinavian girls than English girls. I am now thinking not so much of their appearance— Nordic good looks need no advertising in any case—as of their ability to talk sensibly and respond convincingly to different sorts of experience. You can see at once that they are less repressed, have jobs, are better educated, and are not ashamed of showing their intelligence. Even the richest Swedish girl is brought up to do something—an important consideration in the one country where the birth-rate of the rich exceeds that of the poor, and consequently enjoys herself far more than a debutante vicariously fore-dedicated to the banality of a stereotyped pleasure-cycle; while the lower classes, thanks to excellent state schools, are all better educated than their English counterparts. If I remember rightly, we were far from early in repairing to our bunks, but as Sir Toby Belch puts it, "Not to be abed after midnight is to be up betimes."

After a bathe from the yacht and a late breakfast we took a walk round the village in the morning. There is only one street, a narrow, paved alley, confined to bicycles and pedestrians, running along the sides of the slope between light-painted houses each with its garden of hollyhocks, roses, phlox, and showy annuals behind neat white palings; and on either side are occasional passages leading up to the higher cottages perched on the bare rock, or dropping down to the salmon-tiled *sjöbodar* which line the edges of the vividly blue creek. Further in, where the creek ends in the shape of a fish-tail, the houses give way to oaks and elms; and cornfields, branching between the rounded hulks of pink granite, fall like green glaciers into the water. Only a few miles away, on the opposite jaw of the fjord, is Lysekil, the biggest coastal town of the

province, a rather ponderous place with its solid granite buildings in a very ninetyish style. Apart from being an out-moded
watering-place Lysekil has a factory supplying a large number
of the engines for the fishing-boats of the province. The very
first engine installed in a Bohuslän fishing-boat was designed by
the founder of the firm, who was then a mere fisher-boy. The
inhabitants of the West Coast with thousands of years of ship-
building experience behind them must indeed be fine crafts-
men, for the boats themselves are still built by the local farmers
on detailed instructions from the fishermen, nearly always without drawings or mathematical calculations of any kind. Lysekil
also has the questionable distinction of being the terminus of
a rather quaint narrow-gauge railway linking it with the main
coast line. (I recently had occasion to use it and was sorry to
find a new gas-mask factory in one of the neighbouring
villages.)

A little way up the fjord from Fiskebäckskil is a narrow
passage boring into the hills to the south like a gimlet,
notoriously difficult to navigate under sail except in the
smallest craft. Having decided on this course, we approached
the entrance in a stiff breeze, my companion being responsible
for the mainsail and the steerage, I for the jib and the chart-
reading. The land now rose sheer on either side, now stretched
out in marshland broken up by confusing creeks and back-
waters. Tacking repeatedly, counteracting the sudden gusts
of wind and luckily avoiding submerged rocks, we twisted
in and out of the staff-buoys and guide-stakes till at
last we emerged in a great steep-sided fjord and were
able to relax. It was, we felt, a triumph of alertness and
co-operation.

After sailing up the fjord for a while, we put in at a quiet
island for a bathe and lunch. The slopes here, being comparatively sheltered, were covered with spruce; in the lower parts
there was an occasional oak. Trees in conjunction with water
are something of a rarity in outer Bohuslän, so the sight was a
welcome change. A mile away to the south stood part of
Orust, by far the biggest island of the province. Continuing
our sail, towards Uddevalla, we eventually rounded the

northern point of Orust, came into more open water, and then turned southwards.

But when several miles from our intended haven we found ourselves becalmed. We began to row but felt it was futile; besides, it was making us hungrier. We decided to wait for the ten-o'clock breeze. And so, utterly still and passive, we lay back while the splendid Northern twilight lavishly heaped colour on a sky barred and feathered with enormous clouds. At ten the sails miraculously grew tauter: we slipped slowly into port.

Dinner and dancing over, we retired at the usual late hour to our berths. But not to sleep for long, for a young gale had arisen and *Lasse-Maja* was bumping violently against a fishing-boat, the jetty—anything she could reach. So we took her out to a buoy where she could tug and fret at will.

All day the gale continued, and even there, in one of the most sheltered havens on the coast, the water was chafed into rough edges. Unwilling to sail in such weather, we spent the day ashore, walking inland through rather rich agricultural country, through avenues of trees torn inside out and fields ruthlessly flattened by the windy onslaught, to the houses of some friends where we passed the time talking and eating strawberries. In the night the wind veered, dropped to a half gale, and brought rain. And so it remained for our last day's sail, which involved continual tacking down the long Hakefjord separating Orust and Tjörn from the mainland. Tjörn is the second largest island on the coast, with motor-roads and numerous villages and hamlets. It was here that Karl Nordström was born in the middle of the last century, one of the greatest of Swedish artists and one of the most Nordic. Originally a member of that group of distinguished Swedes who studied in Paris in the eighties and were much influenced by the impressionists and Japanese art, Nordström later evolved a severe monumental style of his own. Unlike Wilhelmson, another fine Bohuslän artist and painter of its inhabitants, he has confined himself mainly to the sterner, more mysterious and dynamic aspects of his province—interpreting its spirit as I imagine only a native could do.

On reaching the mouth of the fjord we began to experience the full force of waves bowling in savagely from the jagged horizon to the west; and *Lasse-Maja*, having rather too much overhang for such a sea, repeatedly received hearty back-slaps as she bobbed up and down. Another hour of rain and spray-douching was enough to prevent me from ever again questioning the use of oilskins in Bohuslän. The feet that we set ashore on the evening of the eighth day were very cold and wet, and mine at last were no longer those of a landlubber.

2 : *Pages from a West Coast Diary*

FOR SOME PEOPLE all travel is travail, and every tour a tour de force. Like Dr. Johnson, who held "It is by studying at home that we must obtain the ability of travelling with intelligence and improvement", they purchase guide-books and mug up in advance the geology or the folk-lore of the countries they are to visit. In my case the question of previous book-browsing did not arise, for my first invitation to Sweden was received at very short notice and as soon as I had packed I was on my way. My approach was direct and natural: without planning it I had the best introduction possible and learned the feel of one particular province in the same way as a man makes contact with a stranger by concentrating on a single topic.

But chances were given me to renew my acquaintance, and my enthusiasm now excited I began to acquire some of that knowledge which has made my subsequent visits both more intelligible and more interesting. Although these of course took me to other parts of the country (there is only one province I have not visited), I have several times been lured back to the incomparable West Coast. The following are some pages from diaries I have kept there spasmodically.

June 28th   *Bovallstrand*
I arrived here this afternoon—ostensibly on bicycle though I really walked pushing the machine half the time, so strong were the headwinds canalized by the defiles on the way. Some

friends have very kindly found me a room not far from their house, in a cottage whose owner I find does the bicycle repairs of the village. As everywhere in the north the place is scrupulously clean and neat, with little of that musty human smell found in most cottages or tenement rooms in other parts of Europe. I shall take all my meals elsewhere, sometimes at the pension, sometimes with the friends nearby. I was just going out for my *middag* when the landlady appeared with an enormous spiced cake and some sherry, both of which I had to sample out of courtesy.

June 29th

To-day I have been taken out in a dinghy to one of the outer islands at the mouth of the Fjord. We landed on a long castellated rock which turned out to be an exceedingly busy gullery. In nearly every cleft and hollow were nests of flattened grass with perhaps a feather or two, also a few eider nests, more shapely and lined with soft grey down. Many of them were empty or contained merely the fragments of broken shells; but in others there were still groups of mottled eggs, some with tiny holes in them which the chicks were visibly trying to enlarge; while overhead the infuriated mothers were forever wheeling and filling the air with their harsh desolate screams. Here and there, almost imperceptible against the background of grey-lichened rock, were younglings, which as far as possible we avoided disturbing, for in one place we discovered the pathetic remains of a youth who had crashed on an unsuccessful maiden flight. It was only after standing for some minutes a little further ahead that I discovered directly below me a robust half-grown gull, still in the mottled stage, absolutely motionless and unperturbed even when I produced my camera (Plate 5). It was a perfect text-book example of protective mimicry. But *is* this camouflage for protection? According to the most recent investigators, it is not: predation, they say, is proportional to numbers. Why then do shape, marking and pigmentation so often conspire to make a living creature inconspicuous in its environment? Is it for aesthetic reasons, or is it sheer caprice?

14

Of all the months June, I think, is the freshest, the juiciest, on the West Coast. Even on an exposed islet the urgency of life (if not the abundance) is surprising. The black or grey-green lichens, speckling the rock with their dry crinkled scales, are not to be sure very lively in appearance during such hot weather as we are now having. Yet, given a rainy day, they expand into pieces of slimy leather than which nothing is more obstinately vital. And it is they who have been the pioneers, the first to gain a foothold on the storm-buffeted sun-scorched granite, clinging to the polished surface with incredible tenacity, slowly and unspectacularly dissolving a way into the brute rock with minute droplets of acid. Partly an alga, partly a fungus, the tiny wind-carried ball of a young lichen can as alga live on dust, air, light and water, and as fungus protect from desiccation with its delicate silver weft the alga which provides it with food. Later on come the seeds on higher plants, settling in the myopic crevices, and finding— a few of them—enough soil in the particles of broken-down rock, remains of lichens and bits of guano to grow up and cover themselves with blossom. To-day they were at their best: the bright yellow stars of stonecrop, pink knob-berries of thrift, white fat-throated sea-campions, together with many species of dwarf grasses. And we merely lay there watching them all, with gulls gyrating above us, and below great rust-coloured jelly-fish swelling and contracting in a vague effortless rhythm, their filaments trailing behind frailly and irrelevantly. A few yards out was a family of fledgling eider riding the light swell over a tiny reef; and, far beyond, vague puffs of cumulus growing, landwards, larger and shapelier like dust from a vehicle in a drawing by Heath Robinson.

June 30th

I have been walking round the *sjöbodar* this morning. It is impossible to tire of these quaint buildings which stand partly or entirely over the water on precarious-looking stone piles and have veranda-like platforms facing the sea with their own flimsy jetties projecting in front where the gulls sit in rows and the fishing-nets are hung out on railings to dry. In some of them the fishermen were mending their nets or cutting up the larger fish—the latter a procedure of special interest to the gulls and the numerous village cats. The morning's catch had been landed long before and much of it had already been sold. The whole village subsists on fish, for with fresh cod, mackerel, plaice, whiting, prawns and salted *strömming* to be had so cheaply there is little need of meat: milk and various kinds of bread more or less complete the staple diet.

> *Is any kind subject to rape like fish?*
> *Ill unto man they neither do nor wish:*
> *Fishers they kill not, nor with noise awake;*
> *They do not hunt, nor strive to make a prey*
> *Of beasts, nor their young sons to bear away;*
> *Fowls they pursue not, nor do undertake*
> *To spoil the nests industrious birds do make;*
> *Yet them all these unkind kinds feed upon,*
> *To kill them is an occupation,*
> *And laws make Fasts and Lents for their destruction.*

To kill them is certainly an occupation here; and, unlike fishing on the East Coast where it is largely connected with agriculture, it is a profession, *the* profession. There is ample evidence of that, even though the main herring-fleet is at present trawling off the Hebrides and Iceland. Most impressive of all is the statuesque testimony of a group of old retired fishermen (Plate 3) who sun themselves every day in a sheltered spot behind one of the *sjöbodar* just off the square, "selling" firewood (though I have never yet seen any business done).

The rival industry is that of granite-quarrying. A whole hill several hundred feet high at the eastern end of the village is being ravished piecemeal and the setts carried away in numerous boats to be laid out fanwise in the streets of expanding cities in Europe and South America.

At the outer end of the village is a stone pier leading out to a rock with bathing-huts and diving-boards. Lying out after a bathe, I was watching some children being taught how to swim by the rod-and-line principle. Some of them were only four years old. According to the law, every child must be able to swim by the age of seven. Although the summers are tragically short, water is so accessible in Sweden that the average standard of swimming is exceptionally high. Which reminds me of a story I once heard about her great swimmer, Arne Borg, who once held all the world records for distances over 200 metres. He was in Bologna about 1930 and had just had some teeth knocked out at water-polo. At lunch-time they were teasing him because he was unable to eat anything. This infuriated him so much that he decided to show them something in the afternoon contest. It was the 1,500 metres. Dashing through the water for the first 100 metres, he equalled his best for that distance; and then churning on with unabated fury, eventually left the next man over 100 metres behind. Stepping out of the water full of life, he discovered he had broken the world record. Moreover, the time for the first and the last 100 metres added together was better than the Swedish record which he had held for the 200 metres.

July 1st

To-day has been too chilly, wet and windy for the usual outdoor bathing. Besides, the water was thick with jelly-fish driven in by the sea winds, great flabby masses of them, to-day comparatively inert: young harmless blue ones, delicate and transparent; obscene flesh-coloured ones with inky splotches; and huge rusty-bunched adults—all with streaming innards, the loose strings of fantastic subaqueous parachutes. So I visited the village *varmbadhus*, stepped into a hot brine-bath half full of bladderwrack, and attempted to make a lather with some green grease provided in a saucer for the purpose.

As the rain lifted in the afternoon I walked inland past half-submerged humps of granite that never looked more like whales or submarines. The bigger hills were all transformed by cascades and freshets which gurgled volubly as I passed by. It was a day for snails. Many large black and some smaller striped ones drawled across the road trailing their silvery mucus. I recalled Shakespeare's interest in snails: how it is their sensitiveness rather than their slowness that interests him:

17

Background to Sweden

A "snail, whose tender horns being hit
Shrinks backwards in its shelly cave with pain,
And there all smothered up in shade doth sit,
Long after fearing to creep forth again."

Only "Love's feeling is more soft and sensible
Than are the tender horns of cockled snails";

and Shakespeare, in associating them with love, again showed
his intuition, for do not modern naturalists consider them the
most voluptuous of all creatures?

July 2nd

We took out the dinghy this morning to do some fishing in
the Fjord. There were several other craft out for the same
purpose and the gulls round the rocks were plopping down like
stones to catch (or, as often as not, to miss) the fish on the rise.
It was a busy time for man and bird this half-hour before
sunset, and with three lines we pulled in enough whiting and
mackerel for several families. Our hands were also rather sore
from touching the filaments of jelly-fish that adhered to the
tackle.

July 3rd   *Festival in Bovallstrand*

This is the first day of the summer Festival, the chief local
event of the year—one outdoing even Christmas and Midsummer in importance. They always insure heavily against
bad weather; this year, the change for the better is just in time.

All day people have been entering the village by car and
motorcycle, cart and push-bike, steamer and sailing-boat;
others even on foot. The harbour is already crowded, for many
of the yachts will compete in to-morrow's races. Still more are
arriving, including several from Norway—superb craft which
slit the water with the precision of a surgeon's scalpel.

And now at sunset we join in the stream of people debouching
on the fair-ground, which is a football field on the edge of a
cove about a mile behind the village. The whole area has been
enclosed by palings for the occasion, flags and birch-boughs

being used to decorate the corners and entrances. Half the ground is occupied by stalls and side-shows. But far more popular is the dancing on a large platform at the end of the field. Here for ten öre you can dance to a real band, sometimes an ordinary ballroom foxtrot or waltz, but more often a sprightlier country dance—a *hambo* in which the couple hold hands and swing round and round extremely quickly, an old Swedish waltz, or a *skottish*.

The night closes in. A cordon of coloured lights circles the field of the merrymakers. The breeze is chilly and the people keep together, pooling their warmth and ponderously acquired animation. There is something pathetic in this group mainly of poor fishermen and country people, taking their brief night's pleasures in a little field hemmed in by the shadowy hummocks of rocks. Something symbolical.

A woman in the band makes a desperate attempt to lead some community singing. But the people of the coast are a shy solemn lot and the response is feeble as well as discordant. They are all, however, enjoying themselves in their heavy undemonstrative fashion. Some who have been surreptitiously pouring *brännvin* (brandy) into their coffee in the refreshment tents are by now a little staggery; the rest, not being able to procure it, are completely unaided by liquor of any sort. The bandsmen are having a rest. There is a general movement towards a huge piece of scaffolding at the upper end of the field, where some acrobats are performing in rather dim light. After their exhibition a model aeroplane is hoisted into the air with a boy in the cockpit; it begins to whirl round and round; a squib goes off; the aeroplane splits in two, the boy descends by a rope. The crude display is apparently a great success with the unsophisticated crowd. It is the climax to their evening.

Some acquaintances drive us to a large village down the coast for a drink. One of them is the local dentist, who tells me that the people here have very bad teeth probably because of the excessive quantities of black coffee they drink throughout the day. If, as he says, they drink more than the average Swede, then the quantities must *indeed* be excessive.

Background to Sweden

July 4th

Every flag in the village is straining at its mast against a light blue cloudless sky. There are scenes of great activity as the yachts line up for the eleven o'clock races. The *festledare* is the village postmaster, a sturdy little man who to-day looks quite important in his white trousers and yachting cap as he checks up the entries and gives the starting signals, whereupon the band strikes up vivaciously, and the yachts tack out to sea magnificently—in a stiff breeze. From the lookout rock I see they have soon dwindled to mere dabs among the islands.

Two or three hours later they begin to come in. The judges on the end of the jetty fire a rifle as the winner in each class crosses the line. The crowd cheers, and since there are almost as many sub-classes as there are yachts everyone is satisfied.

At two o'clock sports are held near the bathing rock, which, completely covered with spectators, looks like an overloaded pleasure steamer. There are swimming races and high-diving, comic dives and a life-saving demonstration—all of a high standard.

In the evening everyone returns to the fair-ground, this time with more visible merriment. The dancing is after a while interrupted for the prize-giving. The postmaster in the best of humours makes a few remarks on each recipient, who bows profoundly and marches off to the accompaniment of a shrill fanfare. The revels, if such they can be called, continue into the early hours; and the Festival of Bovallstrand gradually expires with the approach of daylight as the loving couples repair to the surrounding creeks and gullies.

July 5th

The wild flowers of Bohuslän are, considering the scarcity of soil, a varied and attractive community. Marguerites, popularly known as "priest-collars", rest-harrow and scabious are very common on stray bits of meadow, together with *Arnica montana*, a very fine orange gaillardia-like daisy, which grows only here and in a few neighbouring provinces and looks best in a vase with bugloss (fairly easy to find on patches of dry soil). There are still many roses in flower against the low stone walls surrounding the farms. And meadowsweet is just beginning to come out—a very common flower in Sweden, so common in fact that Linnaeus wanted to use it for food instead of almonds. Cranesbill, harebells and loosestrife are also abundant; with raspberries and strawberries now in the fruiting stage, the latter already ripe. Up in the heather on the damper rock-ledges are white sweet-scented orchids, and right on top white-tufted cottongrasses growing at the edges of the brackish rock-pools. Further south, in the Gothenburg Skärgård and in Halland, I have come across the seapea, the horned poppy and sea-kale, though not yet the rare wild-asparagus or the sea-beet—all the last three edible, though far too rare ever to be used for that purpose. As for the commoner halophytes like sea plantains, *Rumex maritima*, *Suaeda maritima* (seablite), rushes, statice and plants like spurreys, glassworts, sea purslane and adder's tongue, they all seem to be species well-known in England. Taking the country as a whole, the variety in the flora is remarkable for such latitudes. "You see that *maskros*?" a botanist once said to me (*maskros* is literally "worm-rose"), pointing to a dandelion. "Well, we have exactly ninety-eight other species of it in Sweden!" Even in Lapland, the number of flowers blooming in the brief summer is surprising, the globeflowers, saxifrages and orchids being especially fine. In earlier times, it is said, there must have been some easier means of plant dissemination round the Pole, for so many of the same genera are common to all Arctic lands.

July 8th

> *The whole day I've been idle*
> *Beside the round rock's rump,*
> *Watching soft wavelets sidle*
> *Up to his chummy hump.*

> *A race of runic ripples*
> *Stipples the tide afresh,*
> *Trapping the shy wild minutes*
> *In its amazing mesh.*

21

Background to Sweden

On a dark pool in the granite
The cottongrasses wag,
Offering the winds that fan it
Peace with a white flag.

But the little winds have never
Ceased from their clever pranks
Since the day they caught the water
And brought her to his flanks.

Now petalled sunlight glistens
Beyond the plashy cove
While the land leans back and listens
To its long-winded love.

July 10th

In time past Bohuslän has probably had as much to do with wars as any province now a part of Sweden. According to legend it was off Brännö, an island in the Gothenburg Skärgård, that the Viking fleets would rally before their expeditions to the west. The fortresses on the coast and on the Göta River were always being besieged, first by the Hanseatic cities and then in the numerous Danish wars even into the eighteenth century—long after they became Swedish. Marstrand has been alternately rased and raised I don't know how many times in history. Within twenty years of its being finally ceded to Sweden Bohuslän was invaded by the Norwegians, who captured Marstrand, won a battle at Uddevalla in 1677, and for a short while took possession of the whole province except the Castle of Bohus (which apparently retained its Viking impregnability even at that time). How the brilliant young Admiral Tordenskiöld of Denmark-Norway threatened the whole coast in Charles XII's day, won a great naval victory at Dynekilen, and later on captured Marstrand, after gaining entrance to the place disguised as a fish-vendor and thus securing information about its garrison and fortifications—all that is well remembered by the Scandinavians, especially the Danes who have used his head as a trademark on their matchboxes (although he was actually a Norwegian!). Even as late as 1788 there was a Norwegian invasion of Bohuslän and a skirmish at Kvistrum Bro. Finally, in the last war in which Sweden and Norway were involved and the one which resulted in a Union between the two countries, most of the few weeks' fighting was carried on round the fortress of Fredriksten and other places just across the frontier. Bernadotte, then Crown Prince of Sweden, had already forced the Danish king to accede to the cession of Norway, which for nearly four hundred years had been united with Denmark; but the Norwegians, indignant at not having been consulted in the matter, held a convention at Eidsvold, framed their own constitution, and elected the Danish governor as their king. So the country was invaded. As Norway was far weaker on land and sea, possessed no resolute leader, and in addition had her coast blockaded by a British fleet, the outcome was a foregone conclusion. In August, 1814, the armistice was signed at Moss on Oslo Fjord, and the same month the Swedish king issued a proclamation according to which "the Norwegian Kingdom, without being regarded as a conquered country, shall in future be an independent state united with Sweden; and its present constitution shall be properly protected". Since then neither country has ever been to war, though of course both have at times suffered severely when other states have been exchanging blows.*

Bohuslän has more than once been a front-row spectator during other people's wars. Nelson, for instance, is said to have anchored off Marstrand on his way to bombard Copenhagen (or was it after the battle?) And many are the rocks and gate-posts in the province surmounted by mines washed ashore during the Great War, when the local fishermen—as if their lives were not hard enough—were for years confronted with the incalculable menace of drifting mines. In what out-of-the-way places does war obtrude its grisly fingers! This evening I have been taken to the quietest little church imaginable, at Svenneby on the other side of the Fjord, where under guardian trees and a tiny red belfry fixed on top of a sheer rock-face lies

* This was written in 1939.

a grave in the churchyard with a stone saying that several English and German sailors washed ashore in 1917 were laid there to rest side by side.

A few days later I set out for Strömstad, the most northerly town in the province, a terminus of the coastal railway, and one of the oldest-established and more popular seaside resorts though with only three thousand inhabitants. The coastline was of the same type throughout—there was the same invariable variety of rude rocks shattered into peninsulas and sherries, the same random irresponsible distribution of treeless knolls and knosps, humps and hulks, solid, unbudgeable, but always relieved by creeks and *viks* surfaced with a satiny sheen or by landsweeps of greensward and harvest-gold; there were the same toy villages and groups of *sjöbodar*, the same yachts, twitching among the islands, and the freighters with their tanky chunk-chunk-chunk-chunk-chunk, the same statuesque horses standing on the rocky eminences so that the wind would blow the flies away. But a mile or two north of Strömstad the hills become steeper and steeper, forming a sufficient windbreak for trees to thrive, the scenery becomes Norwegian and before very long you are actually on Svinesund, which forms the border, waiting for the ferry to take you over. It was there I crossed over the following day, without stopping on the way to have a look at the creek called Dynekilen where Admiral Tordenskiöld gained that magnificent naval victory referred to above. Since it ought to be better known abroad, I think an account of the battle is worth giving. The year was 1716; Charles's continental campaigns were over; and Sweden was in a deplorable condition, drained of her manhood and resources, there being not even enough money in the treasury to pay for state note-paper and sealing-wax, while recruits were almost unobtainable. Charles, wishing to regain prestige and at least *appear* powerful, turned to the only foe it was then possible for her to attack, Denmark-Norway. So Norway was invaded and Oslo was occupied. By the spring, however, the Norwegians succeeded in cutting the Swedes' lines of communication, Danish reinforcements arrived, and Charles being

24

in a critical position was forced to retreat to the border where he was presently joined by the Gothenburg squadron. A couple of months later he once more assumed the offensive by making a daring attack on the frontier town and fortress of Fredrikshald, often called the Key to Norway.

He succeeded in capturing the town after some very severe fighting, but while he was preparing to make it a basis of operations against the citadel, the inhabitants defeated his project by patriotically burning the place to the ground, and four days later. . . . Tordenskiöld audaciously made his way up the narrow Dynekilden in the teeth of the hostile Swedish batteries, and almost totally destroyed the Swedish fleet and transports lying there. . . .

That is about all we learn from the English biographies of Charles XII (the quotation is from R. Nisbet Bain), but Knut Gjerset in his *History of the Norwegian People** tells us more. Tordenskiöld, he says, drew up a plan for the defence of Fredrikshald and for an attack on the Swedish squadron, and in July sailed for the coast with seven small vessels.

When he approached the coast of Bohuslän he learned from some fishermen that the whole Swedish squadron of over forty sail under Rear-Admiral Strömstjerna lay anchored in the harbour of Dynekilen, about twenty miles from Fredrikshald. This was the fleet transporting siege guns and supplies to Charles XII, on which the outcome of the Swedish king's attack on Fredrikshald and Fredriksten (the fortress) at this moment depended. But could Tordenskiöld with seven small vessels attack so formidable a fleet, anchored in a harbour where the narrow entrance was well defended both by infantry and shore batteries? It was a daring adventure of the kind which always tempted Tordenskiöld. At daybreak, on July 8th, he set sail for Dynekilen, and had almost passed the narrow entrance, which is about three miles long, before the signal of his approach reached the Swedish fleet. But before he could enter the inner harbour he was met with a brisk fire from

* The Macmillan Co., New York.

Background to Sweden

the fleet, and also from the battery of six twelve-pound
guns planted on an island in such a way that its fire could
rake the entire mouth of the harbour. Tordenskiöld did
not return the fire till he could place his vessels as close as
possible to the enemy. The real combat then began, and
the ships were soon enveloped in a thick smoke of gun-
powder which made all manœuvres difficult. After the
incessant roar of cannons had continued for about three
hours, the fire from the Swedish fleet began to weaken, and
when Captain Tönder at about one o'clock captured the
battery on the island, Tordenskiöld closed in on the enemy,
and at three o'clock in the afternoon, after a battle lasting
seven hours, he was master of the harbour. The Swedes ran
their ships aground and fled, leaving a few men on each
vessel to set it on fire, or to blow up its powder-magazines.
But the situation was still critical, as Swedish troops and
artillery had been stationed along the narrow entrance
channel, which is only 160 to 180 paces wide. Also the
capture of the ships, even after they had been abandoned,
could be accomplished only with the greatest difficulty,
as most of them had been ruined or set on fire. But the
work was undertaken by Tordenskiöld's men with the
utmost daring. Nine war vessels and five transports with
ammunition and supplies were towed out of the harbour;
the others had been sunk, beached or crippled. The proud
squadron had been destroyed, and with it disappeared
King Charles's hope of taking Fredrikshald. Upon
receiving the discouraging news he withdrew from Norway.

The victory is the more impressive for having been won
against such notoriously resolute fighters as the Swedes.

In less than a year Charles had raised another army for
a second invasion of Norway. "In order to secure well-
protected depots for supplies", says Gjerset, "he fortified
Strömstad which together with Marstrand and Gothenburg
would constitute a line of communications easily defended.
Neither the Danish government nor the higher military
authorities in Norway understood the significance of this
step but the alert Tordenskiöld saw it, and tried to frustrate
the plan. On May 14th, 1717, he made an attack on Gothen-

26

burg, and on July 19th on Strömstad, but at both places he was repulsed, though the attacks had been well planned." The situation now seemed more hopeful for Charles and Norway was re-invaded in 1718. It was on this campaign that the Swedes transported overland two galleys, five large boats and one sloop a distance of fourteen miles across this extremely hilly country under the direction of Swedenborg—a feat reminiscent of the help which Archimedes with his wonderful engines gave the King of Syracuse when the Romans under Marcellus besieged that city. The prodigious actions performed during that winter in 1718 are hard to imagine. "The example of the King", states Bain, "made it a point of honour with the soldiers to endure the most terrible hardships silently and even cheerfully, and throughout this, his last campaign, Charles fared worse than the meanest of his warriors, frequently returning from long rides soaking wet, and throwing himself just as he was on a wooden bench in some wretched hovel, or even sleeping on the coldest night in the open air, with his weary head resting on a soldier's knee." As for the sufferings, prolonged and heroic of the poor *bönder*, left on their farms, who though not actually conscripted had to make extreme sacrifices year after year, they also deserve to be sung. In December, while watching his soldiers from the siege-trenches around Fredriksten, the King, who had brought all these and other miseries on his people for nearly twenty years, was killed by a bullet; the siege was called off; and the Swedish army began their retreat over the windy hills, about a third perishing from the intense cold on the way, so that the journey has been compared with Napoleon's retreat from Moscow.

It was a perfectly cloudless day when I reached Fredriksten, climbed up the steep hill, walked round the gun-spiked fortress, and eventually sat down on the grass and pulled a book out of my pocket. The Norwegian flag was tugging at its staff in the stiff sea-breeze coming in across Svinesund, which like a great river broke through the steep forested hills in the middle distance. Immediately below me lay the port of Halden (Fredrikshald), on my left the wooded undulations of Sweden. The book I had purposely brought with me was one containing

Background to Sweden

Dr. Johnson's *Vanity of Human Wishes*, a poem I had long wished to read on that very spot.

> *Let observation with extensive view*
> *Survey mankind from China to Peru.* . . .

The powerful lines unreeled, the dignified moralizing couplets in which the various objects of human ambition are considered and their vanity indicated. First comes power, exemplified in the life of Wolsey and others. Then the eminence attainable in learning—and he points to Galileo's end. And what of military glory? Here, as we might expect from one who in his conversation never tired of citing Charles XII as the warrior *par excellence* there is no doubt as to who the chief hero will be:

> *On what foundation stands the warrior's pride?*
> *How just his hopes let Swedish Charles decide;*
> *A frame of adamant, a soul of fire,*
> *No dangers fright him and no labours tire;*
> *O'er love, o'er fear extends his wide domain,*
> *Unconquered lord of pleasure and of pain;*
> *No joys to him pacific sceptres yield,*
> *Man sounds the trump, he rushes to the field;*
> *Behold surrounding kings their powers combine,*
> *And one capitulate and one resign;*
> *Peace courts his hand, but spreads her charms in vain;*
> *"Think nothing gained", he cries, "till naught remain,*
> *On Moscow's walls till Gothic standards fly,*
> *And all be mine beneath the polar sky!"*

If "all be mine" implies a desire to gain territory, then it is a misunderstanding of his character, for (in the words of a later Swedish king): "He certainly had not the true conquering temperament that simply aims at acquisition of territory."

> *The march begins in military state,*
> *And nations on his eye suspended wait;*
> *Stern famine guards the solitary coast,*
> *And winter barricades the realms of frost;*

28

He comes, nor want nor cold his course delay;
Hide, blushing glory, hide Pultowa's day:
The vanquished hero leaves his broken bands,
And shows his miseries in distant lands;
Condemned a needy supplicant to wait
While ladies interpose and slaves debate.
But did not chance at length her error mend?
Did no subverted empire mark his end?
Did rival monarchs give the fatal wound?
Or hostile millions press him to the ground?
His fall was destined to a barren strand,
A petty fortress and a dubious hand;
He left a name at which the world grew pale,
To point a moral or adorn a tale.

So ends the finest passage in the poem—the finest indeed in all Johnson's poems.

"A petty fortress"! Artistically, of course, the "petty" could not be bettered, and perhaps that is all that matters. But historically the epithet is wrong. I have approached Fredriksten from three different directions, by land and on the water, and not once did it fail to impress, standing apart from and above the surrounding hills and valleys, at the head of Svinesund where it angles southwards into Idfjord. "Imposing", "lofty", "commanding" are the adjectives that first suggest themselves, volunteering to protect the dignity of this one-time key fortress which was considered almost impregnable. If only Johnson could have seen it! Or perhaps it is lucky that he didn't.

As for the "dubious hand", that is certainly felicitous in all respects. Historians and scientists are still wrangling over the ghastly hole in Charles's right temple: was he shot by the enemy or by one of his own men? I am glad to see that the most recent professional opinion rejects the hateful latter hypothesis.

How many great writers have been inspired by Charles and used his name for "adorning their tales"! Pushkin in Russian, Rilke in German, Voltaire in French, von Heidenstam in

Background to Sweden

Swedish—to mention but a few. And since painters and sculptors have also surpassed themselves in delineating this hero, one would expect to find on the spot where he fell either some artistically presentable display of their power or at least a dignified tablet. But alas we are outraged: the dingy erection in the style of the Albert Memorial (though even more execrable) bears witness to nothing if not a "dubious hand".

August 6th   *Särö, Halland*

Halland is the coastal province immediately south of Gothenburg. No sooner was the Ice Age over than man stepped on the shores of Halland: the finds in the north of the province, dating from about eight or nine thousand B.C. (according to the stop-press academic news), are the earliest traces of man in Scandinavia. Like the two southernmost provinces, Halland was till the seventeenth century a part of Denmark; but its scenery and inhabitants are far less Danish than those of Skåne. Topographically the very north is a continuation of Bohuslän. but south of Särö the *Skärgård* rather suddenly comes to an end, and the coast, sheltered by Jutland, degenerates into a series of bays, many of them having sand beaches.

Särö has its own special narrow-gauge railway with its terminus in Slottsskogen, one of the large parks of Gothenburg. Being a summer resort of the King, who plays in the important tennis tournament in July, it is a fashionable village in its informal unaggressive way.

Any Sven, Nils or Svante can pay his coppers at the *badhus* for the usual bathing and sunbathing in the nude, and as likely as not will find the King there, chatting to all and sundry.

Most of the inhabitants, or at least the weekenders, are wealthy Gothenburg business men, many of Scottish or English ancestry, whose well-built houses, on the rocky slopes overlooking the sunny bay among the pine trees blown into the shape of umbrella pines, give it a rather Mediterranean appearance. The rest of the village, which would otherwise be very hot (for it lies on the north of the bay), is swamped in dense oakwoods noted for their heronries and in umbrageous avenues of mixed deciduous trees. There are also thickets of yew, a very rare tree in Sweden and since the age of the bow a rather useless one.

August 7th   *On an Islet*

I have just been brought out from Särö to a tiny island an hour away by motorboat where my friends have a weekend cottage. It is the old cottage of the lighthouse-keeper and for a hundred and fifty years its stout timbers have weathered the storms on this exposed rock. Still kept in the condition in which it was bought, it has all the naval prints, half-faded photographs, shells, narwhal horns, china, sextants and other nautical instruments and miscellaneous bric-à-brac accumulated by a succession of lonely keepers. There are also other objects presented by visiting friends: some, like the swords of swordfish, quite appropriate; others, such as a couple of English china dogs and an English plate with the motto, "God has need of a perfect man", rather doubtfully so. Most of the latter are put away in drawers and only brought out before the visits of the respective donors (who, however, sometimes appear unexpectedly).

There are only two other houses on the island, the keeper's and another for two pilots and their families. The population, normally six inhabitants, has lately been doubled, for the terrier belonging to one of the pilots has just had a litter. (Her husband lives ashore.) This event and the tunny news (at present) make up all the local conversation. When one day my friends landed with a tunny rod, line, chair and shoulder harness—an outfit costing about sixty pounds—the excitement rapidly spread throughout the island; and one of the pilots, who had never understood a word of English, sat down and read a full-length English book on the subject with the help of a dictionary. So that when a few days ago they took out their biggest boat and followed some herring-trawlers off Jutland, he appeared to be intimately knowledgeable about everything. They apparently had some success, for the tail of the 440-pounder they were tugging half the night is to be fixed over the entrance to the cottage. "There's nothing in the world", I have been told, "like the pull of a big fish."

31

Background to Sweden

Last night the whole horizon was swept by swivelling lights. Vinga in the northwest, the outermost lighthouse for Gothenburg, is the biggest hereabouts. Ours is a rather small one but nevertheless has its regular work to do. The keeper took me over it, and showed me how the oil is pumped up to give a light of three thousand candle-power, and how a shade, worked by gravity, moves up and down every minute or two. The oil seemed to give off more heat than light; at close quarters it was less dazzling than an ordinary 25-watt domestic bulb. Emerson, I expect, would have found in it a useful simile for one of his moralizing essays: "The good man is like a small lighthouse whose beam though never dazzling at close quarters is yet a guide to the mariner labouring afar" or something like it.

This morning we sailed out in a Koster-boat, a type rather popular on this coast and adapted from the fishing boats of the Koster Islands off Strömstad in Northern Bohuslän. Open clinkerbuilt boats, with the hull below the waterline rather short, sharp and deep, and above broad, flat and roomy, they are less noted for their grace than for being sturdy and eminently seaworthy. There was just enough wind to puff us to a neighbouring desert island, where we alternately bathed and lounged on the scorching rocks, which at the water-edge were studded with feet-pricking barnacles, crisp black lichens and dried-up salt-pools, though elsewhere the crannies were miraculously filled with clumps of purple loosestrife, mauve sea-asters, sea-campions, and even dwarf raspberries whose desiccated fruits were but hot seeds on the parched tongue. Even now, on a hot calm autumn day, there is little languor or softness to be found. Everything is hard and virile from the strenuous muscular granite to the dry crystalline air. And that, I think, is the dominating impression given by any typically Swedish landscape: the dark massive dynamic force of forests and rocks, the masculinity of the groundswell, the clearly defined reflections in water, the large emphatic shadows, the almost black-and-white contrasts in tones and seasons—all denote strength without cruelty, simplicity without easiness, the distinctness of a big well-performed action.

II: LETTERS FROM UPSALA

1: *Introductory*

IT WAS LATE in January when I reached Upsala. Looking out of the window of the electric train an hour after leaving Stockholm I saw on the top of a long forested ridge the severe pink-washed Castle and the twin spires of the Cathedral caught in the afternoon sunlight. Beneath them was the town, already in the shade, straddling the River Fyris, and in the foreground the brown shrivelled plains with streaks of snow lying in the furrows.

The whole town is dominated by this early Vasa Castle and by the great French-Gothic Cathedral, the largest church in Scandinavia, beneath which everything else seems almost homely. Except in these, the architecture is mainly post-renaissance, stone, timber, brick and ferroconcrete in various shapes existing side by side. Though only half the size of Oxford or Cambridge and slightly larger than Canterbury, Upsala is to Sweden what they are to us: nay, more, for not only is it the oldest university and the seat of the primate but it was also the original nucleus of the nation and at one time the capital of the country. How many kings have been crowned and buried here! What momentous councils have been convened here, and acts performed which are remembered in Northern annals! What statesmen and scientists, scholars and poets, it has produced! Ancient and illustrious, it still retains its virility and carries on its traditions as a great cultural centre of the kingdom.

Founded in 1477, Upsala is the senior University of the country. With its 3,500 students it is larger than Lund, the other state University, established two centuries later for students of the Southern provinces which about that time were won from Denmark. In addition to these are two modern private Universities at Stockholm and Gothenburg, the latter very small and incomplete.

Only two or three buildings connected with the University escaped the disastrous fire of 1702 which destroyed nearly the whole city. One of these is the Skytteanum where Johan Skytte, tutor of Gustavus Adolphus, lived during his chancellorship; and another is the Gustavianum named after that great King, who remembered even in wartime the exigencies of learning, gave as an endowment nearly all the landed property of the House of Vasa (360 estates)—to this day the University's main source of income, deposited here the libraries of five foreign cities captured during his campaigns, and raised Upsala from a miserably struggling condition to the status of a university worthy of the nation. Small wonder that every sixth of November the students gather round his statue to fill Odinslund with songs in praise of their famous benefactor.

Although as elsewhere on the Continent the students live in lodgings, there still survives the medieval system of nations—non-residential clubs or fraternities for the natives of particular provinces or groups of provinces. Of the thirteen nation-houses scattered about the town, some like those of Uppland and Västmanland-Dala might be country-houses; some like the Östgöta and Gästrikland-Hälsinge buildings might be laboratories; Norrland's might be a large masonic hall, Gothenburg's a bank; small ones like Gotland's, Småland's and Kalmar's might be ordinary oldish town-houses; while others, like Stockholm's and the new Värmland building designed by Östberg seem more nearly to embody their special purpose (Plate 7). But if most of them had the misfortune to be built in the architectural night of the last century, one at least was conceived in an earlier more inspired period, the little Västgöta building from 1666 whose pink walls and black spire have a delightful setting among trees by the River. All of them have gardens, however diminutive; and the interiors, comprising a hall for occasional dinners and dances, men's and women's common-rooms, a small library and a curator's room, are all distinctive and often very charming. There are several fine halls like Norrland's and Gothenburg's; and the interior of Stockholm's has recently been re-decorated in a most tasteful manner, setting off to advantage a magnificent painting of the Royal Castle by Prince Eugén; but the most remarkable within as without is Västgöta's with its tiny period rooms and its hall covered with exquisite mural paintings illustrating places in the province (Plate 6). Each nation elects two of its students as curators who receive a small salary for managing its affairs and in addition have the honour attaching to the presidency of a J.C.R. (In Lund nations are merely nominal, there being only one club-house, which is common to them all.)

A Swede, having to study three modern languages, will generally be a year or two older than an English freshman on going up to University. The change is far less abrupt: no one becomes intoxicated with freedom when he leaves a day-school (sometimes co-educational) where discipline has been light and self-expression relatively unimpeded. He studies for a profession for four or five years and is in residence for nearly three-quarters of the year.

During his last few years at school he will have acquired the habit of working on his own. Through books and lectures alone—there is no private tutorial system—he accumulates enough facts to satisfy, orally and at rather frequent intervals, his exacting and usually pedantic professor. Or, if he should fail any examination, he can take it again as often as he wishes. There is no rustication, and the less gifted plod on into their thirties in pursuit of a degree. In the absence of restrictions, he can order his time according to his inclinations, taking in his room or the Library "large draughts of intellectual day" (but not of fresh air, for the Swede has the continental's abhorrence of it in winter), rising in the morning and going out for his two and a half meals just when he chooses; and for relaxation there are always cinemas, drink, vapour baths or women. If he becomes stale or run-down he can go off for a short holiday.

In a comparison between the great English and Swedish Universities nothing is more remarkable than the relative poverty of the Swedish student, whether count or *bonde's* son.

Background to Sweden

The average allowance is rather less than £100; and one can take a full part in the life for the whole nine months on perhaps a half of what is required in England. The University is literally a free institution, there being no dues except the entrance fee of a few pounds paid to one's nation. Almost no one has more than a single bed-sitting-room; and even that may be in a hostel—in a uniform series specially planned to reduce expenses to a minimum, simply and modernly furnished with a couch, table, bookshelf, built-in cupboard and a couple of chairs—and kept impersonally, almost morbidly, neat. A substantial meal at any of the numerous student restaurants costs about a shilling. In the matter of dress there is nothing approaching the *négligé*: hatlessness is unknown; one's coat during a call on a fellow-student is always carefully placed on a coat-hanger; while the sobriety and neatness of a suit that may cost as little as thirty shillings would delight even the most fastidious of our college deans. In order to help the needier student, especially if he is aiming at a doctorate (which takes at least ten years from matriculation), there is an admirable loan system whereby the interest has only to be repaid when the degree has been taken. And of course there are scholarships of various kinds.

Nor is the poverty confined to the students. A lecturer may receive only 2,000 Kr. (just over £100 in 1939) and a professor begins with 7,500 Kr; but neither is expected to entertain in anything like the same way as their English counterparts.

There are comparatively few clubs and societies, no theatres, very much less entertaining, a smaller variety of types and interests, more graduates and hardly any foreigners—perhaps one or two Americans or Englishmen doing scientific research, mostly under the great Professor Svedberg. From all this you will hardly be surprised that life here is not the brilliantly variegated and intensely exciting thing that it is in Oxford. Where, for instance, are those stimulating and intimate evening talks which always seem to me the greatest single charm of Oxford? The students here, too conscious of being serious specialists, are willing but rarely to commit themselves outside their own special fields or to indulge in the rich irrelevancies

36

of a general discussion. The horizontal limits of their intellectual adventures have been carefully prescribed by time, the purse and Swedish practicalness. Some of the most interesting students are those reading Languages, for since the nature of their work is less specialized they are brought into contact with a larger variety of ideas. (The *lektorer* or lecturers, as opposed to the professors, in these departments are all foreigners who have a special status for five years, after which they can no longer be attached to the University.)

But the life, if narrower, is less fragmentary, just as it is more individual and probably deeper. In the absence of colleges and restrictions the sexes (there are five or six hundred women) can mingle more freely; many students are engaged, some even are married. I at first thought it regrettable that women should play so large a part in the students' lives, taking up so many of their spare hours, and causing them to miss such times as never recur in later life. But then most of them are no longer children, and there is ample time during their comparatively long residence to make good friends and to enjoy all those delights peculiar to student days—the parties where drink and songs are poured out over the winter evenings, the ancient festivals new at every celebration. You should be here for instance on the Thirteenth of December when groups of students with nightshirts over their day clothes march through the streets at night carrying one of their party dressed up as St. Lucia. Knocking up their friends (or sometimes just anyone), they give them coffee from pots they bring with them, and sing hymns in praise of this fourth-century lady-martyr of Syracuse who by some freak chance is still remembered in Sweden (especially Värmland). *Kaffetåren står och kallnar, stander upp nu och drick!* goes one of the hymns, and the sluggard must perforce leave his warm bed and join the revels.

2 : *Gamla Upsala*

IMAGINE A YOUTH who has never been to boarding-school and who perhaps has never been away from home for more than a few weeks in his life suddenly coming from a distant province to study in Upsala. With no college dinners to introduce him to his fellow-students, no representatives of clubs and societies bursting in at ten-minute intervals, no tutors to ask him to breakfast, he must, unless he already has a friend or two, feel rather lonely for a while. But, unlike that of many of our poor scholars, it is a loneliness that time will shortly cure: he knows that all the others sitting about him in the student restaurant are, irrespective of class, his potential friends; that there are no expensive clubs to shut their doors upon him, or costly entertainments to remain beyond his reach.

For initiation a *recentior* or freshman soon after his arrival is brought before some of the wits of his Nation who ask him absurd questions to test his capacity for repartee and to see what stuff he is made of.

I suppose the first Sunday walk takes him to Old Upsala as inevitably as it took us to Iffley or Wytham. It was a foul day when I went—roads slushy owing to a thaw, and a few flakes casually floating down out of a cloudy sky, settling on the overcoat for a moment or two like bits of mould, and then turning into globules of water. Everyone, excepting myself, was wearing goloshes—all these manly Swedes who consider umbrellas and bath-sponges unquestionable marks of effeminacy! After walking a couple of miles northwards we came to three great tumuli, in popular tradition the graves of Odin, Thor and Frey. According to the professors three kings of the Svear were buried there in the sixth century, Aun, Egil and Adils, who seem to have done some hard fighting against Danes and Norwegians, and to have subjugated the Götar (of South Central Sweden), thus forming a union which was the basis of the Swedish nation. Although in some ways these Svear (or Suiones, as Tacitus called them) were comparatively civilized (they are said to have had a "strongly centralized government" two thousand years ago, and they wore magnificent iron-and-bronze helmets—very rare among any peoples of that time), I found myself thinking of Robert Graves' Ogres:*

---

* *Collected Poems*, 1947 (Cassell & Co.).

Those famous men of old, the Ogres—
They had long beards and stinking arm-pits.
They were wide-mouthed, long-yarded and great bellied
Yet of not taller stature, sirs, than you.

So many feats they did to admiration:
With their enormous lips they sang louder
Than ten cathedral choirs, with their grand yards
Stormed the most rare and obstinate maidenheads,
With their strong-gutted and capacious bellies
Digested stones and grass like ostriches.
They dug great pits and heaped great cairns,
Deflected rivers, slew whole armies,
And hammered judgments for posterity---

I should really, however, have been thinking of the Anglo-Saxon *Beowulf*, for Adils is almost certainly the Eadgils who figures in the poem. Here is an account of his death in one of the Sagas:

> King Athils was at a sacrifice of the goddesses and rode his horse through the hall of the goddesses: the horse tripped under him, and fell and threw the King; and his head smote a stone so that the skull broke and the brains lay on the stones, and that was his death. He died at Upsala and there was laid in mound, and the Swedes called him a mighty king.

Just behind these mounds is a small stone church on the most important religious site in the country. For here in Viking times stood the famous pagan temple of the North, a huge wooden building, partly gilded, where festivals were held every ninth year, great numbers of people coming from all the surrounding provinces to witness sacrifices of animals and human beings to the Gods, to feast, and to propitiate Frey, the God of Fertility, with coarse, voluptuous songs. Only when Christianity was firmly entrenched in the country was the Temple destroyed and a cathedral erected instead. An Englishman named Henry was the first bishop of Old Upsala,

D   39

but belongs rather to Finland, where he accompanied King Erik on a Crusade in the 1150's and was eventually martyred. Not long afterwards Old Upsala was made an archbishopric with another Englishman, Stephen, as its first incumbent; but a century later the seat was moved to the present city, and the old one relapsed into a mere hamlet. Within the church I was shown an even earlier link with our country: an inscription on a stone in one of the walls—a rune ordered in memory of his father by one "Sigurd Englandsfärer".

Before returning we entered the Odinsborg Hotel, found a table in a room filled with smoke and students, and ordered the horn from which several members of the houses of Bernadotte and Windsor have drunk the rather strong mead, claimed to be made according to the original recipe—the Viking mead of inspiration.

3 : *Scientists*

February

TO ONE LABOURING with the labial fricatives and battling with the obscure back-vowels of a strange though not difficult language a home mail (just received) is a welcome relief. I have often wondered what a postman does here, for of course a Scandinavian never writes a letter: he will telephone (in Stockholm there is a telephone for every fourth person), telegraph, cable, come to see you, but never write a letter. Perhaps some persevering Swedish Boswell will one day give us *The Life and Telephone Calls of Torsten Svensson*. The postman, apparently, is here solely to deal with foreign correspondence, and circulars (not even with parcels: you have to fetch those yourselves from the post office). But I must admit that he is at work seven days in the week and that his delivery does not stop at the ground floor: in my street, for instance, where the buildings average five storeys it must be exasperating having to climb five flights of stone steps to deliver a butcher's circular to Fru Nordström (who is probably a vegetarian).

Looking up from my table I can see the bare sun-drenched branches of the limes in the boulevard beside the Fyris; going to the window and looking down I can see old women in black —their long shadows stretched on the cobblestones—selling flowers by the bridge that carries Drottinggatan (the High) over the river. Or flowers they would be if the poor could afford such luxuries in February: actually they are brightly coloured feathers wired to twigs. The sun is so inviting that I simply *must* go out before the shadows grow any longer. The days, remember, are still very short.

A splendid aurora to-night (which means a change in the weather): green bands travelling up the sky with white shafts like searchlights shooting across them from time to time; in the north a fine glow. You have heard of Celsius who (with Linnaeus) invented the centigrade thermometer? Well, it was he who first drew attention to the influence of the aurora on the magnetic needle. A native and student of Upsala, he was an important all-round scientist—geologist, physicist and astronomer. In Svartbäcksgatan is the observatory which he founded in 1740—a classical building, now with a cheap cinema on the ground floor, abutting on the street at the odd angle of forty-five degrees.

Nearby is the Lion drug-store where Scheele worked for several years, the great chemist who anticipated Priestley's discovery of oxygen, as well as discovering chlorine, glycerine, arsenic, prussic acid (which he tasted!) and numerous other substances. While buying some toothpaste one day I noticed a plaque claiming that it was there that he actually discovered oxygen. Too poor and too delicate even to go to school, Scheele was never a member of the University. Although his equipment was even for then extremely primitive and his working conditions definitely adverse, it is acknowledged that his power as an experimental investigator has seldom if ever been surpassed.

One of Upsala's most interesting alumni is Olof Rudbeck, who, in his monumental *Atland* in four huge volumes, claimed that after the Deluge Sweden was the land settled by Japhet, son of Noah, and his descendants. (Some of his followers even went so far as to avow solemnly that both Adam and Eve were Swedes—alas that they weren't!). The Bringing archaeology, philology, and the classics to his aid, he succeeded in persuading most of his contemporaries (scepticism was considered to be treason) that Sweden was the Atlantis of the Greeks. But that was in the seventeenth century, and Sweden then a great power had to give a decent account of her origins. Actually, Rudbeck was a prodigious scholar, an important anatomist, and in botany a forerunner of Linnaeus. It was his botanic garden that Linnaeus took over when appointed to the Chair of Botany—Linnéträgården in Svartbäcksgatan which with the house adjoining it has now been restored to its original state.

In the difficult years after Pultava in the early eighteenth century schools and universities were in a deplorable condition. But the Library at least was excellent, and Carl Linnaeus, a poor medical student from Lund, entering on his studies, was before long discovered and helped by the Rudbeck and the Celsius families. In 1730, at the age of twenty-two and a student of only two years' standing, he took over for a while the younger Rudbeck's public lectures, attracting audiences of two to four hundred when the professors had only eighty! His living-room, turned into a museum and menagerie, became one of the sights of the town. At the age of twenty-four he is said to have completed his revolutionary sexual system: plants henceforth could be distinguished by an examination of the number and arrangement of the pistils and stamens. And why give a plant ten names? Two, he proved, were quite enough. A year later he made his remarkable Lapland journey, riding and walking through country which in parts to-day is still hard to traverse. The *Lachesis Lapponica*, describing his adventures, has long been a Swedish classic, and even in English makes delightful reading. Then followed two and a half years abroad. Fourteen of his books, including the *Systema Naturae*, were published; every facility was granted him for his researches; he was meeting and corresponding with the foremost naturalists of the day, many of whom made attractive offers of wealth and honour if only he would stay.

Boerhaave, for instance, wished to establish him in Holland, and Dillenius the Oxford Professor of Botany offered him half his salary. His system was everywhere triumphant. Or almost everywhere, for there was a certain Russian professor who never could believe that God had the immorality to countenance a vegetable brothel—a flower in which, for example, a single female organ was surrounded by ten male: the perpetrator of such a scandalous theory was, he swore, a blaspheming scoundrel.

Back again in Sweden, he became for a while a medical practitioner in Stockholm, married, and was made the first President of the Academy of Science. 1741, the year when Linnaeus returned to Upsala as Professor, is among the greatest in the annals of the University. Students came in from all over Europe, from Northern Africa, Siberia, even America, to hear the man who had revolutionized natural history. Some of his pupils scoured the world for plants; others were sought after by the leading scientists of Europe. In his time the student population rose from six hundred to fifteen hundred (the same figure it was forty years ago). Masses of these, fired by his enthusiasm, would follow him on all-day excursions into the country and press round while some local wonder was being described. The small low-lying Botanic Garden to which he had added three thousand species became the richest in Europe. I like the story of the sea-captain's wife who rushed some tea-plants from Gothenburg, holding the box on her knees in the carriage all the way. No economic advantage came of that; but his culture of artificial pearls was more successful. In Lapland he had watched lake-mussels being opened for pearls. Experimenting secretly in the River, he inserted globules of plaster of paris through small holes in some mussels, and when five or six years later he hoisted them up there were pearls inside. For which discovery he received a financial reward and the privilege of nominating his son as successor to the Chair.

His popularity among the students was immense. When Inspector of Småland's Nation gatherings were always held in his house, there being no hall in those days. Many students,

43

especially the foreigners, lived with or around him, often receiving their board and tuition for nothing at all. His country house at Hammarby a few miles out was famous for its large parties and the dances held in a barn. His work over, nothing pleased him more than to have his family and merry young people about him. Such was the University's greatest son, of whom it was said "God created, Linnaeus put things in order."

A year after his death, Berzelius, founder of modern inorganic and electro-chemistry, was born. And this Linnaeus of chemistry—he introduced the present system of chemical formulation—was also a student of Upsala.

So of course was Swedenborg, who spent most of his childhood here, his father (who as Bishop of Skara was eventually made responsible for the spiritual welfare of the Swedes in America) at that time being a professor of Theology and later Dean of the Cathedral. His school-days, if we are to believe him, were spent mainly in spiritual meditations.

Nothing much is known about his student life except that he went down in 1709 with a decent degree. He was here during the great fire of 1702 which destroyed, along with most of the town, their new stone house in Cathedral Square. The best friend of his youth was Dr. Benzelius, his brother-in-law, a much older man and Librarian of the University. It was mostly through his generosity that Swedenborg was able to travel in England and other parts of Europe after he went down; and he in turn tried to help Benzelius with a scheme for building an observatory in Upsala. Swedenborg was always impatient of the University's exclusively theoretical outlook, and tried for years to have a Chair of Mechanics established here. When in 1718 he was offered the Professorship in Astronomy, one of the reasons he gave for his refusal (in a letter to Benzelius) was "I thus decline a faculty which does not agree with my tastes and my turn of mind, by both of which I am led to mechanics, and will be in future to chemistry." He was then assessor at the Board of Mines where his work and various researches thereafter kept him in Stockholm and other parts; and it was not till 1910 that he returned to Upsala, his remains being brought from London to rest in a black sarcophagus in the Cathedral where so many of his great compatriots are buried. Swedenborg is probably one of our closest links with Sweden. It was in London that his New Jerusalem Church was first founded, and his impress on English and American letters, though doubtless not always for the good, is immense. Emerson and Blake, as is well known, were profoundly influenced by him; Carlyle's *Sartor Resartus* is "saturated with Swedenborg"; Tennyson, the Brownings, Patmore, Ruskin, Thoreau, Oliver Wendell Holmes were all in various degrees influenced; while Coleridge and Henry James are others who praised him very highly. These, of course, were all concerned with his religion or mysticism: only in the last half-century has he been coming into his own as a prophet of science. I remember some years ago at the *Sunday Times* Book Fair being impressed by the immensity of his volumes on *The Brain*, one of the many scientific works printed by the Swedenborg Society of London who have thus made his writings accessible to scientists in various fields. There are said to be about a dozen subjects which he definitely advanced or would have if his researches had been known at the time. I have been reading a life of him and cannot say what an exciting experience it has been plumbing this practical mystic or true Swede writ large. He seems to be the last of all the great *heterogeniuses*, as I like to call Leonardo and other huge, versatile figures of the High Renaissance. Think, my dear chap, what a man he must have been to found so subtle a new religion and at the same time be the first in a country becoming famous for science to give the right interpretation of erratic blocks (those huge glacial boulders so commonly dumped down over Scandinavia), to publish the first statement of the nebular hypothesis and yet not think it beneath him to make improvements in the common house-stove or invent an ear-trumpet for the deaf!

And to-day the Upsala tradition of science lives on in such distinguished men as his namesake Théodor Svedberg (Swedenborg was a Svedberg before being ennobled), Professor in Physical Chemistry and Nobel Prize winner, whose remarkable ultra-centrifuge for the determination of the molecular weights of compounds reaches a speed of sixty thousand revolutions a minute; and the various medical professors, botanists and others whose latest researches are seized upon by specialists the world over.

WINTER EVENING, UPSALA

The sky is stretched, the air is slightly nervous,
*   The Castle shadow lunges on the town;*
The bridges shrink, drawing the house-clumps closer;
*   While on the stiffening snow I saunter down*

Through Odinslund, the lights of Drottninggatan
*   That come out one by one piercing the high*
And intricate grille of sycamores, and starpricks
*   Puncturing the tautened diaphragm of sky.*

Patterns emerge: the vigorous curves of evening
*   Are drawn as on a graph; all sounds are jotted—*
Tram-rumbles, sledgebells' tinkle, certain voices,
*   Foot-scrunching—and acoustic contours plotted.*

Patterns emerge: a matsal's* sweating window
*   Shows up a group of students. At the door*
I join them, now no longer an intruder,
*   But drawn into the pattern of their spoor,—*

Into their lives and several aspirations,
*   And share in tunes ascending to the head*
Out of the heart.—Above the spired Cathedral
*   Throbs with undying rhythms of the dead.*

* Restaurant.

4: *Games and Spex*

I WAS ASTONISHED to find that here an inter-varsity contest is on a lower standard and attracts far fewer spectators
than an inter-college cupper in England. In Sweden it is not
the students who play games; they are about the only group
who do not: or rather, games and studies are quite separate.
The long winter is devoted to intense study, broken perhaps by
a few weeks at Christmas and a few days at Easter; the tragically
brief summer is spent almost entirely out of doors. That they
can remain fresh, despite the heavy drinking and lack of
exercise, always surprises me. From an early age they seem
to have developed the capacity for bottling energy (which keeps
well in the dry invigorating air of the North).

There is, of course, a minority who exercise regularly. In
the autumn they go in for cross-country running with compass,
a form of sport in which the Swedes were pioneers. Even with
a map it is no easy matter to find one's way from one checking-
point to another through dense moraine-strewn coniferous
forest.

When the snow comes (being in the rain-shadow, we seldom
have very much at a time) one can practise turns on Castle
Hill before breakfast or do some ski-walking further afield.
We had a medium fall last week: horse-sledges, their bells
jangling in the crisp air, appeared as if from nowhere; men came
out with brooms sweeping the snow into huge piles and dumping it from barrows onto the ice in the River: cars, many with
chains round their tyres or skis strapped on to the hood,
crept about as if on tiptoe; even the trams were less noisy
than usual. I went round to find someone for a run. Putting
on our skis by the Library, we passed out of the town southwards, crossed the common by the barracks, plunged into the
woods and eventually emerged at Skarholmen, which over-
looks a frozen arm of Lake Mälar, where we had a meal watching men with saws cutting out blocks of ice among the long
violet tree-shadows perfectly outlined on the white surface.
Returning by tram after nightfall, we witnessed a full orange

moon rise misshapen over fields turned now to a corpse-like blue.

Bandy and ice-hockey played on a large flooded sports ground can generally be counted on for at least a few months. By May the ground should be soft enough for field athletics and football, both very popular in Sweden. As in England every village has its field (which is also in part a running-track), but the season is different: its opening coincides more or less with our Cup Finals, while Norway versus Sweden is played at Midsummer! Betting on English teams is almost as widespread as at home. There are always little groups of enthusiasts (especially workers) round one or two of the shops where the latest League results, tabled in ink, are displayed in the windows, and I have several times come across photographs of favourite teams offered for sale by side-street tobacconists. The pools are state-controlled, and although the betting is mostly in coppers the annual turnover is something like a million and a half pounds, a good portion of which goes to the Government.*

There are two covered tennis courts for the University where at least twice a week I play singles for the very reasonable charge of two shillings an hour. The newer building also houses a gymnasium and a swimming-bath. Modern gymnastics, by the way, originated as a by-product of Swedish romanticism. Some literary men, wishing to reinvigorate the country which had fared badly in the Napoleonic wars and lost her ancient province of Finland to Russia, formed themselves into a Gothic League, studied northern mythology, and wrote history and poems idealizing the past. One of the members was Ling, who devised a system of physical training whereby modern Swedes could achieve a vigour and fitness equal to that of the ancient heroes of his long unreadable epics. In every school gym has long been compulsory (though games are not). Perhaps that is part of the secret of their health. Organized in classes and finishing with a game of handball (a sort of terrestrial water-polo), it can be excellent fun; though a few of the more advanced exercises, which alas I have not

---

* The 1949 figure is about four million pounds.

been brought up to, are generally arduous enough by themselves.

Golf, confined mostly to Southern Sweden and even there little favoured by the young, is soon coming to Upsala, much to the delight of the many Anglophiles. Squash, of course, is unnecessary in such a climate and in the absence of large towns; and the club in Stockholm, the only one in the country, appears to be used mainly by the English colony. In Upsala other forms of exercise are riding (on cavalry horses) and dancing. Folk-dancing, I mean. I was recently taken to a special meeting of Philochoros, the student dance club, to see no less than thirty-five different dances, mostly long and intricate, from all parts of the country. Apart from public festivals in the big towns, it is only on such occasions that it is possible to see such a variety of folk costumes typical of perhaps fifty different parishes from Skåne to Haparanda. Natural and smooth-flowing to witness, the dances actually had years of hard practice behind them; and since the speed of some is very great (in one the man does cartwheels round his partner), the expenditure of energy is enormous. The atmosphere I found surprisingly genuine, with nothing of artificial revivalism about it. The performance, which was quite private (there being only two other non-participants), ended with a cleverly arranged puppet-show: The Pyramus and Thisbe scene of *The Midsummer Night's Dream*, given in English.

Which reminds me that Upsala is at present entirely without theatres. There are cinemas enough—one for every day in the week, with films from as many different countries—but not even a student theatre. Here, in Upsala, which might well be Browning's "mountain citied to the top Crowded with culture"! The nations, it is true, have their "spex", a sort of charade which generally turns out to be a skit on famous men and events of the day; and these are a valuable though limited outlet. For a full-length play one must visit the capital, which costs but little in time and money. But I am always being told the Swedes are a not very dramatic people. Judging from the very presentable playwrights they have produced; from the immense popularity of their great actor, Gösta Ekman; from the acclamation given to good foreign companies; from the brilliant achievements of the film industry before it partly went insolvent; and from the masterly manner in which they arrange pageants, I should say that Swedish dramatic talent is there and only wants encouraging, particularly at school.

The drama in Sweden is of comparatively modern origin, dating from the second half of the seventeenth century. There are traces of a native art in the sixteenth, and before that there seem to have been Moralities and Mysteries; but at Court the stage was more or less monopolized by foreigners. Although some English players went to Sweden as well as to Denmark in late Elizabethan days—we find a troupe acting at a wedding in Nyköping in 1592, for example—it is thought unlikely that they left any influence; while Shakespeare, although acted at the Court of Christina, was comparatively late in coming into his own on the stage over here. It is interesting to find that the country's chief dramatist in the seventeenth century was a learned Upsala professor called Messenius, whose classical plays on the Senecan model, based on Swedish sagas and history, were acted by the students, and that the first Swedish professional actors were some Upsala students who began playing here and then moved to Stockholm in 1686, from which year is dated the inception of the national drama. Five years later, however, they had discontinued; and during half the following century there was no native company at all. Not till the brilliant Gustavan era was there any real permanent awakening. The impetus came from Gustavus III himself, last of the great Vasa kings, a consummate actor and orator, who founded a Swedish theatre about 1770, and wrote some of the first Swedish plays. A disciple of the French classical school, he later founded the Swedish Academy of Arts and Sciences on the model of *L'Académie française*, with a membership of eighteen because (he said) *aderton* was "the most beautiful-sounding of all numbers". Much of his time was given over to writing, producing, designing costumes for, and acting in theatricals. The theatres at Gripsholm Castle and at the Palace of Drottningholm, complete with contemporary stage decorations and machinery, preserve even to-day their

Gustavan flavour. His Court was even more French than
Versailles; his levées, held in *salons* decorated in the style of the
Parisian ones in which he had been lionized, were even more
elaborately theatrical; at one time he consorted with outlandish
spiritualists and fake Swedenborgians; on a visit to Russia, he
played a practical joke on the Chancellor by walking
unannounced into his room as he was dressing; while in
politics his sense of the dramatic was always used to exceptional
effect. And, fittingly, his assassination after he became a
despot occurred during a masquerade at the Royal Opera
House. In the ensuing revulsion against the artificial French
atmosphere, which had been so perfectly maintained for two
decades, the drama naturally received a set-back. But it was
never again in any danger; and gradually more theatres were
opened, as if preparing the country for Strindberg, Hjalmar
Bergman, Lagerkvist and other modern dramatists.

5 : *Notes On Religion*

March 25th

I HAVE RECENTLY vacated the sunny but rather Victorian
room I occupied in Drottninggatan, the owner having returned
from his military service in Lapland. My present digs are further
down Östra Ågatan (East River-Street) at the top of a six-
storey block and well above the trees which line the Fyris.
It is a cheerful room, furnished in modern style by the friend
of mine who first introduced me to the life in Upsala and who
has now gone off for a few months with the Coastal Artillery.
On my right lives a graduate from Hälsingland who gives me
lessons in Swedish and whose fiancée frequently appears on a
visit from the capital. Opposite lives a botany student from the
Agricultural College of Ultuna, just outside the town, evidently
very hard up, but always in the best of health and spirits and
neatly dressed. The room on my right should be occupied by
a gay young baron, but since his mysterious disappearance a
few weeks ago it has been taken by a journalist whom none of
us knows for he spends the day in bed and works all night. We

are all cared for by a cheery and industrious landlady who never seems to grow tired.

This is Annunciation Day, a holiday in Sweden. According to the custom there have been *frasvåfflor*, or wafers and jam, for the last course at dinner. On Shrove Tuesday and every Tuesday throughout Lent we have had *semla med mjölk*: a large bun, apparently a hybrid between a doughnut and an éclair, filled with cream and marzipan and swamped in hot milk—an especial favourite with the children. Naturally, such symbols to-day have no more religious significance than the pancake in England. The Swedes, over ninety-nine per cent. of them Lutherans, are not very religious in the ordinary sense of the word. They don't bother too much about the eternal verities or the supernatural. They have no desire to take more spirituality than they can digest. Like the ancient Greeks they have a sensuousness, attractive because it is frank, healthy because overt; and their idealism (too pronounced politically, I have heard it suggested) is tempered by solid common-sense. If they do right, it is probably intuitively. But that, and the question whether they ought to be more religious, I hardly have authority to touch on. As church-goers they are even more irregular than we are. Except on Christmas Day, when everyone goes to Early Service: in the country you will see a line of sleighs, each with flaring torches, moving towards the village church. (The only comparable sight I have ever seen is a midnight procession of mule-carts also with torches. But that was in Johannesburg and I was told they were sewage wagons.)

Being Lutherans, they attach great importance to Confirmation, for which special clothes are bought. Clothiers' shop-windows are for several weeks monopolized by black costumes, and white shirts and blouses; while photographers, experiencing a seasonal boom, make a feature of child-portraits, whose fair-haired subjects, thus stiffly attired, pose with a pathetically captivating solemnity.

Converted mainly by Englishmen, the Swedes were late in becoming Christianized. Not till the twelfth century can the country be considered definitely Christian. In 1164 it became a church province by itself, Upsala being the archbishopric. The Reformation, on the other hand, was comparatively early, and resembled ours in being politically motivated. Olaus Petri, a friend and disciple of Luther and Melanchthon, was its great protagonist. Through his writings and preachings in the early 1520's the reform doctrines were disseminated. It was he who first translated the New Testament into Swedish, thereby fulfilling Luther's demands that services should be conducted in the vernacular. Though a work of unquestionable vigour and simplicity—Master Olof is said to have created the literary language of the nation—his Testament can hardly stand comparison with ours. The Swedes have been less successful in producing a highly accurate and really inspired translation of the Bible, so that the version commonly used at present dates only from 1917. Thanks, then, to Olaus Petri and Gustavus Vasa, Sweden became a Protestant country in 1527. There were only two later attempts at a counter-reformation, the last being in the reign of the Jesuitical Sigismund, King of Sweden and Poland, who had to be deposed in 1599. How the Swedes under Gustavus Adolphus a few decades later were mainly instrumental in saving the Protestant cause in Northern Europe needs no re-telling; but that Charles XII procured the religious freedom of the Silesian Protestants is not generally known. Only two religious leaders since that have had any importance abroad—Swedenborg, and in this century Söderblom, Archbishop of Upsala, who arranged the greatest religious conference of modern times.

Founded by Archbishop Ulfsson in 1477, Upsala literally grew up in the shadows of the Church, the University from the first being "closely connected with the Cathedral; it is even said to be founded 'in the Metropolitan Church of Upsala'." The original endowment also came "from annexation of prebends in the Cathedral Church". Secularization was slow, theology for over a century remaining almost the only study. Here to-day more than half the future churchmen are still trained, some destined for local work, some for the immense parishes of Lapland, some for missionary activities in farthest Asia.

53

Background to Sweden

This afternoon I have been walking by the River. I was surprised to see at the wharf (for Upsala is a port) a small fishing-boat from the West Coast. It had come six or seven hundred miles at least from Marstrand, near Gothenburg, via Stockholm and the Mälar, to sell barrels and tins of fish.

Further down, in the large boat-yard, pleasure craft of all kinds and sizes were being uncovered for their annual overhaul. The variety of paints and smells was delicious.

Spring is arriving a month early this year. As the last blocks of ice are carried down the River the first gulls fly inward, following the open expanses of water on Lake Mälar and winging up such inlets and streams as are free from ice. Although the snow is still lying in the hollows of the fields and will lie for long in patches in the forests, coltsfoot are flowering in the dingy sapless grass. The puss-willows are beginning to blossom. Dwarf sallows, especially the male ones, seem to be all flowers, and are nowhere more attractive than when spreading their few inches against a rock. Even the *blåsippor* (blue anemones) are showing at the edges of the woods or in the *hagar*. (A *hage*, or cross between a meadow and a wood, is, as Strindberg observed, something typically Swedish.) And so it happens that the year's first flowers are, like the national colours, blue and gold, the blue however being no truer than that of a bluebell. You even have both colours united in the same plant, a wood melampyrum called Swedish soldier, which comes into flower sometime in May.

POSTCARD

Spring explodes like a bomb in the North Countries:
masses of snow-masonry
crash; ice-panes are shattered;
arboreal machine-guns rattle out a rapid round of buds;
as grass-bayonets perforate anachronisms with a wild accuracy.

The expectant ground is picketed with coltsfoot. Blåsippor,
using surprising tactics,

burst through precipitantly. Both are temporarily rebuffed
by late frosts and an east wind.

Straight from the mêlée,
and not without hazard,
I have brought these jottings, registered seismographically.
I want you to notice the handwriting.
No doubt it would be more intelligible if written up afterwards,
but custom is a shock-absorber.

6 : *Some Sovereigns and Alumni*

THE ORIGIN OF this University is closely bound up with
the emergence of national feeling at the end of the Middle
Ages. United with Denmark-Norway in the year 1396,
Sweden had during the early days of the Kalmar Union received
quite tolerable treatment at the hands of Denmark, her senior
partner. But as time went on the Danish bailiffs grew increasingly oppressive and twice during the fifteenth century the
Swedes had risen in revolt, first under Engelbrekt, and then
under Sten Sture the Elder who was made Protector and won a
magnificent victory over the Danes at the Battle of Brunkeberg
in what is now a part of Stockholm—a victory commemorated
at the time by the famous wooden statue of St. George and the
Dragon in the Storkyrkan, and in the present age by Milles's
colossal Sture Monument which towers over the woods on a
ridge near Upsala. It was in 1477, six years after this battle,
that the scheme for a national university—broached several
times during the century—first materalized. According to
the Charter, Bologna was ostensibly the model for Upsala,
although it is thought that Paris, Cologne, Wittenberg,
Rostock or some other university known to Swedish ecclesiastics
was probably the real model. Paris especially had been
frequented by Swedish students, who (like others from the
North) matriculated in the English "nation" and were
sufficiently numerous to have three or four special hostels of
their own. During its first century and a half Upsala never

E   55

became a very glorious seat of learning, partly owing to lack of funds, partly to the apathy of the kings, or in one case (when it was ordered to be closed) to direct opposition. But students were at least spared the humiliation of being dragged to Denmark, as the Danish King desired, where a university was started about the same time (having been founded slightly earlier than Upsala) though not opened till a bit later.

One might have expected that Gustavus Vasa, more than anyone the creator of modern Sweden, would assist this national institution in its early days. But no—learning and most of the arts are among the provinces in which this great man was least interested. A story is told of him that one day when at school in Upsala he flew into a rage with his Danish school-master, saying that when he was grown up he would whack the Danes on the nose. On being reprimanded, he plunged his dagger into his Greek text, told him to go to hell, and walked out. And of course he kept his promise by releasing Sweden forever from the Danish yoke. Some of his connections with Upsala, if not with the University, were pretty close, for this town was still the capital of Sweden till the late sixteenth century: he is reputed to have addressed the *bönder* from one of the mounds in Old Upsala, asking them for support in his revolution; the Castle was originally begun by him—after he became King; and with other towering figures of the North he is buried in the Cathedral. I was recently taken into the Convocation room in the University building to see the original painting from which the likeness that appears on all the country's bank-notes is taken—a powerful and masterly work for the middle of the sixteenth century, executed by a German called Binck, and proving (I am told) the real starting-point for Swedish portraiture.

It was not till the reign of his grandson, Gustavus Adolphus, that Upsala first took its place among the great universities of Europe. Its first Chancellor was John Skytte, who as his tutor had early instilled into him a deep love of learning and who is said to have had a profounder influence on his character than anyone. It must indeed have been a proud day for him as well as for Upsala when the King in 1624 transferred over three

hundred of his estates to the University. Expansion was
immediate: the faculties were enlarged, the curriculum
improved and added to, and in a few years the number of
students was doubled. Apart from this magnificent endowment,
the King also established the country's first gymnasia or high
schools and (shortly before his death) founded a university
in Dorpat. With a wealthy, leisured aristocracy rapidly being
increased, and a desire to appear cultivated spreading in a
country which had so spectacularly come to the fore, education
both higher and lower continued to improve during the
century; and two other universities were opened: Åbo (now
Turku) in Finland and Lund in Skåne (soon after the acquisition of that province). Upsala in the past had, *despite* the
conditions, produced some fine scholars; henceforth she was
to produce even more notable men in various fields to a great
extent *because* of the conditions.

Christina, his brilliant and scholarly-minded daughter,
might have done even more: she certainly took some interest
in its welfare, but it was in Stockholm that she gathered around
her those remarkable foreign men of learning. When towards
the end of her reign she moved to Upsala, Descartes, the
greatest of them, was already dead (it is said that he caught
pneumonia through having to visit her at five o'clock in the
morning in the depths of winter). But she herself, sledging
round the town in a great plumed hat, must have enhanced the
glory of the place. Andrew Marvell, in a poetical epistle to a
friend in the English embassy here, held that Upsala could then
vie with ancient Athens: "*Upsala nec priscis impar nemoratur
Athenis*", as he put it. A few months later the Queen had
staged her sensational abdication in the hall of the Castle.

In case you have never come across the first-hand account
of this ceremony by Bulstrode Whitelocke, who was Cromwell's
ambassador at the time, I have copied out some of it from the
entry under May 11th, 1654, in his Journal:

> Early in the morning the master of the ceremonies came
> to accompany Whitelocke to the Castle to see the manner
> of the assembly of the Rikstag, and brought him and his

company to the Castle to an upper room or gallery, not taken notice of by any, yet had the full view of the great hall where the Rikstag met, and heard what was said. . . .

The great hall, two stories high, was prepared for the Assembly. An outer chamber was hung with cloth of Arras; in the antechamber to that were guards of the Queen's partisans; in the court was a company of musketeers. . . . on each side of the hall, from the walls towards the middle of the room, forms were placed, covered with red cloth, and were all seats for the Members, and were all alike without distinction, and reached upwards. Three parts of the length of the hall, in the midst between the seats, was a space or lane broad enough for three to walk abreast together. At the upper end of the hall, on a footpace three steps high, covered with footcarpets, stood the chair of State, all of massy silver, a rich cushion in it, and a canopy of crimson velvet, richly embroidered over it. On the left side of the chair of State were placed five ordinary chairs of crimson velvet, without arms, for the five Riksofficers; and . . . below them, in a semi-circular form, were stools of crimson velvet for the Riks-Senators.

About nine o'clock there entered at the lower end of the great hall a plain, lusty man in his boor's habit with a staff in his hand, followed by about eighty boors, Members of this Council [i.e., the estate of the *bönder*], who had chosen the first man for their Marshal or Speaker. These marched up in the open place between the forms to the midst of them, and then the Marshal and his company sat down . . . and put on their hats. A little while after them entered at the same door a man in a civil habit of a citizen, with a staff in his hand, followed by about 120 citizens, deputies of the cities and boroughs, who had chosen him to be their Marshal. Then come two hundred of the Nobility, many of them rich in clothes, led by their Marshal. A little while after at the same door entered the Archbishop of Upsala with a staff in his hand, . . . followed by five or six hundred other bishops and all the superintendents and about sixty ministers, deputies or proctors of the Clergy. While they walked up to their places all the rest of the Members stood up uncovered: and when they sat down on the uppermost forms on the left side of the State, and put on their hats and caps, the rest of the

Members did the like; these were grave men, in their long cassocks and canonical habit, and most with long beards.

All the Members being thus sat, about a quarter of an hour after entered the Captain, followed by divers of the Queen's guard, with partisans. After them came many gentlemen of the Queen's servants, uncovered, with swords at their sides and well clad, two and two together. After them came the Riks-Senators in their order, the puisne first. After them the Riks-officers, all bare. After them came the Queen, and kept off her hat in the hall, some of the officers and pages of the Court after her. In this order they went up in the open place in the midst of the forms, all the Members standing up uncovered. The Queen's company made a lane for her to pass through, and she went up to her chair and sat down in it; and all the company, except the members of the Council, went out of the hall, and all the doors were shut; and Members sat in their places uncovered.

After the Queen had sat a little, she rose and beckoned to the Chancellor [i.e., Axel Oxenstierna] to come to her, who came with great ceremony and respect; and after a little speaking together he returned to his place, and the Queen sat down again a little time; then rising up with mettle, she came forward to the utmost part of the foot-space, and with a good grace and confidence spake to the Assembly. . . . The speech, which Whitelocke afterwards learnt was quite extemporary [Oxenstierna had unexpectedly refused to open the proceedings by giving the proper announcement why the special session had been called], was to the effect that she had long made up her mind to abdicate, that it would be for the good of the country, and that nothing could alter her resolution. Thanking them for their loyalty, and assuring them that her intention had always been to serve their "most dear country", she ended by expressing the wish "that all may work to the glory of God, to advancement of the Christian Church [whether she meant Roman or not, is a matter of conjecture], and to the good and prosperity of our most dear country and of all her inhabitants".

After the Queen had spoken she sat down again, and after a little pause the Archbishop of Upsala went out of his place into the open passage, and making his obeisance to the Queen, he, as Marshal of the Clergy and in their name, made an oration to her Majesty which was somewhat long; but which amounted to what one might expect: the reign had been happy, her subjects were contented and loved her; he therefore used all arguments and humble entreaties to her Majesty to desist from her intention of resigning the government,—even if it were "to her own trouble, yet for her subjects' good". . . . After he had ended his speech, making three congees, he went up to the Queen and kissed her hand, and with three more congees returned to his place. Then the Marshals of the Nobility and of the Burgesses in turn made their respective, respectful speeches in the same dignified manner and to the same effect.

In the last place stepped forth the Marshal of the Boors [as Whitelocke renders *Bönder*], a plain country fellow, in his clouted shoon, and all other habits answerable, as all the rest of his company were accoutred. This boor, without any congees, or ceremony at all, spake to her Majesty, and was interpreted to Whitelocke to be after this phrase: "O Lord God, Madam, what do you mean to do? It troubles us to hear you speak of forsaking those who love you so well as we do. Can you be better than you are? You are Queen of all these countries, and if you leave this large Kingdom, where will you get such another? If you should do it, as I hope you won't for all this, both you and we shall have cause, when it is too late, to be sorry for it. Therefore my fellows and I pray you to think better on't, and to keep your crown on your head, then you will keep your own honour and our peace; but if you lay it down in my conscience you will endanger all. Continue in your gears, good Madam, and be the fore-horse as long as you live, and we will help you the best we can to bear your burden. Your father was an honest gentleman and a good king, and very stirring in the world; we obeyed him and loved him as long as he lived; and you are his own child and have governed us very well, and we love you with all our hearts; and the Prince [i.e. the successor] is an honest gentleman and when the time comes we shall be ready to do our duties to him as we do to you; but as long as you live we are not willing to part with you, and therefore I pray, Madam, do not part with us."

When the boor had ended his speech he waddled up to the Queen without any ceremony, took her by the hand and shook it heartily, and kissed it two or three times; then turning his back to her, he pulled out of his pocket a foul handkerchief and wiped the tears from his eyes, and in the same posture he came up he returned back to his own place again.

After all of which the Queen caused a long formal Declaration of Abdication to be read, whereafter the hall was gradually emptied.

Whitelocke was quite right in singling out this homely speech by the representative of the Fourth Estate, for there had always been a close understanding between the monarchs and the *Bönder* class who at certain periods in history appear to have formed the only sound tissues in the Swedish body politic, and who, even in this century of bitter struggles to uphold their rights against an overweening aristocracy, were nevertheless still represented in the Riksdag by an estate of their own. Asked a few days later what she thought of this speech, Christina replied (though not at first): "I think he spake from his heart."

Whitelocke: I believe he did, and acted so too, especially when he wiped his eyes.
The Queen: He showed his affection to me in that posture more than greater men did in their spheres.

And soon the whole world was talking of her abdication. Milton (although a Puritan!), having to compose a State Letter to her successor Charles X, took the opportunity of apostrophizing her as "the Daughter of Gustavus, and a Heroess so matchless in all degrees of Praise and Masculine Renown, than many ages backward have not produced her equal". "She may", he said, "abdicate the sovereignty, but she can never lay aside the Queen". But, as you probably know from episodes in her later life, she unfortunately did.

Upsala's greatest alumni from this time till the nineteenth century were perhaps in scientific fields; whereafter the arts could probably claim just as many and sometimes more famous ones. Sweden was late in the literary field: Georg Stjernhjelm, the "father" of her poetry, was not born till the end of the sixteenth century. First recognized by Gustavus Adolphus, he was later on attached as a sort of laureate to the court of Christina for whom he wrote masques, as well as epithalamiums and a long heroic poem called *Hercules*. Stjernhjelm, like many of his generation, was educated abroad; and it appears that the first poet of Upsala to cause much stir did not appear for a century. Johan Gabriel Oxenstjerna was his name, and as you might expect he was a descendant of the great statesman (who incidentally had once been Chancellor of the University). Only seventeen years of age (he was born in the 1750's), Johan Gabriel was one day defending a thesis, "Why great men are more abundant in one country than another", when the King, Gustavus III, looked in on one of his frequent visits to the University. Being struck by his ability, the latter inquired who he was, and before long the young poet had become his favourite and found himself the brightest of all the brilliant lights at the dazzling Gustavan Court. No one to-day, if he can help it, reads much of his reputedly careless, artificial and Frenchified idylls, and I don't pretend to have looked at a line of his; but historically this poet is rather interesting as having been influenced by Thompson's *Seasons* and Young's *Night Thoughts* and as having produced a translation of *Paradise Lost* which up till about fifty years ago was claimed to be the best in any foreign language.

Fröding, however, whose *floruit* was about the end of the last century, is a different matter. He is still probably the most popular poet in Sweden, both to sing and to read. A lyrical writer of great freshness, humour and melodic charm, he was influenced by Burns and other foreigners, and succeeded in blending the perfection-in-finish of an academic style with the spontaneity of folk-song. I was dining the other night in a room overlooking the little tumble-down wooden building where he lived as a student in the '80's. Although in residence for five years, he never took a degree, owing partly to his Bohemian habits which eventually earned him the name of "drunken Wennerbom".

Another literary alumnus of Värmland's Nation is Geijer, a leader of the romantic movement at the beginning of the last century, whose *History of the Swedes,* written while he was professor here, very soon secured him an international reputation. With a large statue to his memory in front of the University Building, a street named after him and also the little ravine where he is supposed to have written his most famous poem, Geijer is among the most honoured sons of Upsala.

But of Strindberg there is no memorial; hardly one among the numerous foreign tourists who visit the town in the quietness of the summer vacation is aware that Strindberg was once a student in Upsala. It was, to be sure, a very short and rather ignominious stay; but so was Shelley's in Oxford: yet what day-tripper fails to inspect the marble nude under its appropriate dome? How often does an institution that has disclaimed a man of genius turn round when he has become famous and attempt to claim some of his glory! But the fame of Strindberg has never added to that of Upsala. (You probably know of that pretty compromise in the case of Landor who was expelled from Rugby: there is a group of three medallions in the School chapel—memorials to Matthew Arnold, Rupert Brooke and Walter Savage Landor, but Landor's is a blank!)

Strindberg arrived in Upsala about seventy years ago with six pounds and a box of cigars. During his three brief sojourns he learned to play the cornet, founded a club for æsthetics, became a slave to drink and of course made himself hated by everyone. No wonder his spasmodic studies and such a reputation stood in the way of his taking a degree! Once, for instance, on his presenting a thesis in æsthetics, the professor remarked that he considered it more suitable for a women's magazine. Then burst out the true Strindberg, accused the professor of ignorance, said that the university system was all wrong, and dictated his proposed improvements. He had to be pushed out of the room.

On another occasion, after an unseemly dispute with a professor at the æsthetic club, he shut himself up in a room, devoted himself to painting, and wondered if he had gone mad. (Later in his life he again resorted to painting and even held an exhibition. I have seen some of his canvases in Stockholm: gloomy landscapes and seascapes in green, black and white, the paint lashed on with the fury though none of the genius of a Van Gogh.) But he had at least a single brief triumph when the King, who had seen a production of one of his plays at the Theatre Royal, summoned him to the Palace and made him a present.

His first contact with the stage, according to his own story, came about in the following way. Passing the Library one day, he heard some people laughing. They were actors and actresses from the capital laughing at the bookstacks visible from the street. "If they can laugh at learning", he thought, "so can I". And he decided to go on the stage. Although after his failure as an actor he returned to Upsala, it was not for long.

But what of the Library in front of which this decisive incident in the life of the great writer whose own books, now ranked there in long shelves, would, it has been calculated, take two years to read aloud at the rate of eight hours a day? The Carolina Rediviva, as the early nineteenth century building is called, houses the largest and finest library in the country. It was after the rich spoils of the Thirty Years' War had been added to it that it first took its place as one of the great libraries of Europe. Among those spoils was the Codex Argentus, taken when part of Prague was captured by the Swedes, and brought north, removed by Christina when she left Sweden, sold or given away by her in Holland, and later recovered by a wealthy nobleman who returned it to the Library where it is now displayed as its greatest treasure. Every tourist is shown the Silver Bible. What his reaction is I cannot say. The circumstances of its recovery are certainly interesting: The Goths, a people probably of Swedish origin, moved southwards across Europe, the eastern branch founding an empire in Italy. In time a certain bishop translates part of the Scriptures into their language. The Goths eventually vanish from Europe leaving barely a trace. Then twelve centuries later come the Swedes on a similar route, what is the only extant Gothic text of any length falls into their hands and is brought to the country whose monarchs are still styled Kings of the Swedes, Goths and Vandals. So the story behind it is now more interesting than the object itself, a bundle of rather dowdy parchments covered with silver ink that has long ago given up its secrets. Yet every tourist must see it, and "looks at it through two intervening layers, one of plate-glass, the other of his own ignorance". A mere unintelligent relic-worshipper and it would do him good to read Aldous Huxley's essay *Modern Fetishism* with its very right-minded protest against squandering £1,000,000 on the Codex Sinaiticus as the English did some years ago.

Then there is Victor Rydberg, the poet-novelist, who though educated at Lund had a memorable contact with Upsala. He was invited in 1877 to write a poem for the Quatercentenary of the University. He agreed. But weeks passed by, then months, without his receiving any inspiration. The composer who was to have set the piece to music became hourly more desperate. What was to be done? Fortunately a week before the date Rydberg produced his *Cantata*, it was set, and all was well. It was indeed so good that the Archbishop, who was strongly opposed to the over-liberal views of Rydberg, burst into enthusiasm and worked off his admiration in a particularly violent fit of swearing. And to-day the poem is reckoned among the greatest in the language.

I could tell you more of the many Upsala writers from aristocrats like Count Snoilsky, Prince Gustav and Wennerberg (also a musician: well-known for his duets on student themes) to the *bonde* poet Dan Andersson;* but what of writers now living? Two of the present-day authors who are most discussed in Upsala are not university men at all. One is Per Lagerkvist, dramatist, story-writer and difficult modernist poet. You can get some idea of his distinct Nordic power from a good translation of three of his stories published by Jonathan Cape under the name *Guest of Reality*. Equally controversial is Harry

* Andersson, though never a student at Upsala, has celebrated the horse chestnuts by the River Fyris.

65

Background to Sweden

Martinsson, a consumptive sailor whose imaginative prose, remarkable for its brilliant word-coinages and condensed images, is about as untranslatable as Thomas Browne's. And yet I see that his *Cape Farewell* has recently been recommended by a big English book-club. Except for a few unusual similes it appeared to me comparatively tame: I should never have thought from the translation that here was a writer worth arguing about. In Sweden he is sometimes called a surrealist, which label even here is coming to be attached almost indiscriminately to any artist who is at all arresting. There are, however, a few surrealists proper: I am told they actually have a magazine, called *Caravan*, edited by Artur Lundkvist.

In poetry, as opposed to the visual arts, it is the traditionists who hold the field, partly because publishing is monopolized by a few big houses with a conservative outlook. There is only one literary magazine of wide distribution (owned by Bonnier's, the largest publishers); but an extraordinary amount of space in the daily press is devoted to serious reviews by the most distinguished and scholarly critics. Poets like Gulberg and Malmberg, remarkable for a fine ear and formal perfection, have in proportion to the population excellent sales. Translations, necessarily of more importance in a small country, are often surprisingly distinguished. The English Georgians, for instance, exerted a strong influence in the twenties largely through renderings by Asplund and Silverstolpe. Indeed the dominant school at present may perhaps be likened to a group of rather full-blooded, masculine Georgians. Eliot and D. H. Lawrence alone among post-war Anglo-Saxons appear to have had any following; Germans and Frenchmen have been much more influential. I was recently talking to one of the better-known younger poets, a translator of Shelley and Eliot, and was surprised at what he told me of the general apathy among poets towards technical experiments. With a shorter literary tradition they perhaps feel they have not yet exploited to the full the older styles and metres. It is probable that they can learn more about prosody from the ancient classics than we can, seeing that Swedish is an inflected language in which for example quantitative hexameters (though not written nowadays) are almost as natural as in Latin. Compared with the visual arts, Swedish poetry is surprisingly unfuturistic. Or perhaps it is not surprising when one remembers that their culture is still as much pastoral-sylvan as urban, and that the young were less affected by the World War in which they never fought and from which their country was one of the first to recover. Ekelöf, first of the modern sensationalists, whose wilder pieces studded with bizarre sexual images recall the Welshman Dylan Thomas, has now taken on a soberer manner which seems more indigenous. The younger Swedish poets are far less political than ours, less violent and less obsessed with hatred. I should say they have a greater intensity and steadiness of vision, are more human (genre poetry seems to be one of their fortes), more intelligible and much more religious and devotional.*

7 : *Sista April*

THOSE WHO LIKE generalizing on the characteristics of whole nations have in the case of Norway or Sweden to reckon with the seasonal factor. The Swedes in winter are in some ways quite different from the Swedes in summer. The transition, especially violent and abrupt in the case of the young, occurs on the last of April. The ancient Nordic festival of Walpurgis, pagan in origin but taken over by the Christians and named after an English abbess of the eighth century, is celebrated throughout the country, particularly by students who throng the streets of the towns and monopolize the best open-air restaurants, singing and drinking with the veriest abandon. Most remarkable of all are the celebrations in Upsala which attract onlookers from the remotest provinces.

About two o'clock in the afternoon students can be seen moving about carrying round flat objects concealed beneath their coats. A large crowd collects in Fyris Square by the

* Since this was written in 1939 there has been a period of vigorous, restless experimentalism; though just recently there appears to be a return to more traditional forms.

67

River. Suddenly, as the clock in the Cathedral towering above booms out the first stroke of three, a cheer goes up, caps are whipped out from the cover of coats, and a forest of white spurts into being, isolating the dense mass of students in the centre of the crowd. Excitement shoots out like an electric current; caps are flung in the air; some of the students toss their winter hats into the River; most of them move up and down Drottninggatan in parties, shouting, charging into other parties, abandoning themselves to an intense *joie de vivre*. You can see some of them in the enclosed photograph (Plate 9), taken from my former room. Notice how the band of white stretches right up to the Library on Castle Hill. Nor are the side-streets quiet, and any townsman or outsider who might appear to be immune to vernal infection would probably be lynched.

Passing the Student Exam. is the most important event of one's youth, eclipsing in personal significance even a degree and in heartiness at least the celebrations of one's later days such as sixtieth, seventieth or eightieth birthdays (announced in the daily papers). Among the requirements for this equivalent of the Matric. are an ability to speak three foreign languages and to write a really good essay in one's own. The successful candidate, capped, chaired, festooned with flowers and symbolic trophies, and mobbed by friends and family, celebrates for a week or more. In Stockholm you will sometimes see a tram, which new students and their friends have hired for the day and decorated with bunting and spring flowers, making a triumphal journey round the town. Youth is but brief and these are the happiest days. The student now has the title *Kandidaten* and can wear for years the envied white cap. On the Last of April even old men, students of half-a-century ago, will bring out their caps for the day and no doubt dream of lost youth and the athletic figures that once they had, of the first night they got drunk, of the charms of Greta and Karin and Inga-Lisa and the tenderness of early love. The cap, made of white velvet, resembling a light yachting-cap and with a blue-and-gold rosette in front, should be pulled rather engagingly over the back of the head. In the South there is another and less becoming type with a high narrower crown (possibly

68

to make the wearers look taller, for the southerners are a comparatively stocky lot!). And these caps are worn only in the summer. When two students meet for the first time there is a clicking of heels, caps are raised, and each announces his name and student year, as: "Andersson, '28", "Bergström, '30". Then the senior can use *Du* (less familiar than the French *tu*); if he fails to do so, it amounts almost to an insult and the acquaintance is severed.

As evening fell we all assembled in Svartbäcksgatan—four thousand students, men and women, including some hundreds of senior members and alumni returned for the occasion. At 7.30 we began to march, six abreast, arm-in-arm, nation by nation, the standard-bearers of the nations leading the way. Right through Stora Torget (the Great Square) we went and up the whole length of Drottninggatan between the dense ranks of onlookers, slowly, and for those (unlike me) in the front of the procession to the sound of music. Wheeling left at the Library, we ascended the avenue on Castle Hill, wild clangs from the little wooden Katrina Belfry setting the air in vibration. There, under the Castle, where the fate of sovereign and state has more than once been decided, we massed ourselves round the Choir, while the remainder of the procession came up behind pressing us together. The air was hushed. There was a hymn to Spring, sung by the Choir; then an address by a representative of the Student Union. But what did the words matter? It was enough to watch the sprouting trees, their branches touched occasionally by a just perceptible breeze, and to see—beyond the Cathedral silhouetted against the evening sky—the flare of bonfires, fed by fallen twigs and leaves, symbolizing the destruction of Winter. For the religion in this Festival is pagan, the paganism religious. Something vast, inchoate, indefinable, an emanation from a simpler and more primitive age, stirred in the roots of my being. Through clefts in the loosening panels of time and space, vaguely and momentarily, I caught glimpses of the essential unity of man, hints of his mysterious unrealized majesty. . . . Four lusty cheers shot into the air; there was some more singing; then we dispersed.

Background to Sweden

Some of the nations had special dinners of their own; most of us crowded into restaurants to occupy tables reserved weeks ago, my party being in Flustret, the largest, which stands in a park by the River. The students, always great consumers of *brännvin* and gin, are never harder-drinking than on the Last of April. Some of them began before noon; when (if ever) they stopped I have not calculated. And what singing! Never have I heard *Svarta Rudolf* or *Jungman Jansson* sung—no, bellowed—with greater gusto, and that prince of student songs *O Gamla Klang och Jubeltid* (from the German), where the four faculties rise in turn to clink their glasses and party after party rocks to and fro, tables are thumped, and everyone for the great final burst leaps on to his chair or table. . . . The night drew on; we moved round from nation to nation and from restaurant to restaurant, finding friends and acquaintances at their heartiest; till, by general consent, it was time to watch from Castle Hill the first sun of summer burst into a cloudless expectant sky.

8 : *Day by the Mälar*

May 10th

ALTHOUGH THE TERM does not officially end for another fortnight, study is a mere sideline this month. Open-air restaurants, miniature golf-courses (the haunt of many an elderly professor), benches in the open, and open trams—all date from the First of May. The enclosed photograph (the frontispiece) was taken that day. You will see how advanced are the horse-chestnuts, the trees celebrated by more than one Upsala poet. Notice some shrubs on the opposite bank of the river: Forsythia in full bloom! Plants in these latitudes have no sense of chronology. On the same day I also observed elms and cowslips in bloom; sycamores bright with their greenish-yellow clusters of flowers, and the birch in small leaf.

To-day the sun has been so warm that going downstairs into the open I fairly bumped into the hot air. I have been cycling with a norrlänning out to Lake Mälar. Coming from a district

70

with a heavy rainfall, he has experienced spring mainly in puddled roads, grey skies and a damp air, often looking on her merely as the forerunner of mosquitoes and pestilential flies— insects that poison the romance of a Lapland summer. Here in Uppland, it is different; and don't wonder at our almost delirious enjoyment of such a day. Passing by orchards in full bloom, reckless clumps of virginal blackthorn and children with bunches of cowslips; right through large drifts of scent from the bird-cherries of the *hagar*, the clear light ricocheting from patches of celandine and dandelion, or from mixed colonies of blue and white anemones, we came to an arm of the Mälar, tore off our clothes, rushed into the water where but three months before there had been skating, and threw ourselves ecstatically on a grassy bank, gazing now into the deep cloud- less sky, now at the scene around us—stretches of highly varnished ostentatious king-cups and the more intellectual fritillaries. In Oxford, too, the fritillaries will, I expect, be out, "the dapple-eared lily" that is her own special flower. But how different they are there, railed off in Magdalen Meadow or trampled under foot at Iffley, to the unending colonies nodding on the quiet banks of the Mälar!

In Sweden the same word is used for both landscape and province. And happily; for the provinces are, always have been, natural divisions, each (except possibly the North Bothnian provinces) having its peculiar topographical flavour. Uppland is one of the flattest of them all. The terrain is characterized by plains alternating with low moraine ridges, generally wooded, and irregular knolls. Especially typical are the protruding knobs of granite on undulating land—quaint natural rock- gardens, with grass, junipers and perhaps dwarf pines among the rocks—islands that the plough sweeps round, leaving on the dark earth furrows like contours on a map. At present the islands are sprinkled with cowslips; soon, when spring-sown corn is a few inches high, you will see a vivid mass of yellow rock-cress through a white veil of saxifrage.

Who is it who points out the connection between flat country and some of the greatest landscape-painting (the Dutch School, for example, and in East Anglia Constable and the

F   71

Norwich School)? Uppland is flat enough, its skies as interesting as any, but its scenery of the interior does not appear to have interested any painter of note. Liljefors, modern animal-painter, worked mainly by the sea and in the forest; and even when the place happened to be Uppland the paintings are generally too much in the nature of close-ups to betray any of the special features of his native province. But Wilhelmson, a painter from the West Coast, has at least registered the undemonstrative phlegmatic but thoroughly reliable nature of the Uppland *bonde* types. Good landscape-painters generally avoid a picturesque subject: they don't want one of nature's put-up jobs. It is curious that the unobvious beauties of the Uppland interior have been almost unexploited in pigment.

In Sweden there is a definite opening for the young artist of talent. He may not receive much for his pictures, but he can at least sell them; for good taste is relatively widespread, the general standard of living is high, and there are fewer old pictures to dispose of than in countries whose wealth was acquired earlier. Though Stockholm and Gothenburg are, as might be expected, the main art-centres, it is surprising what brilliant work one will come across in schools, hotels and private houses throughout the provinces. But the snag in this is that her art hardly penetrates into foreign countries—her pictures remain at home. With good native teachers and fine collections, there is less need for young artists to study in Paris or Germany as once they did. In Kunstforschung too there has for some time been excellent work, and chairs in art-history are established both here and at Stockholm and Lund universities.

9 : *Parties and Pass-Books*

May 27th

I HAVE JUST returned from a "flower visit"—been calling on a professor's wife who was my hostess at a dinner the other night. Such a call, made within a few days of a party, is an essential item in Swedish social etiquette, and considering the price of flowers a rather expensive one. The Swedes have a fairly strict pattern of formal manners. Even at a small dinner-party, for instance, the placing of guests according to rank and honour is as important as at a diplomatic banquet; drinking cannot begin till the hostess has pledged the company; a lady cannot drink till her cavalier says "*Skål!*"; the guests on rising must thank the hostess for the food; while your next encounter with her in the street must always be accompanied by a "*Tack för senast*". But, just as in a painting by an Italian primitive, the freedom and spontaneity, so far from being crushed under the rigid pattern, often take on an enhanced attraction. Despite sometimes the apparently unpromising material of solemn-visaged northerners, there is no difficulty in making a party go if you really want it to: the difficulty, at least among the young, is often to prevent its going too far. Or so I found the other night when I collected a couple of dozen students (and the supply of drink was, if anything, rather mean): some banisters were smashed and my landlady assured me in the morning that she hadn't slept a wink. (I am now, however, in her good books again, thanks to a box of chocolates and my timely chastisement of some doves, which were attempting to roost in her window-box.)

You will have heard that there is a form of partial prohibition in this country. If a Swede wishes to drink in a restaurant he must have a meal at the same time. If he wishes to drink at home he must either be content with a very light pilsner (which he never is) or take his *motbok* (pass-book) to the local branch of Spritcentralen. There, in a very official-looking building he can buy up to four litres of spirits a month, according to his age, income, and status, and as much wine as he wishes. As no *motbok* is issued for anyone under the age of twenty-four, the younger students here have to procure their drink from friends, who generally have some stored away in the fine old tile stoves which since the advent of central heating (now general in towns) have had no other function to perform. A student is also allowed an extra quantity on taking his degree.

To the casual traveller this, the Bratt System, may appear

73

irksome and ridiculous. But it is found to work very well. The importance of the liquor problem in Swedish history is astounding, for drunkenness has always been a national vice. Among the King's retainers in the fifteenth century, for instance, the per capita consumption of extremely strong beer is said to have been nine hundred and fifty litres a year, or over four gallons a week. But it was about that time that brandy was becoming established as the *vin ordinaire* of Sweden—with what disastrous effects on the national health it is not hard to imagine. Whitelocke, Cromwell's ambassador to Christina, had heard all about the Swedish excesses and at first made himself much disliked in Upsala by his puritanical refusal to drink healths. Swedenborg, writing in the next century, prophesied that drunkenness would result in the downfall of the Swedish people; and Frederick the Great, observing that for centuries they had sought their own destruction by such means, said he was amazed at their failure. But they were well on the road to success. *Brännvin*, as some statistician claimed just over a hundred years ago when the drink problem was at its acutest, had brought more misery on the nation than all the wars in which it had ever been engaged.

All Scandinavians have, of course, been great drinkers from the earliest times. Wasn't Thor's drinking-horn connected with the ocean? That his deep draughts produced a perceptible ebb is, I suppose, borne out by the pretty work of northern scientists on water diminution in the Baltic. Odin, the highest of the gods, is said to have lived on wine alone. And among the booty that the Vikings brought from Normandy wine was always included.

Well might Hamlet, speaking as a Dane, complain:

> *This heavy-headed revel east and west*
> *Makes us traduced and taxed of other nations;*
> *They clepe us drunkards and with swinish phrase*
> *Soil our addition.*

And Thomas Fuller, the historian and divine, said he remembered "a sad incident which happened to Fliolmus, King of

Gothland, who, whilst a lord of misrule ruled in his court, and both he and his servant were drunk, in mere merriment meaning no harm, they took the king, and put him in jest into a great vessel of beer, and drowned him in earnest."

"The Danes", said Thomas Nashe, the Elizabethan writer, "are sots that are to be confuted with nothing but tankards and quart-pots."

But if they have always been a hard-drinking lot, they were the first to do something about it. A Norwegian king in the twelfth century enacted the first known liquor control in the world. The question, however, has always been an extremely delicate one, and was for a century a major political issue in Sweden. "You can do what you like with the Swedish people", said a certain bishop to Gustavus III at the height of his popularity, "if only you keep your hands off their brandy."

To-day many a foreign sociologist is attracted to Sweden to study liquor legislation and whole books have been written on the subject. The Government monopoly system, while eliminating private profits, makes good drink almost as accessible to the poor as to the rich. The main drawback is that farmers and fishermen, rarely able to visit a town, are reduced to illegal distillation or smuggling. *Brännvin*, however, is no longer the menace that it was; consumption of spirits has been much reduced and with it many of the attendant ills; while large numbers of Swedes, including the popular Crown Prince, are now total abstainers.

10 : *Spring Festival*

May 30th

I LOOKED IN at a Doctorate disputation this afternoon, held in one of the lecture-rooms in the University Building. The candidate or respondent sits in evening dress on a dais for a public defence of his thesis. Below him, to his right, are the three opponents, one elected by the faculty, two chosen by the respondent. On the front bench sit the professor and the dean of the faculty, who may if necessary interrupt. The room is often filled to overflowing, especially when the third opponent speaks, whose remarks are purely humorous. The ordeal has entailed some hard study for the opponents also, but all they receive for their trouble is a little honour. The present disputation (in philosophy) lasted from ten to five. Christina, by the way, was very fond of attending these disputations in Upsala, which I understand were even fiercer in those days.

The thermometer has been bouncing about surprisingly in the last week—up to seventy-five one day, and two days later it failed to rise above freezing. But nothing seems to have suffered. All the trees are now in leaf, save only the ash, laggard as ever. Even from a distance the pale green tassels of the spruce are very noticeable, but the pine, most reticent of trees, has to be approached rather closely before its erect sand-coloured shoots become visible.

I had not realized how full-blooded the spring can be in the depths of a coniferous forest till the other day. Now, following close on blue and white anemones, come grasses of intense green, stitchwort, solomon's seal, and exquisite little fern-waves plashing about the ankles of the trees, but especially lilies-of-the-valley—in huge rambling masses which the repeated depredations of the townsfolk seem in no way to diminish: you can go on picking them for ever.

Every year in the middle of May is held the Spring Festival, which opens at noon with a concert in the Great Hall of the University. This year the famous Upsala student choir gave, in addition to Swedish and Norwegian songs, a very spirited rendering of Strauss's *Wine, Women and Song*—the whole of it, unaccompanied, and in German. And there was a pleasant little scene as the new Director of Music took over his duties from Dr. Alfvén, now retiring, a popular figure with the students and known elsewhere as a symphony composer. In the late afternoon, with the banners of the nations flying in the breeze, a procession moves through the Botanical Gardens; there is more singing; speeches are made; and the band of the Royal Uppland Regiment maintains a feeling of liveliness as the young men stroll about introducing their partners to their friends. To be invited to the Spring Ball is the dream of every girl in the country, and now a select few have seen their dreams materialize. In the evening there are dinners in all the nations and dancing throughout the night (but, in respect for the ladies, a certain moderation in drinking), ending, like our own Commems, in time for breakfast, perhaps taken in the garden of one of the nations.

For many the celebrations are prolonged in the form of a boating excursion. I was lucky to get a seat in the unromantically named launch *Gasaccumulator III* hired by a nation and thoughtfully equipped with a piano. Firing salutes from a deafening little cannon, we pushed off from the crowded wharf and began to sing and dance our way down the Fyris in a sort of Zoffany musical-party, now laughing at astonished cows, now clapping when a boy fishing on the bank pulled in a timely catch. And all the time "The river shore Oozes out buds at every dewy pore". Eventually we came to the Mälar, landed further along, and by permission of its student owner picnicked in the grounds of Skokloster, a great castle erected after the Thirty Years' War, never more beautiful than when in such circumstances its black-and-white towers are viewed across acres of blossoming orchards.

II: *Doctors' Promotion*

June 2nd

EVERYONE IS GOING on vacation and so am I. The term came to a fitting close with the Doctors' Promotion on the last of May, the crowning ceremony of the academic year. Awakened at seven by a salute of cannon, I went to the window and looked across the town towards the mounds of Old Upsala hidden behind trees to the north. Down below was the Fyris, flecked with scum and slow-coiling chains of bubbles, more ancient and changeless even than those mounds, born perhaps of some great glacier in the last stages of decrepitude and emaciation as the ice age retreated northwards with man and beast in pursuit—the venerable stream that rocked the cradle of the Svea nation. Fresh and ageless, it flows through Swedish

77

history, passing Upsala and adding its tribute to the waters over which Stockholm its successor has been built. Delightful stream that has whispered its secret to a foreigner, it will always flow through my memory.

The sky was cloudless, lilacs were riotous in the open spaces, the horse-chestnuts almost in flower; and from every staff visible above the roofs and intervening spring foliage flags were streaming in a fresh breeze. It was a day of festival.

Here, in Sweden, the formal conferment of degrees is limited to doctorates. The numbers being small, the dignity of the ceremony can be preserved, monotony avoided, and attention focused on the individual. The processions of the main student body, complete with standard-bearers, are to emphasize the importance of the doctors, introduce some order into the movements of the mass, and form a suitable initiation and rounding-off to the proceedings. About noon, when all outsiders have taken their seats in the great Hall of the University, the students enter in procession, followed by the Chancellor, the Rector, professors, doctors and other senior members in evening dress who move to the front circle to occupy their seats of honour. It is customary to open the proceedings with a semi-popular lecture, and this year a medical professor succeeded in interesting his audience in eye-diseases. That over, the platform is taken by the promoting professor of the Theological Faculty, who speaks briefly in Latin and then announces a name. The candidate in question mounts the stage, and while the promoter holds the doctor's hat over his head a deafening salvo is fired just outside by some artillerymen stationed there for the purpose. A ring is placed on his finger, he is handed a scroll (his diploma), and after a handshake and bows he descends by steps on the right of the stage, bows to the Chancellor and resumes his seat. When, as often in the case of honorary doctorates, a degree is conferred in absence, the hat is held symbolically and the salvo fired just the same. This procedure holds good for the faculties of Theology, Law and Medicine; but in the fourth and largest, that of Philosophy (which includes the Sciences and Humanities), a laurel-wreath takes the place of the hat.

There are generally several jubilee doctors, old people who took their doctorates fifty years ago and return for the anniversary. Each is handed a diploma but need not mount the steps to receive it. *They* are the real heroes of the day, and when afterwards they stand before the crowd on the steps outside the University Building it is they who have to make speeches (Plate 10).

All the formalities, even to a slow-motion descent of the staircase resembling a death-march, are carried out in real earnest: it would be hard to invest learning with more pomp and dignity.—I could also speak of myself, when, feeling like a duchess at the opera—as much to be looked at as to look— I was induced to appear in all the regalia of an English graduate and of course fell an easy prey to the press-photographers. But such exotic elements are exceptional.

III · MAINLY UPPLAND

1 : *Runes*

They came, we are told, from the highest of the gods:

> "*Runes shalt thou find*
> *and letters bearing meaning,*
> *letters most mighty*
> *which the Great Counsellor coloured*
> *and most holy gods devised*
> *and the spokeman of the gods had carved.*"

There are runes in England and Scotland, in Rumania and other parts of the Continent, in Greenland, even possibly in North America; but most of them are in Scandinavia, especially Sweden: Uppland, that centre of gravity of the ancient north, is rightly the province in which runestones are most abundant, where indeed they are sometimes as common as milestones along the roadsides. And Upsala, it is not surprising to find, has produced in Professor Otto von Friesen the leading runologist of our day. I had hoped to photograph him posing beside one of the runestones outside the University buildings, but to-day he lives in retirement elsewhere.

Just as *rún* means "a secret communication, a mystery", so is there much mystery concerning the origin of the runes. Whether the Marcomanni, a South Germanic tribe, were the first to use them, or whether it was the Goths of South-Eastern Europe I am not qualified to discuss. Suffice it that they are said to have appeared in the third century A.D. and to have spread northwards into Scandinavia, and from thence into Britain—Denmark because of her situation being the distributing centre for the north. Derived either from the Greek or from the Latin alphabets, or from both, runes came to be used partly for purposes of magic but also to give a fixed form to the spoken language. Few, however, of the early inscriptions have survived, for many were only marked on the back of the hand or the nail (as a precaution against treachery), others on staves, brooches and swords for all sorts of magical purposes— to protect against evil, to heal wounds, give victory, make a man invulnerable, loose bonds, abate fire or storm, rouse love, guard a woman in childbirth, protect someone against poison in drink, produce eloquence and wisdom, even to wake the dead in order to hear prophecies. But in time they were more and more used on stone monuments, and it is these—especially ones from the eleventh century—that perpetuate most examples of the strange script.

Christianity was just then making headway in the north, and its spread is traceable in a special way by reference to the forms and distribution of runestones. As elsewhere pagan practices continued for some time, many being taken over by the Church, so that Christian runes are hardly a rarity: there are runic crosses and even a runic prayer-book. And throughout the Middle Ages runes continued to be used in Scandinavia as the writing of cultured laymen for private records—in Gotland till as recently as the seventeenth century, although mixed with Latin letters. For occasional notes and calendars they persisted almost to within living memory in the remoter parishes of Dalarna and Härjedalen.

Rock carving, which had already reached a high standard in the north by the Bronze Age one or two thousand years earlier, may still have been a living art by the time runes came into use. Or the older rock-carvings may at least have been an influence. But newer impulses were certainly stronger. In Uppland especially the inscriptions were accompanied by cleverly executed ornamental designs, the patterns of which were taken from wood-carvings, an art that had reached a very high state of development during the transmigration and Viking periods. Both runes and designs called for expert craftsmanship (and incidentally they sometimes called for human blood as a pigment!), so that rune-writing became a profession. Asmund, who worked in the early eleventh century, is said to have been the earliest and most remarkable of these professional rune-writers. Some say he was Osmundus, an Englishman of Scandinavian origin who helped to prepare the way for Christianity. Here is an inscription from one of his stones in Uppland: "Ragnfrid had this stone erected to the memory of Björn, her and Kättilmund's son. God and god's mother help his soul! He fell in Esthonia. But Asmund engraved (this stone)."

When we consider that most of the inscriptions give only the names of the heroes in question and the engraver, or sometimes only the engraver's, it is surprising how much history emerges as a by-product from the remaining stones. Swedes, for instance, are not generally thought of in connection with the Danish raids on England, partly because they were mercenaries, and yet, according to certain stones, many a Swedish warrior died over there. Another stone in Uppland actually mentions Canute: "But Ulf has thrice collected tribute money in England; the first sum was that paid by Toste, then it was paid by Torkel, and lastly by Knut." How north, west and east meet at times in the same spot can be seen in the case of some stones in the parish of Varfrukyrka, carved by a rune-master called Lifsten, which name is thought to be a northern form of the Anglo-Saxon Liufstan, and employing *motifs* which some think may have been introduced from the orient by way of the Swedish trade-routes through Russia. (These *motifs*, intricate, interlaced patterns of lines derived from the movement of animals' bodies—lions, dragons, etc.—also penetrated into Norway, where they are found on some carved panels of a "stave church" surviving from about that period; while similar ones can be seen in the ornament of the famous Oseberg Viking ship). Sometimes we hear of an Uppland sea-captain "who gained great wealth out in Greece for his heir", or of a Captain Tuir who had a stone raised to the memory of his sons: "One was called Aki and he perished abroad. The other who led the fleet to Greek havens perished of sickness (Hewed Iknar these runes)." As if in answer to these, we turn to the inscription on the marble lion from Piraeus (now in

Venice): "Warriors cut these runes. . . . Swedes set this on the lion." Then we can trace a hero called Rodfos "betrayed by the Wallachians". But one of the most marvellous inscriptions is on a stone at Gripsholm: "Tola had this stone raised to the memory of her son Harald, Ingvar's brother. Gallantly they sought gold afar, and sated the eagle in the East: they perished south in Arabia." The Swedes, although they doubtless failed to take part in the great trans-Atlantic voyages, probably did more various travelling than any of the other Norsemen.

2 : *Sigtuna*

ABOUT HALF-WAY BETWEEN Upsala and Stockholm the lake steamers put in at Sigtuna, now with only nine hundred inhabitants the second smallest town in the country. A single street and half-a-dozen alleys of tiny buildings, a diminutive square with an almost myopic town-hall; and here and there ruins crumbling among orchards and shade-trees; lilacs, horse-chestnuts and rose-gardens—that is the Sigtuna of to-day. And yet here was once the finest city on the Swedish mainland.

Reputed at one time to have been founded by Odin, Sigtuna actually came into being about the end of the Viking Age as a successor of Birka (Björkö), the great Viking trading centre on the south of the Mälar which was then on the wane. For two centuries it flourished till in 1187 it was plundered and burned by the Esthonians who must indeed have had some courage to sail so far inland: an opera called *The Vikings* inspired by the story of the siege has been composed by a modern Esthonian, Edvard Aav. It was also an important early missionary centre only twenty miles from the heathen temple of Old Upsala. St. Olof's, one of the first stone churches in the country, was erected here in the eleventh century. A cruciform church with a central tower, it is, like a few other churches in the neighbourhood, of a characteristically English-Norman type of architecture. English missionaries were at that time working in

Background to Sweden

Sweden: King Olof Skötkonung, who founded the town, was actually baptized by one, and introduced into Sigtuna some English mintners who minted some of the earliest Swedish coins to be used. Others think that certain Scandinavians, returning home in Edward the Confessor's reign when Norman influence became very strong, or after the Battle of Hastings, and bringing with them a knowledge of the latest styles of architecture, were directly responsible for the form of these churches. There are, also, however, certain elements in St. Olof's—the basilica which was capped by a cupola and possibly the two round windows—that were derived from the East, from Armenia and Georgia, and evidently introduced through Russia with which Sweden had very close ties, especially in that century: Jaroslav, for instance, who had won the Earldom of Novgorod with the aid of Swedish soldiers, was a son-in-law of Olof Skötkonung.

The diocese of Sigtuna was but short-lived, for it was transferred to Old Upsala in the early twelfth century. A hundred years later the Dominicans established here their first monastery in Sweden. Their abbey church of St. Maria, one of the earliest brick churches in the country—a long rectangular building, unrelieved by tower or spire, but with pinnacles of a magnificent eastern façade—remains in its partly restored condition a specially fine example of the Baltic architecture of the period.

But Sigtuna does more than dream of a glorious past. Behind, on the wooded slopes overlooking the warm sunny bay, are the institutions that prove her alive to-day. One, perpetuating her religious traditions, is the Sigtuna Foundation, a non-denominational centre for evangelical educational work, and connected with it a *folk-högskola* or people's high school. There are also two of the four Swedish schools which are modelled on the lines of a small English public school—expensive and exclusive places but evidently useful in their way, one of them (which I was shown over) with a large indoor swimming-bath, gymnasium-tennis court, and attractive houses (ranging in style from manorial to functionalistic) scattered among the pinewoods. Here, then, is the modern Sigtuna standing youthful and vigorous above the old ruins, but not entirely forgetful of her ancient traditions and connections.

3: *Some Uppland Churches*

JUST AS ANCIENT Greek sculpture is to-day very rarely visualized as painted in colours, so in most countries we have almost forgotten to imagine our Gothic churches in all their pristine splendour of painted mural decoration.

It is remarkable that in Sweden, which in the Middle Ages was a poor country with a population of less than a million, there should still exist about five hundred churches with painted interiors. These are mostly smaller churches of the Central provinces, particularly Uppland in which province alone there are more mediæval wall- and vault-paintings than in any other country except Italy. It would be natural then if foreigners visiting the older churches found this feature of primary interest. Instead of straining the eyesight (not to mention the imagination) over a few square inches of faded pigments adhering to the walls of the Westminster Chapter House or St. Alban's Abbey Church, or finding at best the restored work in Eton Chapel, or a mere medallion (though fine) like the Chichester Roundel, you can in Sweden just enter a church and let the whole mediæval atmosphere settle upon you and from all sides. (Technically, these paintings differ from the English tempera work of the same period in being a sort of cheap fresco executed in lime-colour on the stucco of the wall.)

I remember clearly that rather gloomy day I entered the humble-looking church of Dannemora, a little stone-and-brick building without either tower or spire. Such richness and colour I had never expected: blue, red and white, green, black and dun, combining in elaborate patterns, shot up the fluted pillars, followed the intricate ramifications of the ribs, and flowered like rockets between the quincuncial bosses of the vaults. For relief (relief for us, not for the original congre-

85

gations) were numerous grotesque devils disporting themselves upon the walls. Terrifying perhaps at one time, though evidently executed with humour and considerable relish. And have we really outgrown the need of personifying evil? A taloned prancing demon would probably be easier to tackle than some ill-defined -ism or other modern abstraction.

Although in other parts of the country there will be found paintings from the thirteenth and fourteenth centuries, it is to the fifteenth and early sixteenth that most of the work belongs. The development can be well traced in certain churches in Uppland; and, arming myself with a presentation copy of Professor Roosval's *Den Baltiska Nordens Kyrkor* and with a couple of other books, I set out on one or two occasions to investigate some of these exciting little buildings.

The series of paintings at Tensta illustrating episodes from the life of St. Bridget (Birgitta) are typical of the crude, narrative, unrealistic nature of the early period. In depicting a shipwreck, for instance, there is no attempt to delineate sea or land: an inverted ship hardly bigger than a man is merely placed beside some standing figures, while underneath it are shown (just as clearly) a couple of others having an unpleasant time in the non-existent water. In another painting the Devil is handing up a pair of boots on the end of a long pole, apparently to enable St. Bridget to get down to him from a tree in which she is rather improbably perched. And then she can be seen writing in a very uncomfortable attitude—evidently recording her *Confessions*, which became very popular on the Continent; there are other incidents I have forgotten; and finally her funeral in Rome with coffin, pallbearers and nuns following—all represented in a formalized manner without perspective and with little regard to the design as a whole. Such works, says Roosval, are notable for their decorative quality: they make good tapestry, but as paintings are poor.

The curves and bell-like contours of the men characteristic of this style begin to give way about 1450 to perpendicular lines. Vendel, which should be visited for several reasons, affords an excellent example, especially in a painting of St. George and the Dragon. There is more realism; many of the

86

figures for all their stiffness seem to have true dignity; while idealism is expressed both in their faces and movements.

One of the loveliest churches within and without is at Tierp. The slender corner-pinnacles capped with shingles, the single dentate line under the shingle roof to break the monotony of the long white walls, and the ash-trees (surely planted in a moment of inspiration) in the churchyard give a sense of delicacy all too rare in the exteriors of early Swedish churches. Decorated about 1470, Tierp Church represents the next development in style: a very masterly painting of a basilisk and some busts of the Apostles show how the stiffness has almost worn off, while the typical ornamentation is in the form of a chain with lily leaves.

Realism finds its completest expression in the work of Albertus Pictor, greatest of all the known masters, who decorated fifteen churches in Uppland and adjacent provinces. It is thought that his modernity may possibly be explained by direct Italian influence. His simplicity, firmness of line, and lack of irrelevant detail are mainly attributable to the woodcuts of a Netherlandish Bible which appeared about that time. Härkeberga is the best place to see a fine series of his historical figures, which are typically separated by narrow ornamental borders (Plate 12).

Finally, during the first quarter of the sixteenth century, there is a return to older tradition: realism is largely abandoned and single statuesque figures are often preferred; the general inspiration being strong nationalism, for Gustavus Vasa was at that time securing Sweden's decisive independence. In Värmdö Church there is a reredos from this period with a painting of St. Erik crossing the Baltic (c. 1154), also interesting as a reminder that some of the finest Swedish mediæval paintings are to be found in the churches of that province (Finland) which belonged to her for five-and-a-half centuries.

Just after this arrived the first wave of the Renaissance. Mural paintings not only ceased to be made; they were often covered up with whitewash. But fortunately there was no systematic and thorough destruction during their Reformation as there was in England under Henry VIII and then under

G

Background to Sweden

Oliver Cromwell: the frugal Gustavus Vasa seems to have been more concerned with appropriating bell-metal.

Pictorial art did not die: it became secular though entirely non-mediæval. Young Swedes were sent to learn weaving in Antwerp and returned to decorate the royal castles. It also became "peasant" art, for humble *bönder* continued to do imitative work in the form of woven tapestries, tapestries painted on linen, and finally on paper. And to-day in Dalarna and other parts I have seen many a cottage with its nineteenth century paper tapestries (illustrating Biblical stories) in which the traditions of the Middle Ages are still enshrined.

Italy can certainly boast of more resplendent and refined works; and it has been suggested that such buildings as the Sistine Chapel, the Vatican and the Medici Chapel in Florence were designed largely for the purpose of having splendid paintings set off to advantage. In Sweden on the other hand (as in England) painting was always the handmaid to architecture, a necessary but subservient accompaniment. As the commonest form of window in a Gothic country church seems to have resembled a deep-set Norman lancet, the importance of paintings for providing richness must indeed have been great. "Blond painting" is what one art-historian has called this Northern mural-work, whose tone he says was suggested by "the longing for light in the interior of churches during the long winter days". The general type of Swedish mediæval church is explained by Ragnar Josephson:

> It is the important supply of Swedish stone which has decided the method of building. The fabric of the country church is usually formed by huge thick stone walls of sufficient strength to bear the arches without reinforcing struts. The exterior of these churches has therefore generally been a single surface, and unlike their European contemporaries they have formed a massive fortress-like bulk, and in several cases have actually done service as fortresses. The walls were made high in order that their weight might resist the pressure of the arches, and also in order to give the church a monumental appearance, and were crowned by high roofs. This extreme simplicity of

architecture is undoubtedly due to the climate, as too much detail in profile and silhouette cannot withstand the winter snow and the heavy autumn rains of the North. The low arched interiors of most country churches appear to be constructed with regard to easier heating during the winter.

It can be imagined, then, how important—almost necessary—are these wall- and vault-paintings in such a building.

Another significant feature due to the high latitude is that Swedish churches, contrary to general European practice, were built facing towards the sun—with what Roosval has called the "southward-turned façade": the south front is generally the principal one with large windows and richly decorated porticos, and the churchyard was generally laid out on this side to form an enclosed approach to the building.

> Their churches are built of timber, and the towers of their churches for the most part are covered with shingle boordes. At the doores of their churches they usually built some entrance or porch as we doe, and in their churchyardes they erect a certain house of wood wherein they set their bels. . . .

These words, from Richard Chancellor's account of Moscovie in 1553, may well serve for many of the Baltic and East European lands during the Middle Ages and the Renaissance, and for even parts of those countries to-day. Of the timber churches of Scandinavia I shall speak later. Even more numerous—for they are found in association with brick and stone as well as timber churches—are the "houses of wood wherein they set their bels". Detached belfries, still found in parts of Finland, Norway, Poland and other countries in Eastern Europe, are quite common in Sweden, especially in Svealand, though they become rarer south of the great lakes and fade out altogether in the former Danish provinces.

Since a Swedish village is generally an aggregation of wide-spaced farms, one of the best ways of locating it is to look out for the belfry, which for obvious reasons will be built on an eminence if there should be one. Then, if you are looking for the church, a further exploration may be necessary, for the distance between them may be considerable—anything up to a mile.

Nor need there be the slightest architectural affinity between a church and its belfry which may have been built at different periods, in different materials and in completely different styles, as for example at Vendel (Plates 13 and 15). So various are the types of belfry that I doubt if there is any simple key to their forms. They are all modern, the earlier ones being shingled and usually brown or black from creosote or tar, the later ones (their building was forbidden by law in 1770) mainly in clapboarding of red and white or other colour schemes. The architects, it would appear, had in most cases a fairly free hand, and the results, ranging from glorified grandfather clocks to galleried structures with exquisitely tapering spires, are nearly all worth seeing.

In looking at the brick churches, whether ancient or modern, I was particularly struck by the interesting use of this material whose special nature the northern architects seem to have realized, both in regard to general structural design and for purposes of ornamentation. There are two distinct zones in the Baltic where brick was the main mediaeval material for large or important buildings: the northern one comprising Finland and Mälardalen (Uppland and other districts around the Mälar); the southern one embracing Denmark, the southern-most part of present-day Sweden, north Germany, and the eastern Baltic northwards to Esthonia. Four of the seven mediaeval cathedrals of Sweden, for instance, belong to the northern brick belt (Upsala, Västerås, Strängnäs, Åbo or Turku in Finland), as well as Stockholm's Storkyrkan, the oldest church in the capital, where the kings of Sweden have been crowned during the last two centuries. The stepped gables in the old Hanseatic cities and Danish churches of the southern brick belt have long been admired, while modern buildings like Grundtvig's Church in Copenhagen appear to derive from the same style.

But the remarkable method of ornamentation by means of

recessed whitewashed patterns has apparently never been imitated outside the Baltic where it originated. Uppland has many excellent examples of this work, the most striking I have come across being the Church of St. Maria, Sigtuna (Plate 13). The same work is responsible for much of the charm of Holy Trinity, the oldest of Upsala's churches (Plate 14), where Erik IX (who had led the First Crusade to Finland with Bishop Henry) was at mass one day in 1160 when news arrived that a certain Danish prince had attacked the city. After calmly seeing the service through to the end, he went out and was killed in the ensuing skirmish, a well (according to legend) immediately springing up on the spot where he died. Though not actually canonized, he became the patron saint of Sweden during the Middle Ages. The Cathedral itself, in which his relics are still preserved, afforded before its unfortunate restoration in the last century another brilliant example of the pattern scheme. For although the main plan is French Gothic, the building was modified in conformity with Baltic brick-architecture, which (as old engravings show) was especially distinct in the towers which then possessed no spires. Its effect on large buildings can be seen in the cathedrals of Strängnäs and Västerås, and in various places on the south Baltic seaboard, such as Marienburg Schloss near Danzig, and New Brandenburg; while similar work is found in the Renaissance castle of Gripsholm. At Vendel, which is an example of Baltic Gothic at its very best, not only the Church but the gateways in the wall surrounding it are adorned in this manner (Plate 13).

In a country where forests are still abundant, and where a great deal of building in full-timber is still going on, one would hardly be surprised to find a continuous tradition in wooden architecture from pagan times down to the present day. But such is not the case: the numerous wooden churches still in use in many of the provinces and dating from the last two or three centuries (a good example is shown in Plate 50, taken in Västmanland) are all very different from the earliest Scandinavian churches.

Background to Sweden

In most countries wood was the original building material, but as forests were depleted other materials came into use, and although the outward effect of timbering or half-timbering was sometimes preserved for a while, the new materials were eventually used in forms adapted to their special natures, new styles were introduced from abroad, the early wooden structures perished and their forms were forgotten. Nowhere in Europe, outside Scandinavia, are any fully timbered mediæval churches known to survive. Nearly all these extant specimens are Norwegian: Borgund, Urnes, Torpe, etc.—astonishing buildings which seem to have survived destruction by man and the elements only by a miracle. But there are also a few remains in Sweden (Hemse in Gotland and St. Maria Minor in the then Danish town of Lund) sufficient to allow of reconstruction and showing that "a vaguely national method of building" this type of church was developed over here.

Only in recent years has there been any wide appreciation of these Scandinavian stave-churches, or as Strygowski prefers to call them "mast-churches". This art-historian, who amassed a great deal of information about timbered and half-timbered buildings in various parts of Europe and Asia, has been indefatigable in his efforts to interest his fellow professors in such forms of architecture: "The fallacy persists", he says, "that building in wood is a primitive peasant art: this prejudice is probably responsible for its neglect by those historians of art who consider the association of the words 'wood' and 'architecture' essentially absurd"; and again: "The reason for our neglecting our own northern monuments, regardless of their artistic worth, is the humanistic prepossession: the northern peoples are barbarians, and derive architecture and the graphic arts from the south, the fount of culture. This was accepted as an article of faith centuries ago, and has blinded us to the creative artistry of the North in early times."

The mast-churches are unique in form, differing both from the western "framework" or half-timbered churches (some of which survive in England and Germany) and from the various types of "blockwork" or fully timbered churches to be seen in Eastern Europe from Fenno-Scandia to the Carpathians. The foundations consist typically of four sleepers laid so as to enclose a square or rectangle, the ends crossing at the corners and projecting. On each point of intersection stands a mast, and between these are other masts, all of which form pillars quite separate from the outer walls. The interesting point is that the entire clerestory and roof is supported by the masts, not by the outer walls of staves (vertical beams cut in half and either fixed to sleepers or driven palisade-like into the ground) which were mere screens. Now, such architecture is unknown elsewhere (some portions of a restored stave-wall at Greenstead, Essex, being insufficient to provide evidence to the contrary). Where, then, did it orginate? It would be natural to suggest that it was indigenous, that it developed out of the temple and the hall of pagan times—a theory which evidence seems to support. These famous mast-churches, then, are the descendants of buildings even more famous in the past—the heathen Temple of Old Upsala and Hrothgar's "well-built hall", "the fair earth-dwelling" described in *Beowulf*. "The mast-churches", says Strygowski in *Early Church Art in Northern Europe*, "can only be derived from certain personal qualities of the North Sea peoples. They are not a copy of Christian types of other countries, but had their beginnings either, as I think, on the Scandinavian . . . or on the North Sea coast. They are an expression of the personality of the North Sea peoples at the times of the migrations of the Vikings. . . . The mast-church has an individuality of its own. It may not be the individuality of a simple person or a people, but it is at least that of the Teutonic area whose shipping is centred in the North Sea." He suggests, further, that these great seafaring peoples constructed their halls and temples in much the same way as they did their incomparable ships and that "Christianity coming to Norway in the Viking period itself turned to shipbuilding as a model for church architecture". Comparing the roofs of some of them with the Oseberg Viking ship, he finds exactly the same sort of carpentry in both: the roof is an inverted ship. In one church (now destroyed) where the building is concentrated round a single mast, just as some of the halls are known to have been, the parallel is especially close.

93

Background to Sweden

The ornament on the mast-churches, both Norwegian and Swedish, seems to have received as much attention as the buildings themselves. On the doorways and certain other parts superb carvings are found consisting of an intricately inwoven line scheme derived from the movement of animals' bodies— lions, dragons, and others that cannot be identified. The origin of this motif, found also on contemporary ships, runestones and tombs in many places in Scandinavia, is, however, uncertain.

Although Norway continued to build mast-churches from the eleventh century right into the sixteenth, thus producing in wood an ecclesiastical architecture derived from her pagan art quite uninfluenced by classical models, the Romanesque and Gothic architectures had been growing up alongside them in stone and entirely superseded them at the time of the Reformation. In Sweden a complete change from wood to brick and stone took place in the eleventh century, after which mast-churches ceased to be built. Throughout the Middle Ages timber was of course the ordinary material for domestic architecture and was also used for detached belfries; but when (probably in the Renaissance) it was revived for church building in the provinces, the older tradition was completely forgotten, and nothing resembling the mast-church of old was ever again to be built.

4 : *Roslagen*

THE COASTAL DISTRICTS of Uppland and Söderman-land, together with Stockholm's Skärgård, and the adjacent archipelagos, are still known to the Swedes by the name of Roslagen, literally "the Row-Law". For in early Viking times the district was divided into sections each of which had to supply a certain number of rowers for the longships used by the Svear on their great trans-Baltic expeditions. To the Esthonians these Swedes were known as *Rots*, to the Finns as *Ruotsi* (which is still their name for Sweden); while the Slavs came to speak of them as *Rus*. Masters in time of about half

94

of European Russia and founders of a Swedish dynasty that ruled there till as late as 1598, they thus unwittingly gave the country their name, and in later centuries Sweden was to have many a fierce encounter with the growing bear which she had once nursed and which by Napoleon's day she was forced to admit (by handing over her ancient province of Finland) had become altogether too strong for her.

It was in order to see the north of Roslagen, the coast of Uppland, that I arrived there with a friend from Upsala in early June. We first touched the sea at Östhammar, a tiny town with a shallow land-locked harbour around which were scattered the usual *sjöbodar* (of a different type, however, from those on the West Coast), pleasure-craft and *kallbadhus* jutting into the water. A quiet unsophisticated place without even a metalled road, it was except for the town hall built entirely of wood, white, fresh, with that atmosphere of almost clinical purity so typical of Swedish towns and which sometimes makes one want to stop to ask if real ordinary people do actually live in such places. One is prepared, nay expects, when travelling to find some towns and villages pleasing to the eye; one now and then discovers some that appeal also to the ear, or at least do not torment it; but how few within doors or without fail to offend the nose! Where outside Scandinavia will you find places making the threefold appeal?

We had decided to spend the night at Öregrund, another little fishing town, of about twelve hundred inhabitants, further out, quite popular among Stockholmers (who generally get there by coastal steamer), but little visited by tourists from abroad. The season not having begun, we found the place almost deserted, though in appearance probably at its best, with the avenues that drop down to the small bay in their freshest green, the lilacs that bulge over the palings of every garden and round off the street-corners smothered in flowers, the cow-parsley quivering in the rock-crevices down by the water, and swallows plunging about the treetops and filling the air with their sweet screams. Just such a place and evening as one knows one will always remember, though one cannot explain why and any verbal attempt to do so appears merely irrelevant. It was not that we did anything remarkable: I remember a *middag* which was perhaps rather more sumptuous than usual and which must have required perfectly conditioned physiques working in conjunction with minds utterly devoid of care to be digested as thoroughly as it was, and then we sat on the mole at the harbour-entrance opposite the straggly-wooded isle of Gräsö while my companion told me about the folklore of his province. It was not even due to anything exciting in the scene: the twilight, the particular tone of the water, the casual scented breezes, were all just restful. Things just were and that was enough: it was for me a perfect case of Keats's negative capability—a passivity so hard to achieve in the stimulating, invigorating north.

The following morning we found ourselves the only passengers on the southbound coastal steamer as it moved among islands on what might very well have been a lake. Both air and water were glum, and beside us the invariable ship-wave pushed off at forty-five degrees emphasizing the utter calm of the surface. Compared with the west coast the east is sheltered and tame: every islet and promontory is wooded, bare rock being found only in the outermost fringes. The water, slaty and lustreless in appearance, is fresh enough for making a lather with soap; while waves, though sometimes extremely high-spirited, are but an occasional phenomenon.

From time to time the steamer called at various obscure islands, mooring for a moment or two at what could be called "water-sidings": lonely little landing-stages at the end of a track where we would roll off a barrel of red-paint-powder and perhaps take on some sheep carcasses (which were hung up to drip in the middle of the deck) from a couple of fishermen-farmers whose cottages lay out of sight behind the woods, which everywhere extended to the edge of the water.

After steaming for two hours we came to Grisslehamn, a tiny fishing port at the northern extremity of Väddö, a long narrow island running parallel with the coast. By cycling down Väddö we had intended to have views of the sea on either side, for the island is at its broadest only a mile and a half. But alas! throughout the whole twenty-four miles we had but two glimpses of the sea, and then it was just like a river. We might have been in the middle of the country. Eventually, however, the road ended in the water. It was a gloomy evening, the air damp after several downpours and when we learned from the only house that we should have to wait two hours for the ferry, and then, wet and hungry as we were, cycle another fourteen miles for a meal, it seemed like the end of the world. Which is exactly the feeling one has in many places in Roslagen— Trosa, south of Stockholm, is actually nicknamed the World's End—there is a wistfulness and resignation about them very striking to visitors, though apparently the effect on the natives is the very reverse: the Rospiggor are a hearty zestful people, quite unlike the dull phlegmatic Upplanders of the interior. And all we saw at this remote spot was the mail-plane from Stockholm, a mere speck in the sky, flying out towards the Åland Islands and Finland.

That night we spent in Norrtälje, which with only four thousand inhabitants is yet the main town in Uppland's Roslagen, boasting several stone and brick buildings, granite-paved streets, and mudbaths. Lying in a hollow at the head of a long creek, it is something of a fishing centre. The fishing on this coast, it is interesting to note, is carried on in connection with farming, the proportion of professional fishermen (who live mostly in the Outer Skärgård) being quite small. The varieties of fish, however, are remarkable: there is above all the *strömming* or Baltic herring, on which the Svear mainly subsisted, and which treated in various ways is still one of the more important articles in the Swedish diet; and in addition to a considerable assortment of saltwater fish three-quarters of the Swedish freshwater species are found in the Baltic.

In the morning our ways parted, my companion having to hurry off for a date with his fiancée. Proceeding alone in a leisurely fashion, I followed tortuous roads in a vaguely general-ized direction southwards. The land in these parts is still rising steadily out of the sea: many of the rocky hills were but islets in Viking times, as place-names in "-ö" and "-*holm*" serve to remind one; and the soil hereabouts is often sour from the recency of its emergence. Every road was banked with a

97

smother of cow-parsley; in one place they had already made the first hay—at least a fortnight early; but of song-birds, rare in such latitudes, there were none.

I stopped at the ancient Castle of Penningby, built in the fifteenth century by the great Protector Sten Sture the Elder, soon after his famous defeat of the Danes of Brunkeberg and later owned by the son of Lennart Tortensson, most distinguished of all the generals of Gustavus Adolphus. In plan it is a typical fortress of mediæval Sweden—a severe simple cube of rough-hewn stone—with a couple of corner-towers added at a later period. An atmosphere of great age hangs about the place: enormous deciduous trees shut out the sun on every side, the laminated wash is scaling off from the tough stone walls, and even the keeper is suitably bent and hoary. A friendly old man, he seemed to be much at home in the shadowy basements: in the dungeons, cellars and old kitchens, especially at the well in one of the towers where he keeps a rod and line with a stone at the end to prove that the water is eight metres deep. It was hardly surprising to find in one of the cellars a very long dug-out canoe, reputed to be two thousand years old, which had been discovered in the ground nearby. Accompanying us on a round of the Castle were two perfect examples of the unintelligent tourist, a blank-faced couple who asked all sorts of vague questions about the bric-à-brac in various rooms, stroked a small metal planetarium with apparently no thought or emotion whatever, and were intensely interested in the worst Baroque painting ever executed full of hideous cherubs with stomachs revoltingly distended. I admired the old boy's patience. We waved a hearty farewell.

Further south I came to the wooden church of Roslags-Kulla, built in the time of Charles XII, a beautiful cruciform building with red-brown shingles, a central tower and detached belfry in the same style. Timber churches, except the oldest, are nearly always more interesting outside than in. Which is fortunate, for a Swedish church is generally locked, and much time is often wasted in hunting up the warden or the vicar.

I arrived in Stockholm the same afternoon, having taken a train for the last fifteen miles, which are partly suburbanized though quite pleasant, there being numerous woods and fields to within a mile of the city proper. That, and some sailing in the Skärgård, is all I have seen of Roslagen. And though remaining loyal to the West Coast I shall certainly endeavour to see some more. Historically, Roslagen has been to the Swedish Vikings what the fjords were to the Norwegian; while in later times many a great Swede has emerged from this region: St. Birgitta, who, though better known in connection with other provinces, was born at Finsta near Norrtälje; Gustavus Vasa at Lindholm; and Axel Oxenstjerna at Fönö. During the past century numerous writers and artists have exploited it in their works: it is the setting of Strindberg's exquisite novel *Hemsöborna* (a book still waiting to be translated); of very nordic nocturnes by that powerful royal painter Prince Eugné; of morning and evening studies by Sjöberg and Liljefors, Richard Bergh and Eugén Jansson. But above all one remembers the exuberant Albert Engström (now living at Grisslehamn) whose stories, drawings, and character sketches of Rospiggor are as masterly as they are popular.

5 : *Örbyhus—and a Lengthy Digression*

Him Nature looked askance at; stars
Threatened the rich diversity of his being.

IN SWEDEN THERE seem to be almost as many castles in which Erik XIV was imprisoned as in England there are beds slept in by Queen Elizabeth. But unlike Wordsworth, who appears to have died in at least three different beds, Erik with admirable self-restraint died in only one castle—at Örbyhus in the north of Uppland. A large building, half a mediæval stone fortress and half an attractive country residence built by a wealthy noble in the seventeenth century, it is one of the less visited of the castles.

Who was this King, Erik XIV, and why was he imprisoned? Born in the 1530's and the eldest son of Gustavus Vasa, Erik lived to be the second of the Vasa kings. Like most of the princes of that remarkable dynasty, including Gustavus Adolphus and Charles XI, his horoscope cast at birth showed all the signs of a violent death. Far more disconcerting were the signs he showed as he grew up of a violent life. Brilliant, cultured, handsome and with great personal charm, Erik was in many ways among the most polished of Renaissance princes. His father, always a difficult master to please, had at first high hopes of his heir and began to consult him on affairs of state. Every day, however, his vanity and frivolity became more and more intolerable to the serious-minded creator of modern Sweden who began to have deep misgivings lest all his hard-won labour should eventually be undone. The licentiousness of Erik's court during his early twenties was notorious; "In his sport", says one historian, "it was no uncommon thing to see eyes dashed out and arms and legs lopped off, which only served to provoke his laughter"; while his chosen companion was a base-born unscrupulous man whom Gustavus had dismissed from office and who seems to have brought out all that was worst in the son, a man whose only good points were an undeniable competence in practical affairs and a lifelong attachment to his master.

Even before his succession Erik had decided that for a match with his glittering and handsome self no one was more appropriate than the Queen of England. Probably the most persistent of all Elizabeth's suitors, he first sent his brother, Duke John, at the head of a very costly embassy (the portrait he sent, discovered some years ago in England, was returned as a donation and now hangs in the Castle of Gripsholm); and then, no whit deterred by what amounted to polite rejections, he decided to go himself: he would take her in disguise or captivate her by the most elaborate display of princely magnificence. When about to embark his father suddenly died. After the funeral and a ruinously ostentatious coronation, he turned his attention to Mary, Queen of Scots, who in the meantime had become the favourite mark for the royal suitors of Europe. Without awaiting the outcome he simultaneously wooed the daughter of Philip of Hesse; still later a princess of Lorraine. Finally, his indiscriminate advances having made him a ridiculous figure throughout much of Europe, he took for his queen the serving-maid of a court entertainer, Karin Månsdotter, one of his mistresses.

This, of course, incensed the nobility with whom all along he had been on very bad terms. Morbidly suspicious, Erik lived under the delusion that the whole of the higher nobility, including his brothers, were plotting his downfall, and that the ill-success of his foreign marriage schemes was due to their desire to see him remain without an heir. The ancient and very distinguished family of Sture, nearly allied to the Vasas, was especially marked out for his attacks. Nils Sture, a promising and honourable young man, was suddenly arrested as a traitor, brought before a sort of Star Chamber, given a mock trial, and publicly maltreated in a most shameful manner. Then, noticing the reaction of the nobles, Erik tried to make amends by sending him abroad as his envoy to the Princess of Lorraine. On his return with a comparatively favourable answer, he was immediately arrested along with his father, brother and other innocent noblemen on a charge of conspiracy and imprisoned in Upsala Castle. A few days later Erik, in a repentant mood, secretly went into the father's cell to implore forgiveness for his unwarrantable behaviour. The two families were apparently reconciled, and he went out for a stroll by the river.

But an hour later he hurried past the guards in an excited condition, rushed into Nils's cell, stabbed him with a dagger, and gave orders that the rest of the prisoners should be immediately killed in private. Escaping to the woods, the mad king wandered for several days in disguise over the plains of Uppland till eventually he was recognized. Repentance during his lucid intervals, apologies, pardons, amnesties, compensations—all were useless after the terrible Sture murders: the King was a public danger. In the following year (1568) he was deposed.

For nine years he was kept a prisoner and moved around from castle to castle. At first his wife and his children were allowed to visit him, and only Karin, the gentle and beautiful woman who would sing to him for hours, could soothe his fiery tempestuous mind. But in time even that was forbidden. His tortures, which grew increasingly severe, were often as barbarous as those of our Edward II, for many of his wardens were embittered men whom (often without cause) he had previously ill-treated. No wonder his sane periods were spent in writing letters to his brother, begging to be banished for ever; or, when ink was forbidden him, in scrawling out pathetic self-defences with the aid of coalwater in the margins of books. Finally Erik was removed to Örbyhus, where, one winter's day at the age of forty-four, he was found dead—poisoned by a callous governor.

A remarkably tragic figure; and on first hearing his story I could not help thinking how it would have appealed to many an Elizabethan dramatist. What contrasts they could have emphasized between this brilliantly cultured prince and the crazy and brutal murderer! With what effect would they had employed the humble and devoted Karin, what marvellous songs put into her mouth! How popular among the sensation-craving audiences of the Globe would have been this other crazy prince of Scandinavia with his sudden fits of frenzy, now jabbing a red-hot fire-prong into his secretary for a word against his favourite, now murdering his old tutor for no particular reason; so suspicious that every whisper or smile was interpreted as a gesture of ridicule, and afraid of allowing his pages to dress in pure white in case they should ingratiate themselves with ladies of the court. It is hardly surprising to find that attempts have been made to identify Erik with Hamlet. But the Elizabethans, alas, knew little of their Queen's Swedish suitor; and it was left for Strindberg (himself inordinately suspicious and frequently unbalanced) to resuscitate him in drama. Whatever their merits as history, his plays of *Erik XIV* and *Gustavus Vasa* (in which that great actor, Gösta Ekman, who died in 1938, so loved taking the part of Erik) are without question among the finest historical plays ever written, and will I am convinced receive their due as an interest in Northern history becomes disseminated.

It is certainly disappointing to find that Sweden's rise to political greatness more or less coincided with the decline in our drama. If only it had been twenty years earlier Engelbrekt, Sten Sture and several Vasas would probably be living to-day in the blank verse of Shakespeare and his contemporaries. But the Elizabethans knew little of Sweden or Swedish history, and even if they had wished to write on such themes would never have been able to lay their hands on the necessary source-material. It was from hunting up what has been written on the relations between England and Sweden at that period that I went on to trace them out for earlier and later times. Some of the results, culled from a variety of sources, I have thought it worth while giving below in chronological order.

I have mentioned elsewhere the Swedish element in the greatest of our early poems now extant (pages 232-333 and 285-286); and alluded to the fact, far less generally known, that Swedes as well as Danes and Norwegians took part in the Viking raids on Britain, although I have never seen it suggested that any actually settled over there. In the reign of Ethelred the Unready, for instance, when Olaf Tryggvason arrived in the Thames with ninety-three vessels, penetrated East Anglia, won a crushing victory at the Battle of Maldon (991)—a victory vividly described in an old English poem of that name —and received a large bribe to make peace, his chief colleague was a Swede called Guthmund Stegitansson: in fact so many Swedes took part in this raid that one historian of Denmark speaks as if the whole company were predominantly Swedish. Then about twenty-five years later in the last campaign of Canute the Great there were as many Swedes as Danes; they are mentioned with Götar and Danes in the army that captured York. Connections between the Scandinavian countries were very close at this time—Canute is said to have considered the idea of a Union—and it is difficult to sort out the exact role played by each country. Not only were the languages of the different States far closer than they are to-day (indeed they were closely connected dialects rather than separate languages), but the difference between those and the language spoken in England was also very much smaller. "An Englishman", says the Danish philologist Jespersen, "would have no great difficulty in understanding a Viking, nay we have positive evidence that Norse people looked upon the English language as one with their own. On the other hand, Wulfstan speaks of the invaders as 'people who do not know your language', and in many cases indeed the words were already so dissimilar that they were easily distinguished." The Swedes, however, if they never settled in England, can hardly claim any credit for the profound Scandinavian influence on our language. Being mercenary troops, the first thing they got out of England was money. As far as Gotland is concerned, one writer (an American, H. Goddard Leach, in a study of Angevin Britain and Scandinavia) at any rate thinks most of its wealth was acquired through commerce:

> Of English and Irish coins from the eighth century until 1150 thirty thousand have been unearthed in Norway, Sweden and Denmark, and almost half of them were found on the island of Gotland. And the great mass of this wealth must have been accumulated in commerce, for Gotlanders do not appear in history as viking raiders. Their trade with England, to which they brought large quantities of fur and wax, continued throughout the Middle Ages, even after Low German merchants in the thirteenth century obtained a footing in Gotland, and Visby became a member of the Hansa League. The trade between England and Gotland does not appear to have left any trace in literature. . . .

I have spoken elsewhere about the English missionary work in Sweden in the eleventh century (pages 241-244), about the English influence on certain churches and on coins; and it may be possible to track various indirect influences exerted through Norway a bit later. In the documents and accounts of voyages collected by Hakluyt Sweden is barely mentioned till the fifteenth century: there are the famous accounts of their voyages by the Norseman Ohthere and the Dane Wulfstan as reported to King Alfred; and we learn that Canute the Great, after the death of King Edmund Ironside in 1016, tried to get rid of the latter's sons by sending them "unto the King of

Sweden to be slaine, who, albeit there was a league between them, would in no case condescend unto Canutus his bloody request, but sent them unto Salomon the King of Hungarie to be nourished and preserved alive"; and later on we hear of a number of charters. "In the English Rolls", says Goddard Leach, "we have but one or two records of Swedish merchants in the twelfth century. In 1231 a relative of the King of Sweden visited England and gave Henry III a present of hawks and hares. In 1255 Earl Birger, regent of Sweden" (whom legend says was the founder of Stockholm), "sent an embassy of Dominican Guards to King Henry to make a treaty of peace, and Henry replied by sending a delegation of the same order to 'bind a perpetual chain of peace between us and you and the King of Sweden your son'." We also hear of an English colony in Linköping in the Middle Ages, to whom we can possibly attribute the English influence discernible in some early Swedish mural paintings.

From the end of the eleventh century till Elizabethan times there was little intercourse, apart from a certain trade, between England and Sweden. In those days Sweden was far too insignificant politically to be of much interest outside the Baltic, although in the early years of the Kalmar Union when the three Northern nations, united under a single sovereign, looked as if they might become dangerously powerful, our Henry IV took care to secure their friendship by marrying his daughter Philippa to Erik of Pomerania, King of Norway, Sweden and Denmark, at Lund in the year 1406. She, the only English queen of Sweden, was much beloved of her subjects, and on her death was buried at Vadstena. But nothing came of the alliance, and since Sweden eventually broke away from the Union, our relations with Denmark-Norway remained far closer: to the former, who controlled the entrances to the Baltic, every ship passing through the Sound or the Belts had to pay dues, while our trade with Iceland had at one time to be stopped because some of our sailors had maltreated the inhabitants. The Danish kings too, being slow to forget how their predecessors had ruled in England, more than once thought of following in their footsteps. Scotland, especially, had many

Background to Sweden

ties with Denmark-Norway, which as late as the 1460's was complaining that she had neglected for several years to pay the quit-rent which she had promised in 1266 to Norway for the surrender of the Hebrides and the Isle of Man. When just about that time James III of Scotland married the daughter of the Danish king, the debt was cancelled and the Orkneys and the Shetlands were mortgaged as part of the dowry; but the money could not be found, so the islands became Scottish. In 1520, the year before Gustavus Vasa finally secured Swedish independence, we find Scots fighting in the Danish army that invaded Sweden from the west, penetrated to the capital and for the last time in history enabled a Danish sovereign to become King of Sweden as well.

We have already seen how John, one of Gustavus Vasa's sons, came to England to sue for the hand of Queen Elizabeth on behalf of his brother Erik. That, in 1558, was about the first event to bring the name of Sweden before the average Englishman—or rather, of Swethland, Sweveland, Sweedland, Suethia or Suecia, as it was indifferently called well into the seventeenth century. The second event was the visit in 1565-6 paid by their sister, Princess Cecilia, who having heard so much about Elizabeth and her Court from her brother John, was consumed with the desire to see them for herself. But her visit ended rather ingloriously, for the Princess ran up enormous bills in England, was sued for debt and when her position became intolerable beat an undignified retreat, much embittered by her experiences. Only one of her ladies-in-waiting stayed behind—to marry the Marquess of Northampton. Says E. M. Seaton, writing of the Englishman's knowledge of Sweden in the late sixteenth century:

> The ordinary man would remember the trade in iron and copper; the use of hot stoves, the excuse for many unsavoury jests; as a devoted subject of Elizabeth he would recall how "The mighty King of Sweden sewd to wedde her for his Queene"; and the learned would mention Olaus Magnus whose *Historia de Gentibus Septentrionalibus* was winning recognition as a standard work.

Apart from an unexciting, factual *Description of Swedland* by one

George North in 1561, translated from various Latin books on the North, there was nothing to be read in English during that century. But the learned had, and still have, in the large Latin work of Olaus Magnus, full of intriguing woodcuts, one of the most remarkable books of its kind ever produced. He and his brother Johannes, the last Catholic archbishops of Upsala, had escaped to Italy at the Reformation where they both wrote books on the North, and Olaus made what was probably the first map of Scandinavia showing much accuracy (see Plate 16). It is instructive to note that till then the only available map was one made by Ptolemy fourteen hundred years beforehand, and slavishly copied time and again till about 1550, showing Scandia as an island, just as it had been described by Pliny the Younger, the first writer to mention it, in the first century A.D.! The woodcuts, however, in Olaus Magnus, some of which I reproduce, were made neither by him nor—judging from the palmlike trees, the unlikely architecture, and the impossible skis—by anyone who had ever been to Scandinavia.

Other recorded contacts with Sweden are few before the seventeenth century: we hear of some English actors visiting the country, of Swedish merchant ships in the Thames, and Sir Humphrey Gilbert refers to Swedland and Russia as "countries very populous" where "the rigor of cold is dispensed with by the commoditie of stoves, warme clothing, meats and drinks". We hear that "by reason of the warres of Swethland" in the 1550's the English were unable to carry on their trade with the Muscovites and Liefland (Livonia), so resorted to the Northern route round North Cape. References become increasingly numerous about the turn of the century—"The bloody warres of Swethland" fought against the Hanseatic cities, Denmark-Norway, Russia, the small Baltic States (which had belonged to the Knights of the Sword) and Poland—all before the appearance of Gustavus Adolphus. The Polish wars, probably the most complicated of all these, appear to have been the first actually to involve any English interests. We first hear of twenty-eight English ships being hired from merchants resident in Poland (1598); and then ten years later of another three English ships, which found themselves in a war area, being pressed into the service of Poland together with their masters and crews. The information comes in the form of a testimonial from the Polish Commander which appears in a preface to a very rare book, *The Warres of Swethland and Poland*, 1609, by Anthony Nixon, being an account of "the original ground of these present warres of Swethen" from the time of Gustavus Vasa, enlivened by some crude woodcuts depicting the human butchery that they involved. The scene is Riga in Livonia, over which state Sweden and Poland happened to be wrangling at the time; and the Polish Commissioner, thinking these three English captains might be of help, "held them there, and employed them in the service of Warre for the most excellent King of Poland my most gracious Lord, and they undertook to defend the Dunn, wherein they did behave themselves very faithfully, manfully and valiantly, so that the Swedish Commander was often by them driven back again to his great loss and shame; and likewise he was often assaulted by them, so that he lost not only his strength of men and his courage but also lost some shippes with many men and goods which the said Englishmen with a memorable courage, and to the notable glory of the English Nation, did set on fire and burne". But the following year we hear of a far greater company fighting—voluntarily—on the opposite side, mostly on Russian soil. The campaign is too complicated to explain in detail: suffice it that the Swedes, having undertaken to support the Czar against the Poles who had invaded Russia, advanced into the country with an army consisting partly of foreign mercenaries, captured Novgorod and Moscow, and then when a Polish army appeared were deserted by the Czar and obliged to return; with the result that a Pole secured the Czardom, and Russia henceforth was the enemy not the ally of Sweden. The account of some of his experiences by one of the English mercenaries is taken from Purchas:

> About a fortnight before Midsummer, which was A. 1609, a companie of Voluntaries to the number of a thousand and two hundred soldiers, were at severall times shipped from England to passe into Sweden, to aide the King of that Countrie in his warres against the King of

Poland. To which aid divers other Nations did likewise
resort, as French, high Dutch, &c. Of the English companies that went thither, the first was commanded by one
Calvine, a Scot; who by appointment was made Lieu-
tenant Colenell, and chiefe of the other Captaines over the
footmen.

The narrator, who was put in a Swedish ship, describes how
they landed for victualling in Jutland, where they had extremely
unpleasant experiences, some of their party being murdered or
tortured; how they managed to reach Elsinore, take a ship and
eventually arrive in Stockholm. "Upon our arrivall at Stock-
holme wee met with the rest that had gone before us, and with
divers others of our Countrimen that came out of the Low-
Countries." For want of money they very nearly starved, had
to beg and even fight for food, but one day stopped the King
when he was out riding and he sent them some money. None
of it reached the soldiers, for the captains sent most of it home
to their wives. Setting out again with only one month's provisions they were for some unstated reason

> forced to lye 8 weekes at sea: in all which time we had
> nothing but pickled Herrings and salt Stremlings with
> some small quantitie of hard dryed meates: by which ill
> dyet many of our men fell sicke and dyed.
>
> At the last it pleased God to send us to a place called
> Ulfrasound in Fynland, where we landed (Fynland being
> subject to the King of Sweveland). From Ulfrasound we
> were to goe to Weyborough [that is, Viborg or Viipuri]
> a chiefe towne in the Countrie of Fynland: where we no
> sooner arrived, but our soldiers ranne some one way, some
> another . . . being done only to seeke foode so great was
> their hunger.

He describes how they marched from November to Whitsuntide ill-clad and with little food, how many starved to death,
and "some lost their fingers, some their toes, some their noses,
many their lives: insomuch that when wee all met at Wey-
borough" six hundred had perished out of two thousand: "the
miseries and misfortunes which wee endured upon the borders
of Fynland were almost insufferable." They then marched

109

into Russia, "where wee found both plenty of corne and cattle; onely the people of the Countrey ranne away, leaving all their goods behinde them, but so cunningly hidden, that the best pollicie of ours could hardly find them out." How they marched on Novgorod and Moscow, how seven hundred Poles fled before them, and other events are too confusingly and ponderously described to warrant quotation; and the whole compaign was too abortive to give these mercenaries a real foretaste of what fighting in Swedish armies was to mean a bit later.

When Gustavus Adolphus succeeded to the throne in 1611, a Danish war which he attempted to end broke out afresh; and Christian IV, his adversary, being a brother-in-law of our James I, did some of his recruiting in Britain. So did Gustavus, who, in attempting to raise a revolt against the Danes in Norway, arranged for a Dutch-Scottish invasion of the country in that year. But the Norwegians would have none of it: three hundred of the Scots were captured by them and put to death; and the only result of this obscure little "invasion" was that it helped to rouse the dormant patriotism of the Norwegians. One of the two Scottish corps had been raised by James Spence of Wormiston, who later on became a Swedish baron and undertook much valuable diplomatic work for his adopted country. Whether or not the British mercenaries secured by the Danes actually saw much service in Scandinavia I have failed to discover: the war was over in a year, Englishmen incidentally serving as arbitrators at the peace treaty. Denmark, though still the strongest state in the North, had now reached the peak of her political position; henceforth she steadily declined; while Sweden grew stronger and stronger under her forceful king whose name in the next few years was beginning to be heard of abroad.

The Thirty Years' War had already broken out. Gustavus Adolphus, seeing the alarming tide of the counter-Reformation rolling northwards, was busy winding up wars with Russia and Poland and consolidating his position in the Baltic. Our James I was equally busy diplomatically, attempting to enlist any likely State in the cause of the Bohemian Protestants.

Ambassadors from him arrived in Stockholm and Copenhagen in 1624. Both the Swedish and the Danish kings submitted plans: the former, foreseeing the magnitude of the undertaking, demanded 17,000 men to be paid for out of the English exchequer and four months' pay in advance; Christian, shortsighted and impatient, agreed to intervene for far less, as long as he were given command. So James, being hard-up, promised to support the latter with thirty thousand pounds a month; Denmark entered the war; things went badly with her; the English money was not forthcoming; and in a year or two she was defeated. What with this, and the defeats of Mansfeld, also in the nominal pay of England—a continental adventurer who, appearing in London as the "Protestant hero", had enlisted 12,000 Englishmen in his service, most of whom were through lack of payment very soon unfit to bear arms—what with these, one could hardly have expected much further help from Great Britain (or a promise of it) when eventually Sweden was ready to intervene in the German war. There was certainly no alliance except with the invested city of Stralsund; but in time there were numerous Britons fighting under the Royal Goth. In the very episode which determined Sweden's entry into the War—in the relief of Stralsund in 1628—we find 2,000 Scottish troops (under Major Monroe and Lord Spynie) and another Scot, Colonel Alexander Leslie, in command of the Swedish troops. "Three Scottish and two English regiments at first seem to have followed the King of Sweden",says C. R. L. Fletcher in his biography, which would mean not less than 7,500 men and probably many more. Among these was the Colonel Robert Monroe on which Scott modelled his Captain Dalgetty in *The Legend of Montrose,* and whose diary of *His Expedition with the Worthy Scots' Regiment called Mackey's Regiment, levied in August* 1626 . . . *first under the Magnanimous King of Denmark* . . . *and afterwards under the Invincible King of Sweden during his Majestie's Lifetime* is one of the most interesting inside accounts of the War in any language. Then in 1631 the Marquis of Hamilton recruited another 7,000 (only a thousand being Scots) who were ready to leave in July, three months before the great Battle of Breitenfeld. According to Gardiner:

Background to Sweden

The Lords Lieutenants of the Counties were ordered to give every assistance in filling his ranks, pressing only excepted. There were always vagabonds and rogues enough in England, of whom the official people were anxious to be rid, and Hamilton, as Mansfeld had done before him, at last gathered round him a force of which the numbers were more imposing than the quality.

Partly, I suppose, because so many of the officers were Scots, and partly because the Scots seem to have been better soldiers, we hear more about them than about the Englishmen who served—Hamiltons, Monro(e)s, Sinclairs, Fleetwood, Crawford, Douglas, Ruthven, Ramsay, Barclay, Chalmers are the names that were most familiar—; although there appears to be no evidence suggesting that Scots were actually more numerous, except at first. Hamilton's force, at any rate, was predominantly English: and this is what Ranke, the German historian, has to say of it:

> The English have always affirmed that the arrival of Hamilton with a considerable body of troops contributed materially to the decided successes of this year of the war. And with good reason: for they gave the Protestant princes greater confidence in their cause and made the Emperor anxious for his territory of Bohemia.

So astounding were the exploits of the Lion of the North, so close the sympathy of England for his cause, that in the absence of any contemporary Englishman of sufficiently stirring character the Swedish King became the greatest popular hero in the country. No praise could be too extravagant; and men who a few years beforehand had perhaps never heard of Swedes were now talking about them half the day. In 1632 the popular feeling had become so strong that Charles I had to forbid the gazettes for a while to print any further news of the Swedish successes. And then came Lützen: England may almost be said to have been in mourning; at any rate the brilliance of the victory was obscured by grief for the death of the victor—a death lamented by innumerable writers from the humblest poet-journalists of the day to Henry King, Bishop of

Chichester. A good deal of our early journalism is concerned with the Swedish period of the Thirty Years' War: the "corantos" and tracts, and Sir Thomas Roe's *Swedish Intelligencer* which (with its sequels) appeared twelve times between 1632 and '39. Gustavus was long remembered in England: soldiers returning from Germany kept his memory alive and introduced his tactics into the Scottish and our Civil Wars. Thomas Dekker, one of the great Elizabethan dramatists, who lived into the '40's, actually wrote a play, *Gustavus King of Swethland* (possibly, however, about Gustavus Vasa), which was entered in the Stationers' Register at the Restoration, but is now unfortunately lost. And Daniel Defoe, born only in 1661, who among other things was a keen septentrionalist, later wrote his *Memoirs of a Cavalier*, ostensibly by one "who served in the armies of his Majesty the King of Sweden and afterwards in that of Charles I of England".

Sweden, which for about the first time since the Gothic migrations had profoundly affected the destinies of Europe, emerged from the Thirty Years' War as the most powerful and the most courted of the Protestant states. Her prestige was considerably greater than that of England, which weakened by civil war had come to play a comparatively minor rôle in European politics. But the two countries were nevertheless drawn together closer perhaps than they ever had been. In the 1650's, for instance, England and Sweden found it to their mutual advantage to array themselves against a Danish-Dutch coalition: Bulstrode Whitelocke negotiated with the Swedish Government an important trade agreement in 1654 which did much to facilitate the further step of political co-operation; and two years later another commercial treaty was signed. Most important of all was the Triple Alliance in 1667 between Sweden (then at the peak of her power), England, and Holland, against France (who however won over the former two in time). It is also curious to note that just before our Revolution it was rumoured that William of Orange was bringing over with him to England a force of Swedes—not to mention twenty thousand "anthropophagi Laplanders clad in bear skins, that never lay in bed in their lives"! In 1700, on the contrary, *we* were supporting the Swedes: an Anglo-Dutch fleet which was sent to the Baltic helped to keep open the Sound while the Swedes transported an army to Zeeland, thus enabling the young Charles XII to dictate a peace to Denmark (which country of course had started the war in her usual foolhardy fashion).

Popular interest continued to be centred in the sovereigns: the eccentric Christina attracted a good deal of attention in this country, favourable at first but after her embracing of Roman Catholicism mostly the reverse, though stories of her life in Italy still had a sensational value for Englishmen for many years after her death, and Dryden during the Restoration wrote a comedy, *Secret Love or the Maiden Queen*, of which she is the heroine. The exploits of her successor, on the contrary, Charles X (or as he was generally known abroad, Charles Gustavus), which were hardly less amazing than those of Gustavus Adolphus, created but little stir in England: this King, indeed, eclipsed by other Vasas, has never received anything like his due in this country. As for Charles XI, a ruler concerned mainly with internal affairs, he was of course even less heard of; but after the turn of the century his adventurous son had once again drawn all the eyes of Europe on a King of Sweden. This time England had a war of her own and in Marlborough a striking general; there was no rush to the Swedish colours as in the time of Gustavus Adolphus, although a few Scots appear to have gone; and few Englishmen were at first particularly interested in the cause of Charles XII (even if they thought he had one). In time, however, the fascination of the pure adventurer began to tell: he was on the lips of everyone; we do not have to read far in *The Tatler* or *The Spectator*, for instance, to find references to "The King of Sweden" or to "Bender"; and in 1715 Daniel Defoe published his *History of the Wars, Of His Present Majesty Charles XII*, eulogizing him in the preface as a hero who "might vye with the Cæsars and Alexander of Antient Story"; "He has done Actions that Posterity will have room to Fable upon, till they make his History Incredible, and turn it into Romance". There were, moreover, rumours that the Swedes had intrigues with the Jacobites and intended to support them—a suspicion that George I's hostility to Sweden (on account of territorial disputes in Germany) did nothing to allay; in 1715 there were in fact twelve battalions under a Scottish Major-General Hamilton waiting near Gothenburg in readiness to transport to Newcastle; and in 1717 the Swedes agreed to support the Jacobites with 12,000 men. The threat of a modern Scandinavian invasion almost became serious, though nothing actually came of it except that George ordered Gyllenborg and Görtz, the Swedish ministers in London and the Hague, to be arrested and their papers seized. Here again Defoe is thought to be the author of a couple of pamphlets that appeared relating to these events; he certainly published an *Account of the Life and Most Remarkable Actions of George Henry Baron de Goertz, Privy-Counsellor and Chief Minister of State, to the Late King of Sweden;* he produced an abridged version of his *History of the Wars*; and in 1720 a second edition of the last work with additional matter covering the final years of Charles and his death in Norway.

By this time one would expect the average Englishman to have been comparatively well informed about Sweden and her history; and so he was—better perhaps than at any period before or even since. Having been drawn together politically during the seventeenth century, the two countries not unnaturally exchanged many diplomats; and since the personnel of an Embassy sometimes numbered a hundred a good many Englishmen must thus have visited Sweden. No one at that time thought of travelling in such hyperboreal regions for pleasure; no heir in a well-to-do family ever thought of including Sweden on the grand tour of the Continent he would generally make to complete his education; nor did any but a handful (among whom was Colonel Robert Monro) of the British soldiers fighting for Gustavus actually pass through Sweden; so that these diplomats were about the only educated Britons to travel there, and upon their reports and impressions an Englishman's conception of the country was partly founded. One of these ambassadors, John Robinson, who later became Bishop of London, actually published in 1694 *An Account of Sweden*, one of the most exhaustive and best-informed books on the country (and also because of its tedious informative tone one of the most exhausting). It is very regrettable that Whitelocke's well-written and extremely readable *Journal of the Swedish Embassy*, 1653/4, was not printed before 1772, although it was probably handed round in manuscript. In 1669, however, there was published *A Relation of the Embassies from Charles II to Muscovie and the King of Sweden, performed by the Rt. Hon. the Earl of Carlisle in the years* 1663 *and* 1664, written up by one of the attendants, a Swiss, Guy Miege (not alas! by Andrew Marvell, who was acting as the Earl's secretary). If only because it concerns Sweden during the decade of her greatest political power, it is an account well worth quoting from:

> On the 8th of Sept. the Ambassador made his Entry [i.e. into Stockholm], where he received all possible expressions of an amity extraordinary. True it is, there was not that bravery and ceremony as at his entry to Moscow, but I dare affirm there was much more sincerity, frankness and decorum. And whereas in that the Moscovites made demonstration only of their grandeur and vanity, the Swedes in this made no other expression but of kindness and civility. Their artillery which is so dreadful in the wars was become here the grateful proclaimer of peace and affection, nothing being to be heard about the Town for an hour together but the noise of their cannon and great guns. . . .
>
> The buildings are most of stone, yet some also of wood. Of the first sort there are several very magnificent, and among them that of General Wrangel [who was in command of the army] and the Chancellor's. There are some parts of the town which being built off from the Island stand like parts of Venice upon hills, so that the sea flows under them. [As early as this then, Stockholm was "the Venice of the North".] The Palace [that is, the old Palace, burned down at the end of the century] hath nothing in it very remarkable, saving that it stands on the bank of the sea, and has a fair prospect of several ships that ride hard by and the King's men-of-war. But that which is most considerable in Stockholm is that in so cragged and

unpleasant a place the people should be so courteous and friendly and that amongst so many rocks and uninhabited islands we should find a court so civil and benign. In Moscow we had experience of the contrary. . . . Whereas here in a place that seems the very refuse of nature we found all manner of humanity and politeness. Besides the peculiar language of the country the nobility do with great industry addict themselves to the French, and indeed they speak it as freely as if it were their own. Their humour and manner of living has great affinity with the French also. . . . They are free and open-hearted and no less affectors of gallantry.

The writer has much to say of the "extraordinary pomp" with which they were treated by De la Gardie and other nobles; but had he arrived twenty years later such luxury among the aristocracy would hardly have been so noticeable: the King, whom he describes as a "very handsome" boy nine years of age, had by then become an absolute monarch whose main life-work was to rescue the country from complete domination by an oppressive aristocracy.

More interesting personally are some of the ambassadors that Sweden sent to England: Johan Skytte, the learned tutor of Gustavus Adolphus; Johan Oxenstierna, whose son, a nephew of the great Chancellor, received an honorary M.A. from Oxford in the year of Lützen (and was perhaps the first Swede to receive an English degree); Bonde, who complained of the employment of Milton on his papers: "it seemed strange to him there should be none but a blind man capable of putting a few articles into Latin"; Coyet, "the first known Scandinavian owner of Shakespeare's collected plays" (he bought a Second Folio in the 1650's); and several others.

In addition to the mass of topical and ephemeral literature occasioned by the Thirty Years' War and other events mentioned above, there was not unnaturally a fair supply of books relating to Swedish history—most of them translated from foreign languages, such as Hildebrandt's *Genealogie and Pedigree of the most illustrious and most mighty King of Sweden* from High Dutch in 1632, several editions of Vertot's *History of the Revolution*

in Sweden from the French later in the century, and von
Pufendorff's (all too) *Compleat History of Sweden* also from High
Dutch—not to mention the works, read by a few, that remained
untranslated. With such material available it was now possible
to exploit the past history of Sweden, in more imaginative
forms, and in the early eighteenth century two plays were
written on Gustavus Vasa (attempts which though belated
were in advance of any by Swedish dramatists): *The Revolution
of Sweden* (1706) by Catherine Cockburn; and Henry Brooke's
Gustavus Vasa, published in 1739, the performance of which was
unfortunately forbidden because of a fancied resemblance
between the villain and Sir Robert Walpole, then Prime
Minister. Nor should the works of scholars, probably the most
readable of these books to-day, be omitted. Olaus Magnus's
amazing repository of Northern lore from which, long before
its abridged translation in 1658, writers like Thomas Heywood,
Robert Burton and Thomas Fuller fished out numerous picturesque stories of Lapland magic, of Eric Windy-Cap the
ancient King of Sweden who "could command spirits, trouble
the air, and make the wind stand which way he would" by
virtue of an enchanted cap, of the musical ghost of Rupes Nova
in Finland, and so on; and Scheffer's *History of Lapland*, translated almost immediately after its appearance in Sweden.

Scholarship and art were perhaps after war the channels
through which the Swedish spirit began to trickle into England:
several Swedish scholars were elected Fellows of the Royal
Society in its early days, and several Swedish portrait painters
settled in England at the end of the century: Christian Richter,
Charles Boit, Hans Hysing, but most famous of all even to-day
Michael Dahl.

"The fame which has followed the Swedish arms throughout
the length and breadth of Europe has too often been won at
the expense of our individual happiness", said Gustavus III

during his speech at the opening of the Swedish Academy in
1784.

"It remains for us to achieve another and a greater triumph

—the triumph which waits upon polite literature and bookish arts, the triumph which defies time, and is indifferent to the precarious glory which vanishes with hardly won and lightly lost material conquests."

Yet, he continued, if a long peace is desirable or necessary it too often "develops a spiritual sluggishness . . . men are so constituted that only enthusiasm can inflame them to great deeds. . . . The emulation, the energy, excited by the cultivation of the arts and sciences are the only means in quiet times to nurse that fervour of mind which may be of such service to the commonwealth, and to fashion in the womb of peace those citizens capable of saving the realm when storms arise."

These victories of peace, no less (or perhaps rather less) renowned than war's, were first of all achieved in scientific fields, Linnæus who visited England in 1737 being about the first Swedish scientist to attract much attention over there. Both Scheele and Professor Bergman of Upsala, another great chemist, were heard of in England in the second half of the century: the former received an offer (which he refused) to go and settle there, and some of the latter's papers were published by the Scientific Society of London. Swedenborg, however, exerted his very strong influence solely as a mystic and religious leader during his years in London where the first of the New Jerusalem churches was built and where eventually he died. Literature, which flowered so late up here, was to have no influence on ours till the time of Strindberg; and the visual arts (except through Dahl and his group) not till the present century. Swedes, as everyone now knows, can teach us much about architecture, sculpture, interior decoration and commercial arts; they could possibly teach us something about painting as well.

As far as literary influence is concerned, the tide has been mostly in one direction. First, in the two decades just after Charles XII's (the Great Northern) War, that is, from about 1719, when the two countries were political allies—a period during which our Queen Anne prose-writers especially, and certain of our poets, left their imprint on Swedish literature. Though Fröding and other later poets were stimulated by English romantics, only Scott and Edmund Gosse among our septentrionalists down to this century (a considerable band that included Gray, Borrow, Mason, Southey, William Morris and William Taylor), seem to have been interested in Sweden. Shakespeare, who now exists in two excellent translations, made up for a belated appearance in Sweden by helping to mould the mind and art of Strindberg, also a keen reader of Byron, Dickens, Scott, Marryat, Darwin and many of our social and historical writers. These, however, are in the main isolated instances: cultural traffic between the two countries has been but spasmodic, and the modern arts of Sweden are indebted for their foreign blood rather to France and Germany than to England.

Especially curious is the manner in which Sweden and far-off France have so often in history been drawn closely together. To think, for instance, that Richelieu, a Catholic Cardinal, should have supported the Champion of Protestantism in the Thirty Years' War more powerfully than any of Gustavus's co-religionists! Cultural and often political ties were extremely close between Sweden and France for two centuries or more after that time, especially during the reigns of Christina, Gustavus III (who once more raised Sweden to the rank of a great power in the late eighteenth century), and Charles John (otherwise Bernadotte, the former general of Napoleon's). During the Napoleonic wars Sweden's chameleon-like rôle in European politics was quite bizarre. In 1801, being a member of the League of Armed Neutrality, which league England looked upon as hostile, Sweden was just on the verge of coming to blows with us: Nelson, after the first Battle of Copenhagen, was just about to attack the Swedish fleet off Karlskrona when news arrived from England enabling the engagement to be avoided. Two years later we had reached an agreement with Sweden regarding her trade and the Continental Blockade. In 1808 Russia invaded her province of Finland, and if it had not been for the obstruction of an English fleet might have effected a landing on the Swedish mainland.

In the same year Sir John Moore arrived at Gothenburg with an English force of 10,000 to help Sweden out of her difficulties, but finding it impossible to co-operate with the King, Gustavus IV, a hopeless incompetent (whose second name was, ironically, Adolphus), he decided to withdraw. Not long afterwards this miserable monarch was deposed in favour of his uncle, Bernadotte being elected Crown Prince in 1810. Sweden had by then again veered round to France: along with Napoleon's other allies she complied with his demand to declare war on us and adopt the Continental System. So for two years—the only time in history—England and Sweden were nominally at war, though not a single shot was fired and trade continued much as before. Another curious event was Bernadotte's alliance with Russia against Napoleon himself, partly with the idea of winning Norway. In 1813 Britain, in giving her sanction to the seizure of Norway, promised a subsidy of £1,000,000 as well as the island of Guadeloupe in the West Indies in return for Swedish military aid against Napoleon; while the following year we helped Sweden to acquire Norway by blockading the latter's coast—an act which, however, was far from popular with the English people as a whole. The far-off island of Guadeloupe (discovered by Columbus) was to prove quite useful to Sweden, for two years later at the Congress of Vienna she not unwisely sold it to France. With the proceeds (according to Stromberg) she liquidated her national debt, thus being one of the few countries to emerge without a foreign debt from the Napoleonic wars. This, I might mention, was not her only overseas colony: the nearby island of St. Bartholomew, eight square miles in area and with a couple of thousand inhabitants, ceded to her by France in 1784, remained in her possession for nearly a century till eventually it was re-acquired by France for £11,000. The Swedish settlements on the Delaware in 1638 are better known; and at one time there was a chance that Madagascar might become a Swedish island.

In her last century and a quarter of peace Sweden's relations with us have been above all commercial. From being the country which gave the original impetus to her industrialism we long ago became her chief customer, thereby helping to establish her material prosperity. We in our turn have also learned much from them since the eighteenth century (when Swedish tinplate workers were brought over to England)— from her scientists, inventors, engineers, technicians, sociologists and so forth. Of her political attitude towards us during the Great War I have said nothing: those who were old enough at the time may be better informed on the question than I am; but having read the accounts of many impartial writers I am convinced that Sweden acted as an honest neutral and that any anti-Allied feeling there may have been is quite understandable when the facts are considered, especially her geographical position, and her historical and cultural associations with Germany on whose soil she actually possessed territory till about a hundred years ago.

IV · FELLS

"As soon as I came to the fells I gained new life, and as it were a heavy weight was taken off me."

LINNAEUS, *Lachesis Lapponica.*

―――――――――――

1 : *Härjedalen and Jämtland*

WHERE IS THE middle of Sweden? The provinces from Gothenburg to Stockholm are generally known as Central Sweden. And since they have always been more or less the centre of the country's cultural gravity, and because most of the north has but a meagre sprinkling of people, this definition will generally suffice. To the people of Skåne even the Stockholmers are remote hyperboreans—Samoyeds, as they call them (after the tribe of Arctic Russians). But Stockholm is not the middle of Sweden: *that* is nearly four hundred miles to the north of the capital, about twelve hours' train journey. The bisecting line is the Ljungan, or the Heather River, which rises on the border between Härjedalen and Jämtland, mountain provinces finally won from Denmark-Norway in 1645.

It is there I had arranged to go with a student friend at the beginning of April, in order to do a few days' tour across the fells. The morning came. I was busy packing. Suddenly my landlady burst in waving a newspaper: "Look! Look!" And there I read how a party, caught in a blizzard, had been frozen to death on the very plateau we had intended to cross.

It was the same at the station. Everyone who came to see us off bombarded us with warnings and admonitions. "*Do* be careful!" "You have a really good compass, I suppose?" "Don't whatever you do lie down if you're tired!" "You haven't forgotten your *anorak**?" "For God's sake do what

―――――――――――
* A hooded windproof jacket of light grenfell material.

123

they tell you at the tourist station!" "Have you an extra ski-tip?" "Cheerio, then!" "And BE CAREFUL!" "Adjö!" "Adjö!" "Adjö!" "Good luck!" "Adjö!" "Aaa-jö!"

Upsala platform slid out of sight. Gunnar and I, exchanging half-amused glances, prepared to turn in.

Looking out of the window in the morning, we could see nothing but great snowy forests. At nine we arrived at the village of Åsarna, pulled out our rucksacks, and looked round for somewhere to eat before our bus left in half-an-hour.

For we still had a seventy-mile journey ahead of us to get to Ljungdalen, chosen as the base for our attack on the high fells because of its central position in regard to the main Härjed-alen-Jämtland massif, and also because it is one of the least frequented resorts around those fells. The government bus-services in Norrland, linking the most distant and sparsely populated valleys throughout the year, are one of the wonders of the country. Despite the weather, despite the ice, snow or mud, the diligence with a trailer behind and often a snow-plough in front regularly battles its way to the loneliest villages and settlements whose poor, hardy inhabitants count on it for their mail and for many of the necessities of life.

For four-and-a-half hours our bus, groaning all the while, lurched and slithered through the Ljungan valley, now ac-celerating on a flat easy stretch, now slowing down at a hamlet for the driver to throw the King's Mail out of the window on the roadside. Occasionally we stopped at a village to offload packages or to re-fuel; once, in the middle of the forest, to hand groceries to a bent gnarled old woman huddled in layers of rags—a figure eloquent of the toughness of life in those parts. Sometimes we would see a herd of reindeer shying at our approach, or lumberjacks piling logs at a lakeside; but mostly it was silent unrelieved forest, tree upon motionless tree.

As we penetrated further and further long ranges of spruce-clad hills gradually rose on either side running into the skyline ahead, on which in time we could just discern towards the head of the wide valley several blunt white peaks, serene and remote, resisting the enormous tides of eddying forests. Then once more they would be lost to view altogether and we would be as hopelessly engulfed as ever; but each time we snatched glimpses of them they appeared to be nearer—white buoys anchored in the dark ocean in whose currents we were caught and being moved along. Eventually in the narrowing valley large clearings were encountered, scattered farmyards, and the irregular slant-poles of half-buried fences. Ljungdalen, at last. Twisting to the right the bus pulled up near the head of the valley at an unpainted building which houses the hotel and *diverse handeln* (or village shop). Feeling rather dazed we put on our skis and made off for our pension in air that reminded us of our stomachs as much as it exalted our spirits.

Our meal over, we then set out to explore, aiming first at the slalom slope which we were told lay "over there". Only after prolonged searching among the trees did we find ourselves at the foot of a narrow clearing on the hillside which was evidently the place designated. Though nearly vertical and well peppered with stumps and protruding rocks, it was so well covered with soft virgin snow that we could take it flat out. But as for slalom . . . We managed to do a few telemarks.

While returning after dark we were stopped by a couple of boys who wanted to know if we had brought any drink with us. They were the only beggars I have ever encountered in Sweden (supposing indeed that they *were* begging, and would not have offered us payment if we had had anything to give them). This little incident reminded me how dry the country districts must remain unless they resort to illegal distillation on their own. Perhaps only once or twice a year can these farmers get to a town where alcohol is procurable, and even then the amount is limited by law. So that before they have got home the whole lot will have been consumed. (We had just observed the notices in the bus: "No drinking allowed!") Although the rustics are probably better without any drink, it is the chief fault in the present system that it discriminates unfairly against them. If the townsman, they argue, can get his drink, why shouldn't we?

For several days we wandered about this straggly hamlet of scattered farms and into the adjoining forests on the hillside.

Background to Sweden

Sometimes the children would pass us, dexterously scampering across the fields, now running up a bank, now jumping a half-submerged fence, till they reached the school, slipped off their skis and unhitched the rucksacks which serve them as school-bags. Even up here they all appeared to have the proverbial Scandinavian good looks; but the years that are mostly winters soon begin to tell heavily: they will be old when middle-aged.

In winter the farmer turns lumberman. We sometimes followed tracks into the forest and watched the tall trees which with trickling increment had so slowly and painfully attained their stature and withstood the onslaughts of Arctic storms succumbing in a few minutes to the ruthless blade, thudding to the ground and leaving a gap for their offspring. I was much impressed by the quality of the instruments which the men one day allowed us to use—all made of the best Swedish steel, the finest blades in the world. Care is always taken to clear the snow from the base and to do the cutting as close as possible to the ground. The trees once down are trimmed up, barked with special barking knives and sawn into logs of stipulated lengths, which are placed on sledges to be drawn by horses to the nearest stream. No machines in this part of Scandinavia have yet replaced the draught horse for the purpose of forestry. The breed here as in the rest of Northern Sweden is the *nord-svenska*, a hardy active little animal admirably adapted to the severe conditions, patiently tugging away in his wooden patterns, always contented, always good-natured.

Often as we sat in some sunny sheltered spot in the valley to eat our lunch, magpies, infinitely fascinating against a background of white, would gambol around us busy already with the complications of mating. Though not a native, the magpie is now one of the commonest birds in Sweden. It is also among the handsomest, but that terrible death-rattle of a voice lets him down badly.

The gales being fierce and continuous, we could seldom go above the tree-line. Even in the valley the clouds of snow-dust, driven before the gusts, often restricted visibility to a foot or two. By far the most unpleasant feature of these gales was felt in the lavatory, a lean-to shack very loosely put together and exposed to the full fury of the north. One cannot, I suppose, expect indoor sanitation in such spots; but what an ordeal!

Otherwise our pension was not lacking in comfort. We had electric light, a telephone, wireless, no draught and good round meals—things that you cannot buy in many an English pub boasting of the name "hotel".

Several days passed by. We had not yet reached the plateau which we were to have crossed in three days. Nor, so long as the gales and blizzard persisted, was there any likelihood of our doing so.

But we made one attempt in the company of a couple of young Stockholmers—about the only outsiders then in Ljungdalen. Although climbing against the wind with thirty-pound packs, we at first made good progress. Beyond the tree-line it became more difficult. On one side a long ridge rose sheer above us, its outline blurred by the fierce grey smoke of snow-dust streaming before the wind. It was into this smoke, becoming whiter on our approach, that we gradually mounted. Lashed into blindness and fatigue by the gale's relentless whipcord, our hands, feet and noses threatened by frostbite, and our skis grating and slipping on the arbitrarily corrugated ice, we emptied our entire energy into the effort to grope upward from one half-buried telephone-pole to another. But

> *"Being so caught up,*
> *So mastered by the brute blood of the air"*,

we at length had to turn round, and that within only a couple of miles from Helagsfjället, our objective.

Once again below the tree-line, we rested, warmed and dried ourselves in a cattleshed. For we were wet as well, the fine snow-powder having found out every chink and crevice and wormed itself among the remotest objects in our rucksacks, and even under our anoraks.

We now had but two days left. Storms exceptional in their violence for April had ruled against our tour. "But there is", we were told, "a shorter unmarked route. Though less spectacular it is interesting and will take you to Vålådalen and the Jämtland railway. There's a Lapp boy in the village who will show you the way for a few kronor."

And fortunately the next morning was brilliantly fine. Our little guide turned up in the most up-to-date Stockholm skiing clothes; even his bindings were modern. Apart from a certain stockiness and a sallow complexion, there was not much of the Lapp about him. He was also quite good-looking, possibly owing to a mixed origin. (Härjedalen is the southern limit of the Lapps in Sweden, and a certain amount of inter-marriage has taken place.)

Because of the conditions, we had hardly improved our skiing during our stay. Even in the valley Gunnar, my companion, had broken a couple of his skis, and had now bought the last pair in the shop. Being made of birch, they were not calculated to stand up to really rough usage. As for mine, excellent hickory specimens from Gresvig's in Oslo, protected by brass edges and an under-rimming of some patent celluloid-like substance (made from milk and fitted in London), they were, despite tough work over many a hundred mile, as good as new. Certainly heavy with their brasses for *langlauf*, but very reliable—except at extremely low temperatures, when hickory is liable to split. Most Scandinavians keep two pairs, to be used according to the conditions.

"Gunnar, you *can't* take that!" He had fallen in love with a vast slab of chocolate in the shop, quite four pounds in weight. "Oh, we'll soon get through it." Remonstrating with him was useless. He bought it and we divided the burden.

You forget, when such a still sunny day comes round, that there ever has been bad weather. And so we hacked on exultantly through *tö*, wet sticky snow that weighed down the skis, our guide leading the way. Now and then we saw a hare, and many snow-buntings flitted around us, their forms discernible only when seen against trees or the sky. They would soon be ready for their spring moult and change with their environment from pure white to the neutral browns of the rock and shale.

Reaching above the tree-line a *Lappläger*, or summer camp of the Lapps, we stopped for our lunch. Westwards across the plateau the dark clustered spikes of Sylarna stuck out of the white fell-rim like a decayed molar in an otherwise toothless gum, though to the left Helagsfjället was hiding behind a wad of brownish drift-cloud. These are the highest peaks south of Lapland. Five or six thousand feet may not sound impressive, but a vertical foot in these latitudes is really the equivalent of a yard in the Alps. Nor would I have the fells higher than they are. Given a day or two of fine weather, the skier can conquer even the loftiest; there is none of that topographical red-tape found in the Alps, where half the peaks are out of bounds in winter, despite funiculars. When, after doing your own climbing, you can move along the highest peaks rather than have them hanging intangibly about your head, a far greater intimacy with nature becomes possible, and the grandeur though probably less super-human is more intelligible. (The weather, of course, may limit your activities, but it never keeps a Northerner indoors.) Skiing in Scandinavia is essential horizontal, not vertical.

We were now on the border of Jämtland, traversing the stiff crust of an undulating plateau, whose austere ridges, like the knuckles of an old man, stuck out on three sides. It was hard to believe that any living thing had ever before visited this ice-desert: no stick or suggestion of life was visible, save on exposed crests the shrivelled grasses and lichens clamped as if in a vice.

"What's that?" I wondered, stopping a small object which was bowling along in the breeze. A mouse! A "cow'rin', tim'rous beastie", indeed, encrusted as it was with ice and apparently exhausted, though still alive. Taking pity on it, we wondered if we could carry it with us and release it elsewhere. But how? We had no mind to be clawed and bitten or to have holes nibbled in our clothes or rucksacks. So we left the pathetic creature to an unknown fate. Apart from a distant herd of reindeer, it was the only animal we saw on the high plateau.

Evening had begun to pull out long violet shadows from the

129

fell-sides over a lower plateau now opening before us (Plate 18). Our guide would have to leave us in time to return to the *Lapplåger* before it was dark. So, when we had paid him off and he had pointed out to us a tiny speck, the *fjällstue* (hut) where we were to spend the night, we said goodbye. "He's a decent chap; let's give him some chocolate." We gave him a chunk and saw him return at high speed by the way we had just come.

Being hungry, we began to wonder what sort of food they would give us, and if anyone else would be taking our route on the morrow. "There don't seem to be many people about." "No." And, as we approached, the windows were seen to be boarded up. "I suppose the glass would be blown in without the shutters?" "Look, it's funny they have no telephone." Suddenly it occurred to us that it might be just a rest-hut, without keeper or food.

It was. Having forced open the door, we found two rooms with beds, blankets, benches, a table, even cooking and eating utensils. Above all a stove. And wood, which we carried in armfuls from the shed nearby. We lit the inflammable papery birch-bark, and the room gradually warmed up as the wind increased without. A great little tree, the birch, growing farther north than any other in the world. It is beautiful, even as scrub giving a heavy black outline to the ridges. And it is useful, being in such places the only firewood—trusty, genial, warming hearth and heart. What are those lines from an old Eddic poem?

> *Fire needs he*
> *who enters the house*
> *and is cold about the knees;*
> *food and clothes*
> *the man is in need of*
> *who has journeyed over mountains.*

We now had fire and clothes. But food? Why hadn't they told us there would be no one there? We could have brought all we wanted. "Let's see what we have." We laid it all out on the table and made an inventory: one chunk of plain chocolate, 20-*öre's* worth of milk chocolate, some dried apricots, a few *papper-kakor* (brown biscuits), some raspberry jubes, several lumps of sugar, and a tablet of Wrigley's chewing-gum. Having laid some of these aside for "breakfast", we took what remained of the memorable slab of chocolate (regretting we had given most of it to the Lapp), boiled it down with melted snow, added the sugar, and gulped the steaming liquid with avidity. Then followed a stew of apricots, after which we took to our beds.

No scholar would have been needed to tell us that Ullur and Skadi, patron and patroness of skiing, were extremely parsimonious deities. Our empty stomachs knew all about that. Faint and ravenous, we staggered into the morning's snow-storm. A few cairns at first marked the route down to the forests, but once among the trees we were forced to depend on our compasses. Being rather inexperienced, we soon found ourselves confused by the difficult country, where a straight course was impossible and any landmarks that might have been visible through the trees were blotted by a heavy, sullen mist. I did not know at the time how the Lapps find their way about in any sort of weather without a compass. It is not purely by blind instinct: where there are trees they steer by them, for the spruce has longer branches on the south side and the pine-bark is redder on the same (the sunny) side; or if they are above the tree-line and visibility is poor they inspect the rocks, taking for the south the side on which moss or lichen is most abundant. In time an identifiable stream told us we were much out of our course. So we set our compass for a point where a marked trail (shown on the map) converged on a large stream. After great exertions in the wet snow on densely forested slopes, we at last came on a series of blazed trees making a track through snow just as virgin as before. To celebrate the occasion we recklessly consumed fully half-a-dozen jujubes, the only barrier between us and complete star-vation.

We were still very far from Vålådalen, the nearest settlement. Slogging on mechanically through the heavy snow, now on the flat, we could think of nothing but food, food, food. Only some reindeer at close quarters could temporarily divert our attention. Most of them were on a southwards-facing ridge, cropping the exposed reindeer-moss (which is actually a lichen); a few stragglers were moving to another part, lifting and setting down their heavy wide-splayed hoofs (which are so fashioned as to prevent their sinking into the deep snow and yet enable them to dig for food) with an extreme, almost fantastic delicacy.

Our tramp was made no easier by the early spring. Rivers generally frozen at this time of the year had now but scattered ice-bridges and occasionally had to be forded. At last we discerned signs of habitation, and after doing some aerobatics on a broken suspension bridge we more or less collapsed in the arms of the manageress of Vålådalen hotel at 5 p.m. In point of mileage I have done many a better day, but never have I undertaken a more exhausting journey.

On the following morning, though loath to do so—for the company was good and this small hotel had an exceptionally agreeable and intimate atmosphere—we ordered a taxi, and after paying our modest bill which included 50 öre (about 6d.) for our previous night in the *fjällstue*, and buying one of Vålådalen's special red woollen caps with a pom-pom on top, drove off to Undersåker, a station on the trans-Peninsular line. We had no time to visit the large Lapp school which is the most up-to-date in existence, being housed not in pyramidal Lapp-huts as elsewhere but in an ordinary Swedish school-building; for we had to catch a train—a very modern Diesel-engined smartly upholstered railbus. An hour or two later we found ourselves in Östersund, the only inland town of any size in Norrland. Apart from being the capital of Jämtland and a market town of some 15,000 inhabitants, Östersund is a big railway junction whose strategic position gives it great potential military significance. In winter some rather famous international motor-car races are held on the ice of the Lake (Storsjön) on which it stands. With lots of stone banks, offices, shops and well dressed people in the streets, it is a fairly convincing urban centre, though the stone or brick buildings, like those in Luleå, Piteå, and other Norrland towns, had the misfortune to be built during the least inspired architectural period of the last century.

Lying between the 62nd and the 69th parallels, Norrland with Nordland in Norway is probably the most northerly cultural outpost in the modern world. Even Iceland only just touches the Arctic Circle (66° 30′). Alaska and Siberia are the sort of countries found in such latitudes, and Alaska and Siberia have not as yet produced any great men or exported their culture. But Norrland can claim men who are unquestionably great—not one as a mere *tour de force*, but several. Take Per Wargentin in the eighteenth century, born at Sunne in Southern Jämtland, who being an astronomer by profession is said to have pulled off some rather tough tables for the satellites of Jupiter. But his main achievement was in the founding in 1756 of the world's first institute of statistics. Utterly unheard-of abroad, this is the man who was in a sense the forerunner of Cassel and Wicksell, Bertil Ohlin, Erik Lindahl, Gunnar Myrdal and other modern economists. A professorship in economics had, it is true, been established in Sweden as early as 1739; but Wargentin was the man who arranged for the collection of figures which are the raw material of the economists. "No country", said Samuel Laing, a British traveller who wrote a well-informed book on it exactly a century later, "is so rich in statistical facts as Sweden". Or take Peterson-Berger, one of the best-known Swedish composers, a native of Ångermanland, who now lives on the island in Storsjön which he has celebrated in some of his songs and operas. There may of course be men of comparable talents who have hailed from similar latitudes elsewhere, but where are they? We have yet to hear something about them.

Westwards this railway continues to Trondheim in Norway through a wide valley in which many of the chief skiing resorts are situated: Åre, the most fashionable, the only one with much Continental sophistication, and with a very shapely mountain all her own called Åreskutan; Storlien, close to the frontier, the most popular in the country; Halland; Enafors; and many other smaller places.

I had visited Storlien in February. In spite of having struck a very bad patch of weather with only one fine day in ten, it was always possible to make some local run, if only down to Teveldalen through a wooded gully where the wind was kinder and in even the most blinding snowstorm one could more or less guess the turns and somehow or other emerge without having fallen. The popularity of this run was also due to the strong Norwegian beer which could be bought at the *Stuga*, just over the border, and you don't have to eat at the same time as you do in Sweden when consuming drinks of comparable strength. This beer is reputed to be the strongest in the world, and from the effect of a single bottle on the student friend I had gone with—a youth noted for anything but a weak head— I should be the last to doubt it. On other days we would practice on the rather good slalom slope, or go off in various directions, sometimes in parties, sometimes alone, to explore whatever was visible through the clouds. Sometimes we would practise away from marked tracks with a compass, and one day arrived so late at our destination that we decided to spend the night there. It was a *fjällstuga* right on the edge of a high plateau; and in the morning, which turned out to be the best they had had for two months, we walked up to the top of Blåhammar the peak nearby and looked across the plateau of dazzling sheet-ice towards Sylarna, Helagsfjället and other peaks in the far distance. At our feet were amazing ice-flowers up to a foot in height, like glittering knobby polyps, while between us and some rounded peaks at this end of the plateau was our hut, inhabited the whole blustering winter through, and almost buried in solid ice streaming off for twenty-five feet to the leeward: the whole exciting scene caught in a deluge of impartial sunlight (Plate 20). The run down that morning was the best we were destined to have.

Apart from the station and a few cottages, Storlein consists of a large hotel with three hundred and twenty beds (many, I imagine, double ones). Caught there for ten days in bad weather, one could hardly be indifferent to one's fellow-guests. There were, I suppose, some fifty or more—mostly families taking advantage of out-of-season reductions in prices. About the only young people (barring tiny tots) were some conscripts around the age of twenty who were out all day doing pretty severe training, each carrying up to seventy-seven pounds in pack and rifle, with which load they have at times to cover forty miles a day, although they never did so there in that weather. On the spring manœuvres, I am told, the cavalrymen carry ingenious foldable skis which are used in snow which is too deep for horses. I am now sorry that I failed to watch these conscripts more carefully when they were building igloos and bivouacs not far from the hotel; but so it often happens when one is travelling: one is caught up in the fun of the moment, and when eventually one decides to go into some matter worthy of study—to cover it—it is too late. These lads kept mostly to themselves indoors, and after their long days would retire early. One night, however, they decided to entertain us, and in their different turns, songs and make-up gave us a moderate performance. It was certainly better than dancing which took place on other nights and generally drove us to a corner of the lounge with whatever book we could lay our hands on. I don't say we were bored with the long evenings, but I can't remember when I have been less willing to dance, in this country not unnoted for feminine charm. So, unless we were talkative, I dabbled in Swedish grammar and even one night (or was it two?) thought my time decently spent in producing the following:

White Darkness

Said Director Maelstrom, stamping his foot like a pile-driver
in the bar of the High Mountain Hotel, Storlien,
"Hell! but I haven't journeyed a thousand miles
just to be balkt by bad weather. A comfortable doctrine
indeed!—Well, if you won't *come. . . ." And wheeling*
he made for the door, leaving Engineer Lundquist
to share a drawled "Så-å-å?" of incredulity
with the barmaid.

Background to Sweden

The air is breathtaking; clouds white
and shapeless are torn carelessly over the snowed fellscape
as Director Maelstrom fumbles with his ski-bindings
and wind-propt starts to climb across the slope.
What with large snow-goggles and a tightened
anorak, all that is visible of his head is the nose
protuberant and a half-mouth (part of the smile
rippling away beneath the anorak's hood).

Now is the ridge reacht: ribbed before him
is a monotonous plain spotlit through cloud-gashes
down which the wind pushes him, his skis now wrencht
round ruthlessly by ice-corrugations, now rasping
against the frozen dribble of a rock.
"O it is grand!" Effortlessly the prowed parallels
slither the glazed waves, carry him, carry him
at madspeed. "Ho, wind, what fun! Ground,
rush under, gallop and cavort!—Blizzard,
be off! How can a man see . . .?" . . . A man
can feel, feel rock, feel rotten;
see ski snapt, and black for white.

Gets up, puts down a weak ankle on O-
what- hard ground, turns round, begins
footslogging into flickt finepowder and dust
enfiladed from rimblades. Scuffles and rough-
wrestling drain toughness, take it out of him.
Struggles also with loneliness: remembers Christmas:
his scarlet-mittened children—his wife's posterior
swaying before him like a safe balloon.

Slogs on,——limps,——sways dazed, unthinking:
legs are pistons, slow, stiff.——Sinks
down; now feels drowsy——how ground
receives him like a bed! in what hard down
and gives him wife of winds, too——snarling darling,
too frigid yet too fierce-affectionate.
Or sodomy? It's the homosexual North,

magnetic and arresting, whose embrace
escape from those who can!

Total immersion
in bled-white darkness: Director Maelstrom sleeps——
spasms and gasps and mistbegotten groans
are gathered in a NOT. No feeble smile
filters through the tight lips of the icy mist——
no wrist wrests life from its grim grip:——
the dust whirls past, a swirling commentary,
with something of the after-melancholy of a Hungarian csárdás.

2 : *A Word For Lapland*

WHEN OUR LEARNED King Alfred translated the General
History of Orosius into English, one of the pieces of his own
material that he inserted into the text was the narrative of the
voyage made by the Norseman, Ohthere, from his home in
Northern Norway round North Cape into the White Sea and
back. This explorer, who visited the Court of Alfred about
890, said that the country

"wherein he dwelt was called Helgoland. Oether tolde
his lord-king Alfred that he dwelt furthest North of any
other Norman. He sayd that he dwelt towards the North
part of the land toward the West coast: and affirmed that
the land, notwithstanding it stretcheth marveilous farre
towards the North, yet it is all desert and not inhabited,
unless it be very few places, here and there, where certaine
Finnes dwell upon the coast, who live by hunting all the
Winter, and by fishing in Summer. . . . At the same time
that he came up to the king, he had of his owne breed 600
tame Deere of that kind which they call Rane Deere of
which number 6 were stall Rane Seere, a beast of great
value, and marveilously esteemed among the Fynnes, for
that with them they catch the Rane Deere. . . . Their
principall wealth consisteth in the tribute which the Fynnes
pay them, which is all in skinnes of wilde beasts, feathers

of birds, whale bones, and cables, and tacklings of ships
made of Whales or Seales skinnes. . . . The mountaines
be in breadth of such quantitie as a man is able to traveile
over in a fortnight, and in some places no more then may
be traveiled in sixe days. Right over against this land, in
the other side of the mountaines, somewhat towards the
South, lieth Swethland. . . ."

And he described how the sun up there failed to set in summer,
how the people carried boats on their backs, and how wars
sometimes broke out between Norwegians and "Queenes",
another people living to the north-east. This is the first English
account of Lapland, a country stretching through the North
of Norway, Sweden and Finland into Russia, and it is interesting to notice that even then the inhabitants paid tribute to
their more civilized neighbours. As William Burrough remarked, one of our Elizabethan explorers (who made a
remarkably accurate chart of the coasts from Trondheim as
far as the White Sea and Nova Zemlya about 1576), "Such
is the simplicitie of this people the Lappies that they would
rather give tribute to all those that border upon their country
then by denying it have their ill willes."

Many an Elizabethan in search of the North-East Passage
encountered Lapps when putting in near Vardö or Petsamo.
Sir Hugh Willoughby and his brave company, probably the
first Englishmen to winter in Lapland, were frozen to death
there before the spring in 1554. Several others left interesting
first-hand accounts of the country. A couple of years later,
for instance, a servant of Richard Chancellor's describes

"a land called Lappia: in which lande be two maner of
people, that is to say, the Lappians and the Scrickfinnes,
which Scrickfinnes are a wilde people which neither know
God nor yet good order; and these people live in tents
made of Deares skinnes; and they have no certain habita-
tions but continue in heards and companies by one hundred or two hundreds. And they are a people of small
stature and are clothed in Deares skinnes and drink
nothing but water and eate no bread but flesh all raw.

And the Lappians be a people adjoyning to them and be much like to them in all conditions".

He also speaks of the Kerilli, evidently the Carelians. Anthony Jenkinson a year later, though also describing these peoples as nomads, and averring that "there is nothing seen of them bare but their eies", speaks of them as "half Gentiles". Hakluyt gives a letter written in 1575 by one James Alday to the Moscovie Company "touching a trade to be established in Lappia": The English, he warned the Company, were too slow and were losing excellent trade opportunities: they had bought up only 300 barrels of oil whereas foreigners had bought no less than 1,183 barrels. Having wintered there with four other Englishmen, he evidently knew what he was talking about; and one of these men, Roger Leche, he recommends as an expert on those parts, who had travelled three hundred miles one winter, knew the language and the customs of the Lapps. Another good account of Lapland was left by Giles Fletcher the Elder, author and diplomat, who went to Russia as ambassador in 1588. The whole country, he said, consisted of lakes and mountains ("called Tondro" towards the coast), with forests inland. Of the Lapps:

> "Their diet is very bare and simple. Bread have they none, but feede onely upon fish and foule. They are subject to the Emperor of Russia, and the two kings of Sweden and Denmark,which all exact tribute and customs of them."

Some of them were Christians, though all were "utterly unlearned". "For practice of witchcraft and sorcerie they passe all nations in the worlde"; and he gives the story of their buying and selling winds to which there are so many references in the literature of the period—a superstition described by Thomas Heywood, for instance:

> "*The Finnes and Laplands are acquainted well*
> *With suchlike spirits and winds to merchants sell,*
> *Making their covenant, when and how they please*

> They may with prosperous weather cross the seas,
> As thus: They in an handerkerchief fast tie
> Three knots; unloose the first, and by and by
> You find a gentle gale blow from the shore.
> Open the second, it increaseth more
> To fill your sailes. When you the third untie
> The intemperate gusts grow vehement and high."

In a time when old and deformed women were burned as witches in English towns and villages men were naturally curious about these Northern hags and sorcerers who could perform such feats; who fell into trances, changed men into cows, snakes and birds; snatched away knives from dinner-tables; and used magic drums, darts that would split rocks, and malignant balls of cow's hair.

In 1674 they were able to read about such matters at length, their *kåtas*, drums, *pulkas*, reindeer and so forth, in Scheffer's *History of Lapland*—which still remains about the best book dealing with the country. Written in Latin, by an Upsala professor of Law and Rhetoric who had travelled there, the work was translated into English almost immediately by an Oxford undergraduate as "an imposition set him by Bishop Fell for courting a mistress at an age which the Bishop disliked . . . the Bishop was however pleased with the translation". Taking the *Germania* of Tacitus as his model, Scheffer produced what a living English archæologist has called "the most complete ethnological survey of a single people to be compiled before the science of anthropology had been systematized in modern times". And it is one of those books that is of interest alike to layman and scientist, specialist and dilettante. With such a work still fairly easily procurable, and a whole host of more recent ones (among which Turi's *Book of Lapland*, written by a Lapp, may prove the most enduring) there would appear to be little excuse for anyone not thoroughly acquainted with the country to write more on this subject. But a province that occupies nearly a third of Sweden cannot be entirely ignored; besides I shall speak chiefly of the less celebrated southern portion.

According to Scheffer, the country "was subdued and made a province of Swedland" in the time of King Magnus Ladulås (c. 1277), but the boundaries for many centuries were extremely hazy, and numerous disputes arose down to quite recent times, among the nations that claimed different parts of Lapland, concerning taxation of the inhabitants. Some attempt seems to have been made even at this early date to obtain the nominal conversion of the Lapps, but Scheffer agrees that their Christianity till the sixteenth century consisted merely in the rites of marriage and baptism, and even those probably being confined to the more accessible tribes. Although Gustavus Vasa sent priests there at the Reformation, the first churches were not built till the early seventeenth century. Little progress was made till Gustavus Adolphus and Queen Christina established schools there and had certain books translated such as primers and parts of the Scriptures.

> "By the benefit of these aforesaid books they began to understand what they prayed for, and some of the youth of Lapland having studied at the University of Upsal made so good progress . . . that they were intrusted with the ministry."

That the Lapps were still far from being thorough orthodox Christians at the time Scheffer wrote in the 1670's is shown by his chapters on "some remains of paganism", "the heathenish gods" then worshipped, and their "magical ceremonies". When Linnæus travelled there fifty years later they were still using their magic drums, which however were not long afterwards ordered to be destroyed, so that the one he brought back with him is among the very few surviving specimens to-day. Then about a century ago a missionary called Leustadius succeeded in kindling a good deal of religious fervour in his congregations and a wave of "Leustadianism" swept through Swedish, Norwegian and Finnish Lapland. But despite all this many of the original superstitions linger among the less sophisticated Lapps: lots of them still believe in *uldas* (a kind of trolls), use charms, and have (as I once had explained to me) a terrible fear of being photographed.

Background to Sweden

The fact that no Swedish king had visited the north of his domains before 1694 and that even he did not penetrate the Arctic Circle helps us to realize the utter remoteness of this province till recent times: it is as if William II had been the first English king to enter Yorkshire. *A Voyage of the Late King of Sweden, &c.*, by a bishop who had accompanied him describes this journey of Charles XI, a king ever absorbed in the internal affairs of his country, father of Charles XII. Having heard it said that there were twenty-four hours of sunshine in summer in the north of his kingdom, he—being a monarch who delighted "to make the exactest scrutiny into all things"—became "desirous to try with his own eyes" if it were true. So (I am quoting from the contemporary English translation) "He was then in Torneo in Westro Botnia situated about 65° and 43′ of latitude". But it was after the solstice, and woods and mountains obscured the horizon towards which the sun would dip down low at midnight. "However the undaunted heart of the most invincible monarch never fatigued by any labours conquered all these difficulties. A little tower being showed to us of about a hundred feet high on which the bells of the church of the city are hung, he gets up into it by ladders and those very steep accompanied by some eminent persons", where he satisfied himself that the sun remained above the horizon the whole night—at least it disappeared for only a few minutes and then behind a cloud. "The most serene king himself did not disdain to put down with his own hand into his table-book this observation", and the next year he sent off some mathematicians further north to do some work on refraction, variation in the magnetic needle and so forth.

At the beginning of the present century the world's first Arctic railway arrived at the monstrous iron-mountain of Kiruna-Vaara, where a carefully planned town of ten or eleven thousand inhabitants was created in a few years. Electrically lit and heated throughout the long winter by means of the Porjus Power-station, which also provides the power for working the mines and the Narvik railway, Kiruna is among the most up-to-date towns in existence. Telephones, buses, motor-boats, and aeroplanes are also in regular use in this boreal province which has now been brought within a day's comfortable and not-too-costly train-journey of the capital. But romance and mystery have not yet been driven out of Lapland: the intrusions of modernity have been fairly localized, and many of the Lapps continue to live the same sort of nomadic life as did their forbears in the Stone Age.

As described earlier in the chapter, I had, after skiing with a friend in Härjedalen and Jämtland, arrived at the town of Östersund. Having arranged to join a party of students for Easter, we left the same day for Hoting, just south of the Lapland border, where their train was due early the next morning. It was now the second week in April, and the snow at these low altitudes lay only in streaks and patches, though the lakes were still for the most part frozen over. A few hours' jolting over flat forest-and-bog country, broken occasionally by clearings with lake- or river-side hamlets, brought us to this aptly named junction of Hoting (pronounced Hooting). A nondescript village set in the middle of forests it has no interest for the casual traveller except as being the place where the world's oldest ski has recently been discovered in a bog. But more of that later. Among the group of houses just numerous enough to form a couple of streets at right angles we came upon a pension where we could spend the night, and, after drinking some coffee in a room full of local people being warmed up for the holidays with *brännvin*, retired rather early.

We had just finished our breakfast in the morning when the Swedish Students' Union's special train from Stockholm steamed into the station. Every compartment was full of young people vibrating with life. There were medical, dental and economic students from Stockholm University, linguists and historians from Lund, law students from Upsala, art and language students from Gothenberg, students from the College of Forestry, a typically hilarious Dane and a couple of young Czech engineers. I found myself among half-a-dozen of them apparently at the top of their form, and the miles slipped by like telegraph poles as we sped northwards by the Inland Line of Lapland (which runs parallel with the coast and the Norwegian border and midway between them both). In two hours' time we had crossed the great Ångerman River and were following it till it opened into a lake where the large village of Vilhelmina stands on a hillside facing the south. The air was clear and dry as we jumped out into the brilliant sunshine reflected from walls, snow and birches. And this was actually in Lapland—this sunny, sheltered modern-looking village where (as I noticed) lilacs appeared to be perfectly at home—at about 65° N., which is the latitude of Central Iceland or the Behring Straits.

We immediately began to transfer crates of skis, suitcases, boxes of oranges and rucksacks to the buses and lorries waiting at the station, and after a second breakfast (or perhaps it was lunch) moved off in parties for Saxnäs, our destination in the fells. For five hours our bus with its heavy trailer groaned along the wide open valley of the Ångerman, which most of the way was not a river at all but a long very graceful lake called Malgomäj, beyond whose whitened expanse, broken once by a herd of reindeer, the forested foothills unselfconsciously pandiculated. Whenever we skirted the Lake we could see near its edge the winter bus-route which had been abandoned only a week previously owing to the spring thaw. Huge cracks were visible in the ice; in the more open parts of the forest the collapsed crystalline snow was broken by patches of heather and bilberry; and the road was already a series of quagmires and puddles. Bumping and slithering along, we had our journey considerably shortened by singing and the heartiness of some southerners. I can never tire of these popular songs of Sweden, many of them written by her greatest poets, but owing to the influence of folk-song neither too heavy nor too foolish to catch on among the common people, though students of course memorize a larger number than they do. England must have been like that about three centuries ago when no country in Europe could outdo her in the musical field, yet nowadays who sings the lyrics of the Elizabethans, Herrick or Blake, Shelley, Bridges or Auden outside the concert-room? We have living composers to be proud of and more poets than are recognized, but any songs that may have caught on either have embarrassingly execrable words or are by Americans, Scots and Irishmen.

In the North of Lapland the mountain-chain of Scandinavia, known commonly as "the Fells", officially as Kölen or The Keel, flowers in a cluster of lofty massifs gashed by sheer-walled valleys and huge glaciers which sweep down from the highest peaks in Sweden. But southwards the massifs become less monstrous and more detached: the scenery is less spectacular. Our situation at Saxnäs was free and open with fells of various heights scattered at random over a billowy plain which averaged about a thousand feet above sea-level. Here was a scratchy cluster of dwarf birch, there a dark smudge of spruce forest; on the flatter parts occasional scrawls of fences, in the more sheltered places on the south slopes curious storeyed frameworks for drying hay; beside us a lake, a white spotless sweep curving round the fell-bases to the northwest to collect the Arctic winds, and beyond it the icy epaulettes of Marsfjället glittering in the sunshine.

Our invasion of the village was pretty thorough: the pension by the lake, three of the four houses nearby, the school about a mile away, and even the summer coffee-stuga belonging to the pension were occupied by our party of sixty-five, some of the villagers having betaken themselves elsewhere for the time being.

There was little time for skiing the first evening, but the next morning after splitting into three groups according to our experience we went out with our group-leaders—lads who had passed special skiing tests—to practise our turns on various slopes in the vicinity: stem turns of rather questionable purity, stem-christies, christies, but no telemarks (which are now used less than in Norway, and in any case are intended for the deep snow found earlier in the winter). Sometimes we made all-day tours to the tops of the neighbouring fells, which though not more than five thousand feet in height were often difficult to conquer on account of winds and long stretches of hard white crust or pure sheet-ice. Once or twice my skins came in useful on these climbs and I was surprised to find that two of the others also possessed some. For skins are still rather rare in Scandinavia owing to the terrain: they are hardly worth the trouble of putting on and taking off several times in the course of a run which generally consists of a series of ups, downs, and flats. They are commoner, I found, in the more Alpine parts of Norway such as Myrdal, but even there most of the owners appeared to be foreigners. Waxes—or what the Americans call "dope"—are used instead. For climbing, a small patch at the back of each ski is generally smeared with a sticky wax which balls as the ski is put down at each step, thus preventing it from sliding backwards, and before going downhill the ball is easily knocked off and the run down not interfered with at all. There are waxes for every conceivable *före* or surface; for climbing, slalom, walking on the flat; varying from paraffin wax, smeared on in a moment or two, which wears off in a few hundred yards, to *klister*, a thick brown treacly substance which takes an age to spread and even longer to scrape off. It often happens that by the time one has smothered the skis with *klister* the stiff crust it is meant for has changed with a slight rise in temperature to a terrible gluey *före*; the *klister* has to be removed and the skis waxed all over again with *valla* or some other slithery substance. Further complications arise when the snow changes in nature (as it usually does) from one place to another—from icy above the tree-line to sticky below and so forth. Transitions from one kind of *före* to another are often so violent that descents that would otherwise be tame are made extremely treacherous. A patch of gluey snow occurring in the middle of an ice-slope will, as I know from experience, suddenly grab the skis and throw you over. Or consider the end of a schuss on to a lake where you have to allow not only for the check on flattening out but for what may be either additional retardation from a sticky surface or acceleration from an icy one. No wonder a certain well-known Swiss ski-instructor had to be taught how to ski when he came to Lapland.

One day we visited a *Lappläger* (Lapp encampment) where the *kåtor*, though conical like the traditional portable tents, were solid fixed huts made of spruce-poles (Plate 22). Though dressed for the most part in their native dress these Lapps had several western-European articles of clothes such as caps and gloves which were probably made in Stockholm, and many modern utensils such as knives and china cups used for drinking coffee (now a very popular beverage among them. Sugar is placed in the mouth not in the cup.) Their reindeer were grazing out of sight in the forest; but there were some goats tethered nearby and the inevitable dogs which are seldom friendly with outsiders. Originally the Lapps never milked their reindeer: only when they came in touch with the Nordic Scandinavians who kept cows did they learn to do so, and thereafter reindeer milk became an important article of their diet. Quite recently however they have begun keeping goats instead, which give a higher yield (though poorer milk) and are less trouble since they are always at hand when required. The Lapps never make butter—only cheese and *messmör* (a sort of sweet cheese made from the remains after the ordinary kind has been separated). I learned that a good deal of the land round Saxnäs—forest, grazing and farm land—was owned by "forest Lapps" who lived in ordinary Swedish *stugor*, farmed, did lumberwork and dressed for the most part like ordinary Swedes, and as far as I know owned no reindeer whatever. Our servants were all of this type, apparently from the poorer families, for some families are large landowners and comparatively well-to-do. There are to-day fairly distinct types: the nomadic mountain Lapps, who carry on as they have always done; the forest Lapps, most of whom have settled down and own land in forest districts, who engage in forestry and farming and may or may not own reindeer as well; and poorer sedentary Lapps who live mostly by fishing. What proportion each type is of the total number I was unable to discover, but hazard the guess that about half the Swedish Lapps belonged to the second comparatively sophisticated type. There are less than thirty thousand altogether: about nineteen thousand in Norway, some of whom cross the Swedish frontier during their migrations; seven thousand in Sweden (not confined to the provice of Lapland); and some three thousand in Finland and the Kola Peninsula in Russia.

Our food at the pension was excellent and consisted largely

of local produce. The lake trout, caught through holes in the ice, were especially delicious; and so was the *hjortron* jam, made from the cloudberries common on peat bogs in Norrland, and from time out of mind the Lapps' main antiscorbutic (since it is about their only source of vitamin C). The very small sausage-like potatoes, the only variety that will grow in these latitudes, more than made up in palatableness for what they lacked in bulk, and were much the tastiest I have ever eaten. There was always an abundance of butter, cheese and *messmör*, while other typical Swedish dishes like *filkjölk* and a fairly various *smörgåsbord* were always forthcoming. We had poultry, pork, meat balls, and once some reindeer flesh which tasted like venison, but otherwise there was more fish than meat. I would however gladly forget the pudding made of pigs' blood, looking like, but certainly not tasting like, fried plum-pudding, for I thought it both primitive and disgusting. About the coffee, as I happened to observe (though the pun was completely lost on my victim), there were no grounds for complaint whatsoever.

For Easter Saturday some ski competitions were arranged, the star event being an obstacle race. Holding an egg in each hand you had to make a tortuous course, do a small jump, climb under some ski-sticks, and run up a slope to the finishing-post—all as fast as you could and without breaking the eggs. In the evening we had a special dinner in a room festooned for the purpose and decorated with brilliant caricatures by an artist member of the party. The menu was excellent and included unlimited quantities of ice-cream; speeches were made, and there was prize-giving. We then repaired to a large room out of which the beds had been removed, and were joined by some of the local Lapps, one of whom played the concertina, and we all began to dance. The room grew hotter and hotter, and the waltzes brisker and brisker, even the heavy box-like figures of the Lapps—all with their hats on and ugly expressionless faces—being caught in the irresistable maelstrom of music and motion. Going outside during an interval, we discovered, just as if it had been on the programme: "10-45—Aurora", a brilliant display of the Northern Lights—long rays like searchlights meeting in an apex overhead, but forever changing kaleidoscopically into other curious and dramatic patterns. Different at every performance, the Aurora is an inexhaustible source of wonder even to those who have always lived in the North. I can speak at least for the Scandinavians who from the earliest times have been noted for their intense love of nature and for their exceptionally strong tendency to personify natural forces. Probably more than any other Europeans they have preserved this love of nature both in town and country. No large cities have divorced them from nature or killed in these practical efficient people their sense of wonder; and—what is even more remarkable—nature has never grown stale to the country people who have to earn their living from the soil. Here if nowhere else De Quincey's observation, "The great despisers of rural scenery, its fixed and permanent undervaluers, are rustics", becomes manifestly untrue.

I was furious at being unable to compete the next day in a slalom competition organized by some other club whose members arrived by bus in the morning. It was one of the hardest courses I have ever seen—incredibly steep and being a north slope very icy. Even the best competitors—and they weren't bad—fell several times; in fact negotiated all the trickier parts in more or less prostrate positions. I couldn't help regretting that I didn't damage my ankle on this spectacular slope (as I'm sure I should have done) instead of having done it beforehand in a completely tame manner—an accident I put down partly to my unbreakable skis and their kandahar bindings. Every day skis were being broken; there were ten in a single day, I remember.

The leader of the party, a forest officer (*jägmästare*) in the Government service, told me one day about a tour he had made for Skidfrämjandet (the Society for the Promotion of Swedish Skiing) and for two Stockholm newspapers. Starting in Northern Värmland in the middle of February, he travelled northwards over the fells for 120 Swedish miles (about 744 English) and arrived in Central Lapland a month later. He had one companion and three dogs to haul their *pulka* with tent, provisions, etc. They are fine creatures these Lapp-dogs

149

—wolfhounds that are about three-quarters wolf, being blacker, having longer hair and bushier tails than ordinary wolfhounds. I once had a very exciting drive at Storlien in a sledge hauled by a team of seven, and I shall always remember that evening as we swung through the crisp air with the driver standing behind on the sledge-runners cracking a long whip. Their main disadvantage for long ski-tours is that they cannot climb too steep a slope, for which reason many a fine route may have to be avoided. But of course there are Lapp dogs and lap-dogs.

To-day there is nothing very unusual in making ski-tours lasting about a week, even in places where there are no rest-huts. Some parties take tents; some, sleeping-bags, which can be used without other protection. I have heard of a young comparatively inexperienced skier who once made a tour all alone, sleeping out in a bag fitted with a hood which enabled him to read by torchlight. A large party will often depend for shelter entirely on igloos, which of course take some time to build. A bivouac, made with the help of skis, is more suitable for smaller groups. No one, it is said, has ever been frozen to death who has made a bivouac beneath the snow: if ever you are unable to reach your destination, you know what to do (and take a candle: that will raise the temperature another degree or two). The advice is excellent; if followed, it would probably have saved most of the lives lost in the fells. But how, I always wonder, can a party trapped in a blizzard and more or less exhausted dig themselves a shelter in snow almost as hard as rock? The answer is probably a memorial stone, like one I have seen in a desolate part of Jämtland. But for all that I have an agreement with a Swede to cross the Jotunheim some day (the great plateau of Norway), probably with the help of a sail.

Nansen was not the only explorer of the last century who helped to popularize skiing. There was Adolf Erik Norden-skiöld, Sweden's greatest explorer and the discoverer of the North-East Passage, who arranged in 1884 what I think must still be one of the most remarkable langlauf competitions on record. On an expedition to Greenland the previous year a

(above) *Bovallstrand, a typical west-coast village* (below) *Smögen, one of the larger island villages*

(above) *Sjöbodar in Smögen* (below) *These old salts will never again cross the North S*

(left) *Torsk, did you say?* (right) *A Fjord near Uddevalla*

(above) *Across the creek, Fiskebäckskil* (below) *Portrait from a gullery*

Västgötas, the oldest nation-house dating from the seventeenth century

(above) *The Skytteanum and the music room* (below) *Värmlands the newest nation-hou.
designed by Ragnar Östberg, architect of the Stockholm town-hall*

(above) *The Gustavianum, lying under the Cathedral, is named after Upsala's greatest
benefactor* (below) *Upsala is also a port: Steamers from Stockholm on the Fyris*

Sista April, Upsala : scene in Drottninggatan after the students have brought out th
summer caps

(above) *Doctors' promotion   A Jubilee Doctor speaking from the steps of the University building after the ceremony* (below) *Valpurgis Night.   Choirs on Castle Hill singing hymns to the spring* (*photograph by Hasselblad's*)

(left) My Swedish teacher and his fiancée in their Hälsingland folk costumes (photograph by Sten Wahlberg) (right) Runestone from 1050 a.d. at Bokstad, Uppland. Notice the hunter on the skis to the left (photograph from Skidfrämjandet: "Finds of skis from Prehistoric Time in Swedish Bogs and Marshes," E. Munksgaard, Copenhagen, 1950.)

A vault painting by Albertus Pictor from the 1480's Harkeberga Church, Uppland of Jonah and the whale (photograph by Kungl. Vitterhets-Historie-och Antikvitetsakademien etc)

(left) *St. Maria Kyrka.   The Baltic-Gothic western façade* (right) *Baltic-Gothic at its best : a gateway in the churchyard wall, Vendel*

(left) Tierp, a mediæval church with corner pinnacles (right) Holy Trinity, the oldest church in Upsala, is a good example of Baltic-Gothic

(left) *The bells of Sigtuna clang out over the Malar* (right) *Tierp New Church. A typical modern country church*

Map of Scandinavia by Olaus Magnus 1539, from the Carta Marina. (Reproduced by permission of the Trustees of the British Museum)

(above) *A village in Härjedalen* (below) *Ljungdalen : the hotel*

(above) *Evening in the Fells.* On the *Härjedalen-Jämtland border* (below) *Shine and shadow, Saxnäs*

Jämtland ski-terrain

Early morning, Blåhammar

Lapp-dog with pulka (photograph by Dr. B. Record)

A Lapp couple at their Kåta (photograph by Erik Jonsson)

(above) *Stone-age rock tracing, Rödöy, Nordland, Norway (after Gjessing)* (below) *Stone-age rock tracing near Lake Ladoga, Russia (After Raudonikas)*

e) *A Norwegian ski-trooper by J. H. Senn circ.* 1800 (*after Einar Stoltenborg*) (*below*)
A seventeenth-century ski-picture, from Scheffer's History of Lapland

(left) *A Bothnian farmer-lumberman* (right) *The Forest Gateway*

(*above*) *Log-pile on the banks of the Angerman* (below) *Logging in winter* (*photograph by Anders Eriksson*)

(above) *Timber floating on a Swedish river (photograph by V. Lundgren)* (below) *Skogsele Students from the State College of Forestry in their special green-and-scarlet waistcoats*

*ve) The first Riksdag met in Arboga (below) A fine stand of Scots pine in a state forest ;
and Kopparberg Church, a good specimen of shingle work*

(above) *A town in Bergslagen : Kopparberg* (below) *Läckö castle on a island in lake V*

e) *A Bergsman's home in Västmanland; and a cow roaming at will in the forest* (below)
Typical Lower-Värmland scenery

(above) *Sidestreet in a town, Middle Sweden; and the Swedish East India Company buildin*
the German church, Gothenburg (below) *High summer in Middle Sweden*

(above) *The swimmer by Carl Eldh (photograph by Almquist and Cöster)* (below) *St. Bridget: wooden statuette by a Swedish master circ.* 1500, *Brahe Church, Visingsö ; and Folke Filbyter by Carl Milles, part of the fountain, Linköping*

(above) *The Northern vapour-bath (after Olao Magno)* (below) *In Dalarna, the maypole is left standing throughout the summer ; and mill on Alvaren*

(left) Halltorp, once a royal shooting box, is now a home for the old (right) My villa in Borgholm, with fruiting vines over the gateway

(left) *Harbour study* (right) *Kalmar : Castle and harbour*

(left) *Kalmar Cathedral: The principal Baroque church in Sweden* (right) *Interior of the Cathedral, showing the altar-piece by Precht*

couple of Lapps he had sent out to reconnoitre returned after fifty-seven hours saying they had accomplished twenty-three miles (142 English). Knowing that a Lapp-mile generally varies according to the Lapp's fancy, he was rather sceptical and decided on his return to hold a test over a measured distance. So a course of 142 miles was decided on in Lapland (Jokkmokk to Kvikkjokk and back again) and only Lapps were allowed to enter. The winner completed the course in twenty-one hours, twenty-two minutes! I myself was quite proud of doing between ninety-five and a hundred miles in three days (in Norway), which perhaps is not too bad for an Englishman with exceptionally heavy slalom skis.

Every March a fifty-six-mile race is held in Dalarna over a course which is hallowed ground. For it is the route taken by Gustavus Vasa four centuries ago when, having apparently failed in his attempt to raise a rebellion against the Danes, he was escaping on skis into Norway. But the Dalesmen had meanwhile thought better of his offer: some skiers were sent from Mora and overtook him at Sälen. He returned, eventually became the liberator of his country and one of its greatest kings. So the Vasaloppet from Sälen to Mora, probably the most remarkable ski Marathon in existence, is now as much a national event as the Boat-Race or the Derby is for us. Such is the interest in it that reporters will often run beside favourite competitors to learn from their own mouths how they feel and so forth. Some of the runners have not only frequent drinks *en route* but quite substantial meals also. The record is held by Gösta Andersson, who completed the course in five hours, eighteen minutes, forty-three seconds in 1944.

A typical form of Swedish competitive skiing developed during the last thirty years or so is *budkavelöpningen*. Comparable to the autumn cross-country running with compass, it is a kind of ski-relay of perhaps thirty miles run in three parts, the competitors finding their own routes from one control-point to another. And here as in Finland distance and endurance are generally at a higher premium than speed.

Our last evening at Saxnäs was further enlivened by the arrival of half-a-dozen students who had spent their Easter

L 151

week on a long tour over the fells. They were tough, experienced lads even more bronzed by the sun and wind than we were. They had some amusing stories to tell about their adventures—how they had once carried all day, in addition to their heavy ruck-sacks, enough birchwood to make a fire in the *fjällstue* where they spent the night, and how they sometimes slept in cattlesheds among the cows and hay.

It was a wonderful holiday this week in Lapland, and often when the sordidness of everyday life threatens to overwhelm I shall dip into the memory for these blue-and-white porcelain days.

3 : *For Bengt*

The fells here have grown old with waiting,
Bearded with fosses and insidious screes;
The reindeer has outlived the days of mating;
His antlers shagg'd with mosses
Copy the wizened, wind-wrenched, withered trees.

The fells here have grown cold with waiting,
Their backs are stiff, their arteries are rigid;
Nude bones gnawed raw protrude
Against whose frigid grit
Our skis, grating and rasping, grasp the top
On which we stop and sit.

This marvel you have shown me.—How the sky
Bulges like a spinnaker! The ground
Tosses in whitened waves limitlessly,
The mind now nearly drowned
In the undertow of sound,
But always rising to the crest
And in motion finding rest.

For me you have decoded
This sunscript on snowparchment. Let to-day

Be like this rock, be special and apart!
And let it be unaltered, uneroded,—
For the heart
A monumental pillar, though the rest be swept away!

4 : *To a Ski Jumper*

Only you can get behind
The cumbrous scaffolding of flight
To worship Form in all her pure
Abstraction from the filtered air.

Only you have learnt to fix
The keystone of a reckless bridge
Whose beautiful and breathless span
Would baffle any alidad.

The flawless jewel of your flight
By the diamond-dust of ice
Is polisht, and intensely flashes
Through the dark of human wishes.

You can swing on a trapeze
Where man himself is the machine:
And from aerial outcrops wrest
Nuggets of otherworldliness.

You only among men can fly
On pinions of posterity.

5 : *The Birth of a Sport*

THAT GREAT AND versatile Norwegian Fridtjof Nansen,
in speculating upon the origin of skis and skiing in his book

Background to Sweden

The First Crossing of Greenland (1890), may almost be said to have invented a new science. Ski research, thus initiated, has been taken up with much enthusiasm and seriousness by the Scandinavians who have formed remarkable ski museums in Oslo and Stockholm and have called upon some of their foremost philogists, geologists, ethnologists and archæologists to help them solve the problems involved. Becoming interested in the subject myself, I began to read up all the relevant publications I could trace, and in this I have been much helped by Major Artur Zettersten of Stockholm and particularly Statsadvokaten Helge Refsum of Nordland, Bodö, Northern Norway, who have so kindly sent me various pamphlets and articles, some by themselves, and referred me to others. It is mainly from these that I have compiled the following account which I hope will be of interest, seeing that English attempts in the same field (such as certain chapters of Arnold Lunn's *History of Skiing* and E. C. Richardson's *The Ski Runner*) are now rather out of date owing to numerous recent discoveries.

Like all ancient and romantic arts skiing has an uncertain origin. No one has yet discovered who were its first exponents nor where exactly they lived. The theory that it originated among the Finno-Ugrian tribes in Russia is no longer tenable now that highly developed skis have been found in Scandinavia dating from times considerably earlier than the first few centuries B.C. when the Lapps and the Finns first began to occupy their present homes around the Baltic. From almost the earliest times the inhabitants of Northern Eurasia from the North Sea to the Behring Straits have traversed fell and tundra by sliding across the snow on planks affixed to their feet. For them as for many of their descendants to-day, whether Scandinavians in the west or Chukchees and Korlaks in the east, skis were used essentially as a means of locomotion and for the chase. Some of the earliest ski pictures known, the Late Stone Age rock-tracings discovered near the White Sea and Lake Onega in Russia, represent men hunting reindeer (Plate 23). In another curious carving from the same period (Plate 23), one of those found at Rödöy in Nordland, Northern Norway, the skis are for some unknown reason far bigger in proportion to the human figure than any could ever have been in real life. Most of these tracings show the skiers in the running position with bent knees in the best Telemark style, though it is consoling to find that even at such an early date rabbits were not unknown in the skiing world: at least the headdress which this prehistoric Norseman seems to be wearing (probably made of the ears or horns of an animal) certainly gives him that appearance.

From about the same time as these carvings dates the ski I have mentioned as having been dug up from a peat bog at Hoting in Ångermanland, Northern Sweden, and which is now in the Ski Museum at Fiskartorpet, Stockholm, catalogued as No. 152: "at least 4,200 years old and probably 5,000 . . ." (according, that is, to a pollen analysis—a method I have described elsewhere).

The earliest literary mention of skiing is probably the reference to a race of Scrid-Finnar by the Byzantine historian Procopius in the sixth century. These people, a branch of the Finno-Ugrian family, dwelling more particularly in the North of Norway, are equivalent to Lapps rather than to Finns in the modern sense. (The Old Norse term for Lapp is "finn", which is even now used in that sense in Norwegian.) Though often mentioned in geography and literature from the Dark Ages onwards (in the Anglo-Saxon *Widsith*, for instance, probably our oldest poem), there is seldom any evidence that the meaning of their title was understood. *Scrid*, as Paul the Deacon, the eighth-century Lombard remarked, refers to their custom of gliding over the snow by means of some instrument fastened to their feet. Saxo Grammaticus, the Danish historian who recorded the legend of Hamlet in 1204, is more explicit: "This people", he says, "is used to an extraordinary kind of carriage, and in its passion for the chase strives to climb untrodden mountains and attains the coveted ground at the cost of a slippery circuit, for no crag juts so high but they can reach its crest by fetching a cunning compass. For when they first leave the deep valleys, they glide, twisting and circling, among the bases of the rocks, thus making the route very roundabout by dint of continually swerving aside, until, passing along the

winding curves of the tracks they conquer the appointed summit." In Northern mythology skiing is connected with the
names of Ullur (Ullr or Ull is the Norwegian form), the god
of winter and hunting, and of his wife Skadi, a beautiful
giantess and goddess of winter who had formerly married
Njord the summer god but finding co-habitation impossible
very wisely decided on a separation. Both Ullur and Skadi
travelled on ski; the latter in fact is also known as Ondur-dis
(the goddess of Ski); and skiing, according to the sagas where
it is frequently alluded to, became one of the necessary quali-
fications of a hero.

Not far from Upsala is a runestone (plate 11) depicting
rather crudely a Viking skier hunting with bow and arrow.
This carving, executed about A.D. 1050, is apparently the only
known ski picture between those from the Stone Age which
we have seen and the woodcuts made to illustrate the works of
Olaus Magnus. His *Opera breve*, 1539, is probably the first
book in the world with an illustration of a skier. What artist(s)
he employed for his cuts has never been discovered; for the
illustration in question is inaccurate and his artist may never
have seen a ski. Titian, it is said, based a ski painting on these
cuts; while some of the drawings published in the next century
were also misleading, such as an illustration for a book by the
great Danish scholar Ole Wormius showing skis turned up
behind (1655), as well as in front. Scheffer in 1673 took care
to secure reliable illustrations for his *Lapponia*, and the only
inaccuracy one can detect in Plate 24 is possibly too great a
thickness in the ski. "Their shoes, with which they slide over
the frozen snow", he writes in the chapter *Of the Laplanders'
Weapons and other Instruments of Hunting*, are made of

> "broad planks extremely smooth; the Northern people
> call them *skidder* and by contraction *skier* (which agrees
> something with the Germans' *scheitter*, that is, cleft wood).
> . . . The way of going in them is this: they have in their
> hands a long staff, at the end of which is a large round
> piece of wood fastened to keep it going deep into the
> snow, and with this they thrust themselves along very
> swiftly. This way of running they not only use in plain

and even, but in the most rugged grounds, and there is no hill or rock so steep, but with winding and turning they can at last come to the top . . . and that which is a great miracle will slide down the steepest places without danger."

Although travel books containing descriptions and illustrations of skiing become more numerous from this time onwards, we have to wait long for the appearance of one by an Englishman. Neither King Alfred, who had what must be Halogaland, Finnmark and Scridfinnia described to him, nor any of our early northern traders and explorers who encountered the Lapps and Scridfinns have left even the barest mention of a ski: the first English book is Sir Arthur de Capell Brooke's *A Winter in Lapland and Sweden,* which appeared in 1827 with drawings by a Norwegian; if, that is, we omit Pinkerton's *Voyages and Travels* which mentions Siberian skiers in 1719.

But if the exact district where skiing originated cannot be definitely fixed on, neither can the evolution of skis themselves be described with certainty. Though most authorities are now agreed that they could never have been developed from snow-shoes or pattens which are probably older, the possibility that a sledge-runner provided the precedent does not seem to have been rejected. Pattens, used throughout the world by men and animals for crossing snow, sand, mud, etc., and mentioned for example by Xenophon (c. 400 B.C.), have existed side by side with skis down to the present day in Northern Europe. They are used especially in logging operations when only short distances have to be traversed; at the end of the day the lumberman may put them in his rucksack to return home on ski.

It is thought by some that the real prototype of the ski was a shoe of fur with the hairs of the skin on the undersole running from toe to heel. The Arctic Type of ski at any rate is held (by Prof. Nils Lid) to have been developed from this. Short, broad and covered with skin, which enabled a hunter to approach his prey without disturbing it by a noise, skis of this type were in former ages used throughout Northern Asia (it is the only Asiatic type) and Arctic Europe.

Background to Sweden

The second main ski-type distinguished by the late Professor Wiklund of Upsala is the Southern Type whose distribution extended from the Urals westward through Central Russia and the Baltic states to Southern Scandinavia. Long, broad, without skin but with side-pieces for bindings and usually holes in the tip for a rope (which on the run was held in the hand for steering, or tucked in the belt, and used for towing the skis behind in bad conditions), this is the ancestor of the modern racing ski used the world over. Indigenous to Scandinavia, this ski has been there since the Stone Age, eventually reaching its highest state of development in the mountains of Southern Norway (especially Telemark). The Finns, who were the first to search for and collect skis from peat bogs, have discovered a by-no-means-primitive specimen of this type at Riimäki north of Helsinki dating from about 1,500 B.C.—some thousand years, that is, before their race reached Finland. It is the type still in use in the Baltic States, and even in South Sweden its development has been so arrested owing to the infrequency of heavy snowfalls that skis like this (with tip-ropes as in the Baltic States) have been used there down to the present: the *bonde* would slip into his grandfather's as into a pair of shoes, and if new ones were required they were made in the traditional form.

But in the middle of Scandinavia, with a strip through North Finland to Russian Carelia, at the boundary between the Arctic and the Southern Types, occurred another, the Central Nordic Type, apparently a compromise between them and unique in having one ski longer than another: a short, generally skin-covered ski or *ondur* for the right foot and a long grooved steering ski without skin for the left. Such skis, an entirely Nordic (Norwegian-Swedish) invention, probably originated in the first centuries of our era, spread to the Lapps and by them were introduced to the Finns in whose literature they are mentioned in the Middle Ages. It is the type described by Olaus Magnus and Scheffer (Plate 24), though neither mentions that only one ski had a skin: "These shoes", says the latter, "they cover with young reindeer skins, whose hairs in their climbing run like bristles against the snow and keep them from going back". Nor do any of these writers speak of the very important groove on the steering ski; de Capell Brooke, describing Norwegian skis of unequal length "hollowed in the middle on the under-side to prevent lateral slip", may have been the earliest to mention this point. Sometimes flat, sometime concave, occasionally even convex, the underside of skis has varied greatly according to time and place—a shallow groove, so wide that the undersurface is best described as having two side-ridges, being the prototype of the narrower and deeper groove, generally found to-day.

Footrests and bindings have also undergone considerable modifications or changes at various periods. The more advanced kind of the former, consisting of a cavity (*saetet*) cut out for the foot leaving side-ears much like the metal ones in modern bindings, has been found in many skis of the Southern Type as early as the Riimäki example and the Furnes Ski (a Bronze Age Norwegian specimen), as well as in steering skis of the Central Nordic Type down to fifty years ago in Romerike north of Oslo. But in another form of the Southern Type the footrest was heightened so that bindings could be drawn through the whole ski laterally. For the bindings themselves, leather, used at an early period, eventually gave way to osier or twisted birch twigs which though less durable had the advantage of being more rigid and for a time held its own in the North when the leather bindings were reintroduced within living memory. As for sticks, the use of two at a time, which at first seems to be a Finnish idea, has become general only during the last sixty or seventy years, and even now has not really caught on among the Lapps. Skiers formerly used but a single pole (which was longer and stouter), or (if they wore skis with tip-ropes) no stick at all.

If one of the main intellectual pleasures of skiing in the North lies in knowing that you are taking part in what may well be the world's oldest sport or in one which at any rate has there an unbroken tradition from the Stone Age, another is in finding that skiing has still far from outgrown its original utilitarian purpose. Beauty, as Hopkins insisted, is flashed off valour: is a by-product of action like the unselfconscious charm of children playing or the trainsong which does not enter into the calculations of engineers. But this is not to say that the by-product is undervalued in the North, nor even that it has not come to be rated in importance with the main product itself (utility). If the very animals at the Zoo love sliding down chutes into the water, how much more must men from the first have found exhilaration in the speed, the unique rhythms and (when they learnt them) the turns of skiing. Even the most phlegmatic hunter living in the flattest tundra wastes must now and then have sensed the thrill of speed when moving with a strong wind behind him or on some approximation to a slope, yet how tame is such a thrill compared with that possible in the mountains! Says Olaus Magnus, speaking of the Scric-finns who "pass over the feet of the mountains with a crooked motion round about, and so turn to and fro until they come to the highest parts of those winding hills: sometimes they do it in the heat of hunting and sometimes to try their skill and to contend for mastery therein, as those who run races to win the price". In 1767 we hear of competitions among Norwegian ski troops; in 1845 there was a championship meeting at Tromsöy where it is recorded that the first prize was won by Johannes Steen, afterwards premier of Norway; the first ski club in Norway was founded in 1861 in Trysil; and in 1863 a skiing exhibition took place in Trondheim.

But the year 1868 is best taken as the date which marks the beginning of skiing as a sport. In that winter two *bönder* from Telemark went to a competition in Oslo (then Christiania), where "a small circle of wise sportsmen" had taken up skiing during the '60's, and from then onwards Telemarkings were frequently seen in the Norwegian capital. Crichton Somerville, an Englishman, has left the following account of a meeting held in 1879 on Huseby Hill, which was the slope used before the famous Holmenkollen was chosen on account of its better snow:

"The leaping competition proved most highly interest-ing, though in some respects quite comical. Every man except the Telemarkings carried a long stout staff, and on that, so they thought, their lives depended. Starting from the summit riding their poles as in former times like witches on broomsticks checking the speed with frantic efforts, they slid downward to the dreaded platform or 'hop' from which they were supposed to leap, but over which they trickled as it were; and landing softly beneath finally reached the bottom somehow, thankful for their safe escape from the dreaded slide. Then came the Telemark boys, erect at starting, pliant, confident, without anything but a fir branch in their hands, swooping downwards with ever-increasing impetus until with a bound they were in the air, and 76 feet of space was cleared ere, with a resounding smack their ski touched the slippery slope beneath and they shot onwards to the plain where suddenly they turned, stopped in a smother of snowdust, and faced the hill they had just descended! That was a sight worth seeing and one never to be forgotten, even if in after years such performances have been in a way totally eclipsed."

It is amazing to find that although these Telemarkings' skis—long narrow ones based on the Southern Type thickened at the footrest for holes for bindings—were essentially the same as the modern touring skis, they were entirely without grooves underneath.

But now let us sketch the way in which skiing spread throughout the world.

In Asia, of course, it has probably existed as long as in Europe. Hunting on ski is said to be mentioned in the annals of the Chinese dynasty Tang (A.D. 907); Pinkerton in his *Voyages and Travels* speaks of skiing among the people round Lake Baikal in 1719; it even reached the Japanese islands.

Did it cross the Behring Strait into America? Everyone has heard of Canadian snowshoes, winter companion of the aboriginal Indian; no one of Indian skis. But skis were found among the Eskimos of Northern Alaska in the 1850's: a pair from near Point Barrow is now in the British Museum. How did they reach Alaska—from the east or from the west? They must have come from the east, from Greenland where the sons of

Background to Sweden

Hans Egede, the Norwegian who brought Christianity to the Greenlanders, introduced skis about 1722. Brought westward by the Eskimos, skiing eventually reached Alaska early in the last century. The example of these remote people had no influence on men living to the south, whether Indians or European settlers; and the real pioneer of American skiing was "Snowshoe" Thompson (1827-1876), who carried mail over the Sierra Nevada in California from 1856 regularly for twenty winters. Emigrating from Norway at the age of ten, he had probably seen at home some of the "post-farmers" or "Royal skiers" mentioned as early as the seventh century, just as he had certainly learned to ski there himself. To other Norwegians belongs the credit of organizing a ski club as early as 1876 in Plumas County in the same state; though skis were always known as "snowshoes" in California and the club as the Snowshoe Club. In the 1880s, some ski clubs were founded by Norwegians in Minneapolis, Ishpenning and Eau Claire; the first jumping competition being held in 1887. In Canada some professors at McGill University were among the pioneers. On the American continent, it is interesting to find, professionalism has been carried further than almost anywhere else.

The history of skiing in Central Europe has been written on exhaustively. It is curious to find that, according to a book by a German, Valvasor, in 1689, the peasants of Krain, a province in Southern Austria, practised the sport (on rather short skis) at that date; for it apparently died out, and the next mentions we have of Continental skiing are of some workmen in the Riesenbirge (Austrian Bohemia) in the 1840's, of a Norwegian at Mitlödi (Canton Glarus, Switzerland) in 1868, and of a well-known French climber Duhamel who practised at Grenoble in 1879 on some Swedish skis which had been shown at the Paris Exposition the year before. Although there were other spasmodic attempts in the next twenty years or so, the real impetus was provided by Nansen's *First Crossing of Greenland* (1890) describing his classic ski journey two years earlier with an enthusiasm that startled the keener mountaineers—whether Swiss, German, Austrian or English—who now discovered a means of climbing in the winter months.

That the Alps before long became the winter playground of Europe is common knowledge: from the barren slopes of snow sprouted a new industry.

To the British, who were among the early Alpine skiers and have achieved considerable success in a sport they can but rarely practise at home, the possibility that skiing has an ancient tradition in the British Isles should be of especial interest. In the Stockholm Ski Museum is a pair of old skis found in the North of Scotland conforming in some respects to a type once used in Western Norway. Now, as Major Zettersten points out, there existed from the tenth century till 1196 a Scandinavian colony at Caithness ruled by a Norse earl (jarl) in Wick; while Ragnvald Kale, a certain Norwegian-born Earl of Orkney who died in 1158, is actually known from a literary reference to have been a good skier. It would seem that the Norsemen, crossing the North Sea in those longships which the Sagas sometimes call "skis of the ocean", introduced skiing into these Islands about a thousand years ago. What is more, the tradition may have been unbroken: there was skiing in Devonshire in the seventeenth century; *Lorna Doone* (1860) mentions it; miners in Yorkshire, Cumberland and Durham went to their work on ski in the middle of the last century, and children in those parts going to school in snowy weather brought out skis which some said they had inherited from their grandfathers—all of which points one way when we remember that a Scandinavian kingdom once existed at York.

Skiing in the southern hemisphere can hardly be said to have been established till about the turn of the century, though a Norwegian gold-digger used skis in Australia in 1853. In 1890 fifteen Norwegian engineers emigrated to South America, where they used skis when working on the Trans-Andean Railway. Norwegians again were the first to ski in 1904 in the Atlas Mountains, where a ski club was founded the following year. But what years the first skis were used in the Himalayas, South Africa and New Zealand I have not discovered.

So we see that what in the shadowy past originated as a humdrum means of locomotion in Northern Eurasia has quite recently spread as a sport to all the world's mountain ranges or districts where snow settles on the ground. In nearly every case the initial impetus has been given directly or indirectly by Norwegians (as the words, "ski", "telemark" and "christiania" or "christy", universally borrowed, serve to remind us), for it was among the descendants of the rabbit skier of Rödöy that the art first came to be highly developed. In Norway to-day skiing, though still partly utilitarian, is the national sport to an extent impossible elsewhere for geographical reasons: in no other country can skiing be indulged in everywhere every winter. Unless it be in Finland or Iceland. Sweden comes next, for although the southern third of the country is outside the area of regular snowfalls, so many schools, families and parties visit the fells every year that only a small proportion of the populace can never have tasted the joys of a run.

And what have been the effects on skiing at its source now that the sport has flowed round the world and the waters in some measure found their way back to the original springs? First of all, skiing in the North has become more purely a sport than it has ever been, and continental systems are being adopted, modified or blended with older techniques. The Scandinavians, however, for all their successes in racing are less addicted to competitions than to touring, and in consequence enjoy themselves far more intensely. The international nature of the sport has also made for standardization in the ski itself: whereas half-a-century ago almost every valley in Norway and Sweden had its own special type, to-day standardized factory skis, whether touring or racing, are rapidly ousting the older local forms. In regard to bindings, however, the Scandinavians still prefer merely a simple toe-grip for touring purposes.

There is still one major aspect of skiing I have failed to mention: the ski on spreading from the North has not been used solely for sporting purposes. I am not thinking of its infrequent use as a means of communication or for hunting, or even as an auxiliary for polar exploration; but rather of military skiing.

Skis probably figured in warfare long before 1200 when we know for certain that they were used by patrols in the Battle of Oslo at which that brilliant and lovable King, Sverre Sigurdsson, defeated three separate convergent armies, each stronger than his own. In all the main Scandinavian wars from the time of Gustavus Vasa the ski seems to have been used in the winter and spring campaigns. In 1718, the year of Charles XII's death, both Norwegians and Swedes introduced ski-training into their regular army curricula. Not only patrols but whole regiments moved on skis, the possibility of which must long have been realized by nations famous for the mobility of their armies. Ski troops in short may be called the winter cavalry of the Northerners—every spring, indeed, joint exercises for skiers and cavalry are held in the Swedish and the Norwegian armies. The first printed instructions for ski troops is a pamphlet issued for the Norwegian army in 1774. About 1806, when a single ski stick was still the custom, the Swedes decided to cap it with a bayonet but whether they carried rifles as well I have failed to learn. Pictures of Norwegian ski-troopers from the war of 1808 show some with rifles, some only with sticks and swords. It is surprising to find that no attempt at camouflage was mentioned before the present century, when white overalls made their first appearance. With such a long tradition behind them it is a matter of small wonder that the Northerners, including the Finns (who not only had to repulse Russian armies at home but also served in Swedish armies abroad), have developed military skiing to so high a pitch.

Although the Prussian army had ski troops as early as the eighteenth century, the Russians do not seem to have trained any till some fifty years ago. France and Switzerland (which now have such fine Alpine ski-fighters) and other continental countries followed suit only at the beginning of the present century: some of these troops were in action during the Great War. Even Canada trained a detachment about that time. But as yet this form of warfare does not seem to have been carried on in the Far East. Or has it? Perhaps someone will enlighten us. At any rate, I shall now wind up this desultory reel of (mostly secondhand) information; and wait for that blissful day when the whole northern hemisphere is at peace* and I set out on the first ski journey round the world, beginning in Scandinavia (where I should like to collect some of the older forms of handmade skis before standardization has completely replaced them), and ending . . . where, and when?

*This was written during the War.

V · FORESTS

"Svithiod is a great forest land, and there are such great uninhabited forests in it that it is a journey of many days to cross them."
SNORRE STURLASON'S *Heimskringla* (early thirteenth century).

I : *Sylvan Backdrop*

WHEN AT THE end of the last glacial epoch the ice-sheet began to retreat from the North of Europe a tundra vegetation established itself—certain mosses, lichens, ferns and dwarf willows. Gradually, as the climate improved, flora and fauna grew richer; forest trees like birch, pine and aspen invaded vast areas; and man himself followed in the wake of the ice. Britain, at that time (some ten thousand years ago) united to the European mainland, was part of a great forest whose northern limits were gradually being extended till they reached the Arctic Ocean. The climate changed from period to period and with it the nature of the forest, which became denser and denser and to the south and west composed of more and more species; until, about 500 B.C., we find a climate very similar to what we now know, and a Europe substantially what it would be to-day had man remained in the hunting stage— one immense forest, coniferous in the North, stretching from Russia to the Atlantic, uninterrupted save by bog, moor and mountain.

But man did not remain in the hunting stage: as soon as he had axe and plough clearings were made, populations expanded, the standard of living was raised, and forests began to shrink. Depletion was especially rapid in the west. By the end of the Middle Ages England had begun to import timber in quantity; by Tudor times new buildings were only half-timbered; at the Industrial Revolution the Weald, last of our extensive woodland tracts, had been reduced to a skeleton; while to-day a mere twentieth of our original forest area remains—a sprinkling of spinneys and copses, neglected game-coverts and plantations of (mainly) exotics. For us, with a smaller proportion of forest area than any other European country, a forest is a park punctuated by macadamized roads, selected camping- and picnicking-sites, notices and baskets for litter. Arden and the haunts of Robin Hood are not to be found in the hedgerows. Those who think of trees at all think only of the individuals. Some, it is true, may have sampled the jungle or the Schwartzwald, and others may live near timber-yards; every day we may pass by factories that convert cellulose into paper, silk-stockings, or munitions, or hear "the hum of printing-presses turning forests into lies"; but such is all foreign, purchased material. It is only with an effort that we can imagine being brought up in a timber house on the fringes of forests stretching almost unbroken to the skyline in every direction, within sight of lumberjacks and floating logs, the sound of sawmills and the smell of resin, and yet having telephones and radios, central heating and electric refrigerators, a paper every day, a democratic government and the fused amenities of an ancient culture and a modern civilization. Such, however, is the lot of the average Finn and Swede, who still live like moths in the scarcely nibbled collar of that enormous garment which once clothed most of Europe. And to understand them it is necessary to see them against this background which has remained almost unaltered since the time their ancestors settled there; to remember that they are still children of the forest, largely dependent on it for their livelihood, aware of its mystery and power, its solemnity and primitiveness. The dryads have long since vanished from Greece, and with them the woodland goddess, Diana; but the culture of the North is yet mainly sylvan. The woods are not without their trolls and wood-sprites; Finns and Lapps even to-day have not forgotten their gods of the Forest.

From what Sir James Fraser shows in *The Golden Bough* it

would appear that in no other civilized country are there more relics of tree-worship than in Sweden. In early times most Europeans were probably tree-worshippers and evolved certain customs and rites like the May-pole and processions of leaf-clad mummers. These in most places have gradually faded out or lost their meaning: in certain villages in Upper Bavaria, for instance, the May-pole is renewed only once every few years, while in England it became in time a permanent fixture —a dead pole left on the green indefinitely. But in Sweden a freshly cut spruce is stripped, decorated and raised amid great celebrations every Midsummer, and the villagers dance around it into the small hours. In Stockholm, I am told (though I have not actually seen it), is a great open-air Leaf Market where decorated poles from one to twelve feet in length can be bought. On the last day of April, also, lads will be seen in several parts of the country carrying round bunches of sprouting birch-twigs. Headed by the village fiddler, they make the round of the houses singing May songs and collecting eggs in a basket, and wherever they are well received fixing a leafy twig over the doorway. "The intention of these customs", says Fraser, "is to bring home to the village and to each house the blessing which the tree-spirit has in its power to bestow." Sometimes, as in the case of the Swedish Maypole, the tree-spirit is conceived as incorporate or immanent in the tree. But often it was represented anthropomorphically. In certain villages around large forests—in Bohemia and Alsace, Northern Bavaria and Carinthia—the tree-spirit is still represented by the may-tree and by a man and a girl dressed in leaves or flowers; while among the gypsies of Rumania the Festival of Green George is the chief celebration of Spring. Sometimes, however, the spirit was represented by a living person only. Hence the English Jack-in-the-Green and other leaf-clad mummers: the Little Leaf Man in Thuringia, the Lazy Man in Würtemburg, Green George in Russia, and the May Kings, Queens of the May, and Whitsuntide Kings found in various parts of Europe. Or they may be called Bride and Bridegroom: as in certain parishes in Blekinge where the Midsummer Bride and the other village lassies can choose themselves temporary bridegrooms, the marriage apparently being intended to promote the growth of vegetation by homœopathic magic. (This is the origin of St. Bride's Day in Scotland.) So, civilized man, still more of a tree-worshipper than he realizes, is nowhere more so than in Sweden—not even in Finland, home of Tapio, the woodland god whom Sibelius has celebrated.

What physical relationship, then, has the Swede had to this forest background in the past? In the early Stone Age he would have to enter it for the purpose of hunting and to procure the small quantities of wood necessary for his rude temporary huts, fuel and a few boats. A nomad, subsisting solely by hunting and fishing, he effected no change on his environment. Then with the advent of agriculture and the introduction of domestic animals in the later Stone Age, settlements became fixed and small clearings were begun. Through the Bronze Age, the demands on the timber of the forests were increased, while axes being made of metal were much more efficient than flint. During the Iron Age, when local metal came to be used, the production of iron from bog-ores required large quantities of wood-fuel. More timber too was used for boats, some of which were eighty feet long with planks up to forty-five feet in length; while in Viking times there was, of course, an even greater consumption of boat-timber. Farmsteads at that period comprised no less than fifteen to forty buildings, all constructed of unhewn logs. But it was in order to meet the needs of an expanding agriculture (due to increasing populations) that the first considerable clearings were effected—in the third and fourth centuries—clearings on a greater scale than any during Viking times. In the seventh century a certain Olof, the banished son of an Upsala King, received the surname Trätälja or Tree-Cutter, on account of the clearings he effected in Värmland, where according to the Ynglingasaga he settled and attracted other colonies from Norway and the lands of the Svear.

Then—as the accessible forests elsewhere in Europe became steadily depleted, towns grew up and trade increased—Sweden began to export some of her forest products: pitch, Stockholm tar, masts, spars and a negligible quantity of firewood, all of these being taken by the Hanseatic Cities who at the close of the Middle Ages controlled the commerce and navigation of Northern Europe. During the following four centuries there was little change in the nature and not very much in the quantity of the exports (tar and pitch for naval stores; and masts, spars and logs in the round), which were taken in turn by the two great maritime powers, Holland and England. A British traveller in Sweden just a hundred years ago has left us a description of tar-making as he saw it and had it explained to him in Norrland:

"The machinery of the world", he observes, "could scarcely go on without tar; yet we seldom think of enquiring how it is made. Fir trees [*Pinus silvestris*] which are stunted, or from situation not adapted for the sawmill, are peeled of the bark a fathom or two up the stem. This is done by degrees, so that the tree should not decay and dry up at once, but for five or six years should remain in a vegetating state, alive but not growing. The sap thus checked makes the wood richer in tar; and at the end of six years the tree is cut down and is found converted almost entirely into the substance from which tar is distilled. The roots, rotten stubs, and scorched trunks of the trees, felled for clearing land, are all used for making tar. In the burning or distilling the state of the weather—rain or wind—in packing the kiln will make a difference of 15 to 20 per cent. in the produce of tar. The labour of transporting the tar out of the forest to the riverside is very great. The barrels containing the tar are always very thick and strong, because on the way to market they have often to be committed to the stream to carry them down the rapids and waterfalls. . . ."

Not till the nineteenth century, when the Industrial Revolution was well under way, was there any great expansion in export markets for forest produce. But that we must consider later.

Meanwhile there had been changes in the internal demands on the forests. The development of the mining industry in the fifteenth century—chiefly iron-mining in Bergslagen—called for an ever-increasing quantity of fuel and charcoal. So important was mining that the government took active steps to ensure an adequate supply, farmers for instance having sometimes to furnish charcoal instead of taxes; while the mining companies eventually acquired large areas of forest land, thus establishing that close connection between the industries still persisting to-day.

Simultaneously, though very much more slowly, the sawmill industry was being established. The earliest mills, driven by water-power, were located right up the rivers, and though cruder in form were probably not very different from the little mills owned jointly by a few farmers that one still sees by foss or fall even now. But with the advent of steam sawmills about a century ago and the vastly accelerated European demands for sawn timber, large mills sprang up throughout the country, especially at the mouths of rivers. And since on the sea steam was faster than sail, more voyages could be made each year to the Bothnian ports (ice-bound in winter), thus enabling larger exports to be made; hence further settlements were established in Norrland, where much forest hitherto virgin began to be exploited.

So right into the last century the Swedes were colonizing their own land, experiencing many of the dangers of overseas pioneers and not a few of their thrills. The best and more accessible tracts were of course occupied first, but even down to a hundred years ago land for new settlements could in certain parts be had for the asking, whereas in North America the settlers had generally to pay at least a nominal fee. Farmers from the very first had grazing rights within the forest, just as in many places they have to-day, while an ample supply of timber was always at hand for their own purposes. As in time enclosures became necessary the farmers began to acquire woodlots of their own. A wood, though not very profitable, was an essential part of a farm: the *bonde* was, and is, farmer and woodman in one, possessing those self-reliant, individualistic, conservative traits that the ownership and working of the soil inevitably engender. At present about half the forest area is owned by farmers, though much of this is of later acquisition, dating chiefly from the period 1810-30, when most of the Crown forests in the South were given away or sold at extremely low prices, and in the North vast tracts were divided between Crown and private owners, the Crown rights long being neglected so that much of the land passed to the farmers.

But why, it may be asked, was the State so neglectful? The reason was partly ideological: it was thought at that time that the State could not successfully carry on business enterprises. But when in the middle of the last century there was a steep rise in the prices of forest products, with consequent speculation in forests and much thoughtless cutting, the State began to realize the value of forests and that it ought to preserve and utilize them. So it thereupon set about repurchasing considerable tracts till to-day nearly a quarter of the total area belongs to State, municipalities and other public bodies.

We have seen then how the Swedes very gradually penetrated their forests, taking what they needed for their own small population and later on exporting certain of the products. From time to time there were changes in the nature of these products: at first tar and pitch were the main exports, later it was lumber; and these changes, like the rise and relative decline of the domestic demands for charcoal, had effects on the industries within the forest. But not till about 1850, when the swarming industrialized populations of a deforested Europe suddenly began clamouring for timber, which the Baltic, not so far off, could supply, was there any rapid and extensive exploitation. Sawmills, pulpmills, paper-mills and match factories sprouted into being; and Sweden, though not forgetting her mines and agriculture, discovered that the forest was the greatest of her natural resources. And so it remains, providing one-seventh of the national income and almost half of her exports.

2 : *Spring Balance*

These big pink snow-blobs,
Yearning to be delivered of their transitoriness,
Yell out for the broad canvas of Fjaestad.

Background to Sweden

He *would remove them bodily,*
Take them up lovingly in his large hand
And lay them tenderly on the taut cloth.

No colour whatever would come off in the transference—
No, not that delicate pink that clings only to fresh snow
At spring sunrises.

Nor in the fiery removal would there be the veriest vestige
Of melting
Or shape-shuffling.

Not even a single diamond would be found missing
By the scrupulous Head Jeweller
Or the astutest Crystal-gazer.

And the huge pink lumps would go on hanging forever,
Weighing down the soul's dark branches with an intolerable load of
loveliness—
Just not falling.

3 : Småland Woodnotes

With fleet feet borne by, buoyed by neddledown
(Groundswell's nave-mat made for matins)
I thrill to the sun through dun pine-passages
Thick with the mingled incenses of brine and resin,
Catching the swished messages of wave-washing, snatches of light-morse
Tingling among sky-bossed plastic groin-shadows
*   till the mullioned forest opens*
On the middle of a vermilion sunrise veined with lark-strains.

Light flakes, bright flakes flung from water,
Bung the eye-holes, try the ear-holes,
As wave upon weak wave quavers in over the Baltic,—
Glare-drenched shape-whiffs sound-ringletted and quiveringly musical-
luminous
With the glucose embroidery of looped lark-lays, the dewy effluvia of
brine-resin.

4 : *The Forest Tarn*

Don't you remember, Gösta, it was high
Summer? We had been tramping the whole day
Through forests when a tarn got in our way.
Those clouds—don't you remember how they lay
Among the lotuses like fantastic feathers
Dropped from a bird of legend in the twi-
lit nest of night,—how we cried out together,
Threw off our clothes and dived into the sky?

5 : *The Trees of Sweden*

THE FOREST LIKE the Sea may be a single theme, but there
are more variations on it than the uninitiated might suppose,
even in Northern Europe and Canada where straight solemn
conifers repeat themselves with the regularity of cornstalks,
the individual being merged in the mass, the many in the one
—the vast, vague universal Forest.

Turning the map of Sweden on its side, and marking off the
forest zones, we find it a great triptych, the middle panel of
which has a coniferous *motif*, the small side-panels deciduous
ones. The analogy is not too accurate geographically in the
case of the mountain deciduous zone (which would have to be
shifted from the Norwegian to the Finnish frontier), but it will
do. The central panel of pine and spruce comprising four-
fifths of the whole forest area is our main interest. Beginning
in Northern Skåne and ending in Northern Lapland, these
two trees sweep through most of the fourteen degrees of latitude
occupied by the country, now rising with the Småland highlands, now thinning towards the great lakes and the agricultural
plains of Middle Sweden; then gathering strength for the final
austere progression through the undulations and flat stretches
of Norrland. Though mixed here and there with hardwoods,
they are always the same dark conifers. The same, but with
what important differences! How different the sparse stunted

trees on the heaths of the Småland plateau from the tall dense woods on the deep loams of Södermanland! Equally significant are differences due to latitude, differences that make it necessary to recognize two coniferous zones which merge somewhere in the middle of the country. In the southern coniferous region, where summers are longer, the trees grow taller and more rapidly, attaining maturity in sometimes half the time of those in Upper Norrland. But the timber, being coarser-grained, is less valuable for sawing than that of mature trees, perhaps 120 years old, more widely spaced (in order to receive all the oblique rays of the sun) in the far north. The slowness of their growth is due rather to the brevity of the vegetative season than to laziness during that season, for in the brief summer plants actually work overtime and almost non-stop, cereals in places being sown and harvested within six weeks.

Sometimes in pure woods, sometimes mixed, the pine and spruce exist in almost equal numbers. The former, *Pinus silvestris*, is the ordinary Scots pine (usually misnamed "fir") native to Great Britain. But in Sweden there are two sub-species recognized by botanists (*lapponica* and *septentrionalis*), which meet in Middle Sweden giving rise to a number of hybrids. Researchers in tree-breeding are at present sorting out and classifying these hybrids, for the purpose of finding some variety which will embody the good qualities of both sub-species: the slender branches and therefore better wood of the northern with the rapid growth of the southern. It is the pine which provides two-thirds of the timber for the saw-mills, the deal which you can see being off-loaded at almost any port in Europe to provide the scaffolding and roof-timbers, doors and window-frames, floors and boxes of the majority of the populations; as well as many of our telegraph poles and railway sleepers.

The spruce on the other hand, *Picea excelsa*, commonly known to us as the Christmas tree and not a native of the British Isles, is to-day used mostly for pulp. Only eighty or ninety years old, this industry has shot up with remarkable rapidity to keep pace with the growing consumption of paper, cardboard, wallboards, artificial silk—to mention but a few of the uses of wood-cellulose. The earliest pulpmills were, like the early sawmills, erected near waterfalls, in order to obtain cheap power for grinding up the wood by the mechanical method I have elsewhere described.* By the 1870's complicated chemical processes, the sulphate and sulphite methods, were being perfected by Swedes and others, whereby the wood is cooked in liquors which dissolve all the material except the cellulose fibres. Though more expensive, these methods produce far cleaner fibres which can therefore be used for better paper. Mechanical pulp, however, mixed with one-fifth sulphite pulp, is good enough for ordinary newsprint paper. A certain amount of paper is manufactured in Sweden, but most countries prefer to make their own. Only the United States and Canada out-distance her in pulp production, but as exporters of chemical pulp she leads the field, providing forty per cent. of the world's exports. Half of this goes to U.S.A., most of whose forests have been so ruthlessly destroyed—with what disastrous effects is only now beginning to be realized. Whereas half of Sweden's lumber goes to Great Britain, the percentage of pulp (except that for newspaper) is much smaller. And what effect has this upstart industry had on the forest itself? Apart from making it worth while to exploit the more inaccessible woods, it has enabled smaller material to be used than sawmills are willing to take. For pulp, then, trees can be felled when younger—an important consideration in forestry where the time factor counts more than in most other businesses.

Now and then during these long dark coniferous periods we are thrilled by the pure silver of the birch; which in the north panel of our triptych actually becomes dominant, mounting into the fells' severe perfection, daring single-handed encounters with Arctic winds, feeling its way to the sources of rivers, touching the perpetual ice of glaciers. Although there is much difference between the crooked scrub-birch of the fells and the thick-boled wide-spreading trees of the south or the long clean, polished shafts of those in Dalarna, the birches are all alike in their lyrical excitement. If delicacy is the quality one generally associates with the tree, then it ought to be the delicacy of a

* See page 226.

177

pliant metal rod. A birch, admiring her pendulous branches in a lake-mirror, may appear extremely graceful, but are not those the very branches of broom-makers and harsh school-masters? And notice how during a storm she lashes out at her unfortunate neighbours with a truly feminine spitefulness. More resilient than most trees, she bends before every wind. In adolescence she is often pulled down by the weight of snow on her head and clamped to the ground till the spring thaw releases her, though it will be a year or two before she recovers from an arching spine. She is also the hardiest tree on earth, and will be found with dwarf willows at the tree-limit, generally managing to outbrave other adventurous species like the aspen, the mountain-ash or the grey alder by conquering a few extra vertical feet of ground in the inhospitable fells. With her black upper twigs and bolelenticels in sharp contrast with the snow, the scrub-birch coarsely scrabbles the fellsides, giving them a heavy double-crayoned outline. Since the Lapps wandering there with their herds of reindeer take from her their fuel and often the wood for their tent-poles, the tree is not exploited commercially in the mountain zone. But elsewhere it com-prises thirteen per cent. of the timber stock, which is much more than that of the other hard-woods put together. In recent years it has been much used for plywood, especially in Finland where birch, only a short while ago the cheapest of all woods, now fetches better prices than any other. After the spruce and the pine it is in fact the only tree economically important throughout the country and were it easier to float would probably become more so. Domestically it is still the coal of the average Swede, and how much is used even in Stockholm may be guessed from a stroll along Strandvägen when dozens of sailing ships will be seen offloading their bulky cargoes of firewood. All that yellow furniture so typical of the Swedish home comes also from the same tree, which is thus a source of light and freshness within even as it is without. Nor is it surprising to find that ᛒ in the Runic alphabet stands for birch. But the birch stands for more than ᛒ : a birchwood is a shining synopsis of the North.

Neglected till now because of its complexity is the other

small panel of our dendrological triptych: The deciduous forest region of the South. There is nothing very Swedish about it. Nor is there anything profound. A rather lightly scattered series of mixed woods such as might be found in half the countries of Europe, it is confined mainly to the western littoral, Skåne, and southern Blekinge, although there are spasmodic appearances on favourable sites in many other parts, even in Middle Sweden. Technically, its natural limits are found to coincide with a line drawn through places where the mean daily temperature exceeds 8° C. for 155 days in the year. This line forms the southern limit of the spruce: south of it deciduous forests preponderate, north of it coniferous, the change from one to the other being sharp in the coastal parts. In this region beech is the dominant tree and is sometimes grown in pure woods as in Denmark (where it is of great importance as a windbreak and for providing the wood for butter-crates). Used for furniture, building and other purposes, it is (like the oak) not sufficiently abundant to-day even for the needs of the local population, which in this region is denser than elsewhere. It was on pieces of beechwood that most of the runes were carved in Scandinavia, as the modern Swedish for letter-of-the-alphabet, *bokstav*, reminds us (*bok*—beech; *stav*, stick); and hence also the English *book*. The oak, like the lime, elm, alder, maple and aspen, goes farther north than the beech, its upper limit being the Dalälven (though it is rarely seen near that river). Being exceptionally prized for its numerous good qualities, it must always have been heavily cut, while the natural succession of beechwood further reduced its extent. The last of the big oakwoods were destroyed for ship-building in the seventeenth century. The aspen, on the contrary (which a certain forester told me is not indigenous, but was introduced from Finland three centuries ago), has only come into its own since the rise of the match industry, for which a light, clean, fissile wood is essential. As for the ash, elms, sycamore, hazel, birdcherry, a touch of hornbeam and yew, and a sprinkling of exotics, they are all very delightful to encounter, but are economically negligible. Excepting the birch, the entire group of hardwoods accounts for no more than a twentieth of the growing stock of timber. (But I cannot help mentioning another tree for a different reason: the *flögrönn* or flying-rowan—a mountain ash which grows on another tree, on a roof, in a rock-cleft—in other words, midway between heaven and earth. This, if any, is the tree emblematical of the Swedes, and here and there you may still come across people holding the ancient superstition, that a man who is out in the dark ought to have a piece of *flögrönn* to chew, lest he should be bewitched and unable to stir from the spot.)

And all these species, together covering more than half the country, have been there for thousands of years, some longer than others. But how do we know? It is comforting, for example, to learn that the spruce first arrived in Sweden about 10,000 years ago; or that between 7,800 B.C. and 5,600 B.C. the vegetative period was fifteen days longer than to-day though the winters were more severe; or that the vegetation when man arrived on the scene was of such and such a type and the time so many millenniums ago; but how do we know such things? We know them because Swedes like Gerard de Geer, Erdtman, Munthe and von Post, Lagerheim and Sernander have devised and worked out extremely ingenious methods of studying prehistoric conditions. Among the most illuminating is the analysis of pollen grains—minute objects only identifiable under a lens—which because of their lightness are blown great distances, some of them into bogs where they become preserved in the peat. By examining the quantity and types of pollen at various levels it is possible to tell what sorts of vegetation existed at various periods, and when for instance an archæologist now makes an interesting find, an examination of the pollen in the layer where it was embodied will help to determine its age. Even more brilliant are the researches of de Geer, the geologist who discovered among other things the age of man in the North. As the ice retreated northwards, the glacial drift, he concluded, must with every seasonal thaw have left successive layers of deposits similar to the annual rings of a tree. So he investigated and counted these layers in the earth from the southern tip of Sweden to the present remains of the ice-cap in Jämtland, thus working out a record of post-glacial time for Northern Europe. Other Swedes have worked on the post-glacial oscillations in the levels of the Baltic, examining the shells embedded in the littoral deposits; or have studied the plant remains of different periods; or like Montelius have made remarkable advances in archæology; so that all these lines of inquiry used in conjunction have provided those interested in such matters with an abundance of exciting information. History, confined in the North of Europe to briefer and even more recent times than in the South, covers so small a portion of man's sojourn on earth that no one can afford to be indifferent to the nature of prehistoric epochs, however remote they may appear from present realities.

6 : *Science in the Forest*

WE HAVE SEEN how the Swedes about a century ago embarked for the first time on a wholesale exploitation of their forests. With immense markets opened up before them and attractive prices offered for their timber, forest owners, especially private individuals, were tempted to cut recklessly merely for immediate gains. But the stocks would not last for ever; a forest cannot be regenerated over night, and most of the land if not forested would be useless for agriculture or other purposes. So the State, realizing that forests were a national asset, and able by its nature to be more far-sighted than farmers or companies, began to take active measures for their preservation. It first set about re-appropriating as much forest land as it could, some of which had only just come into the hands of private owners in the way we have already seen. It was not enough, however, to increase the area owned by the State: laws had to be made restraining the owners of the rest, and men had to be provided to manage forests on scientific lines in order to ensure a sustained yield of timber. A number of technicians were brought over from Germany, where forestry as a science had first developed, to manage estates both private and public. But the German methods had to be adapted to the different conditions found in Sweden, and there was a definite need for native managers. In order to provide administrative personnel for its own forests the State took the initiative in forest education, founding in 1828 the Institute of Forestry, one of the earliest in the world. There had from the sixteenth century been a Venery Service concerned mainly with hunting and hardly at all with forestry, and it was out of this that the Institute emerged. Very crude at first, it gradually evolved a special curriculum suited to the country and the age. Much enlarged from time to time, always adding to its range and complexity of subjects, and in 1917 reorganized into the College of Forestry, it has remained the medium of higher forest education.

All the public forests (State, municipal, etc.) are administered by the Board of Crown Lands and Forests which came into being later in the century, and which absorbs many of the College's graduates. The larger forests belonging to iron mines and iron works, pulpmills, sawmills and so on are also managed by trained foresters. But the farmers, who own half the country's forest area, cannot afford either to employ fully trained men or to undergo a thorough training themselves. So it is for them that the Forest Commissioners perform an especially valuable service. Controlled by a central Board in Stockholm, these Commissioners have been active for some thirty years disseminating a knowledge of forestry and helping owners to manage their property in the best way possible. Every county (*län*) has one of these Commissions which is composed of three unsalaried members, one appointed by the Government, one by the County Council, and one by the provincial agricultural society, and which is assisted by a paid staff of trained foresters and others; the funds being obtained by a 1.3 per cent. tax on the stumpage value of all timber felled. These Commissions are responsible above all for the enforcement of forest laws. Although there was a certain amount of local legislation in the past, it was not till 1905 that the first general forest law came into force. Any timber cut must, it stipulated, be replaced by new growth within a reasonable time after cutting. As a safeguard against profiteering and carelessness which had hitherto reduced many estates to a deplorable condition this measure has been of inestimable importance. But during the Great War when the demands for timber were greatly increased it was found necessary to make several provisional laws to prevent the felling of young forests; so in the Forest Conservation Law of 1923 a further restriction was added that immature stands must not be cut except for improvement thinnings. As the marking of trees for these thinnings requires a greater knowledge of silviculture than the average farmer possesses, he generally applies to his Commission to have his trees marked, and in Lapland where conditions are most difficult he is actually compelled to do so. With several hundred trained men in their employ, these Commissions work untiringly, drawing up management plans; supervising planting, marking and so on; providing inexpensive seeds and plants from their own nurseries; giving financial assistance for the drainage of swampy land; laying out sample plots beside main roads; arranging short courses in various branches of forestry; writing and distributing free copies of simply written pamphlets; and in other ways disseminating valuable advice and information. Through them land is being reclaimed, timber production increased and quality improved —to the ultimate benefit of both State and private owner. They also have been partly instrumental in making Sweden the forest-conscious country that she is.

To-day a certain acquaintance with the elements of forestry has become a necessary part of the education of most young Swedes, who are expected to realize that timber is the true backbone of their country. Someone brought up in Lapland, for instance, told me that the children there a generation ago would cause serious forest fires by the habit of burning twigs to drive off the troublesome mosquitoes--a practice that has now stopped altogether, thanks to the right education.

Having at one time studied forestry myself, I was anxious to see how the Swedes receive their specialized education in the subject. For men in subordinate positions—forest rangers (*Kronojägare*) and foremen—there are five lower forestry schools, each with a one-year course, in different parts of the country; while a number of pupils, including farmers and their sons, take shorter courses provided by various agricultural schools and Forestry Commissions. For Foresters (*jägmästare*) there is a four-year course at the State College of Forestry, housed in a large building in extensive grounds outside Stockholm. There are some eighty students in all who come by the day from their homes or lodgings in or around the capital. Before being admitted every applicant must have passed not only his Student exam. (University matric.) but also strenuous tests in swimming, gym, skiing and shooting; and his first year is spent on probationary work in the forest itself. Theoretical instruction is then taken in the College, which also arranges excursions and practical work in the vacations; till eventually the student graduates with the much-coveted title of *Jägmästare* (literally Hunting Master) which survives from the old Venery Service. He will then be sent off to manage some State forest, probably in Lapland, beginning with a salary of about £225 with eight days leave in the year, and being responsible to a Chief Forester; or he may be absorbed in one of the Commissions; or perhaps he will enter private service (generally a company), which may prove more remunerative but will carry rather less prestige. As a profession for the intelligent practical man forestry in such a country has many of the attractions that the Colonial Service has for certain types of Englishmen, and is without the worse drawbacks like unhealthy climates and lengthy separation from home and Europeans. An extremely active out-of-door life, it provides opportunities for administrative ability and scientific work as well as for sport and hobbies of various kinds.

I was much impressed both by the thoroughness of the training and the excellence of the museums, laboratories and finely-equipped lecture-rooms at the College of Forestry. Here were magnificent collections of native birds, beasts and insects in their various forms with specimens of their nests, eggs, fæces, spoors and so forth; of fungi, and of the damage done by means of these; for the forester is first of all a naturalist, an ecologist, responsible for maintaining the biotic balance in his woods. He is also a business man, must be able to take stock of his possessions, measure timber standing, in the round, or sawn up; understand his business well enough to increase production and ensure a sustained output; assess the financial value of his forest land and timber; estimate working costs and profits. Examples of plans and tables of figures, photos and charts for such instruction were all shown me. Of wider interest were the scale-models of buildings and engineering works (bridges, dams, flumes, timber-shoots and so on) which the forester must know how to construct; the exhibition of implements used for felling and extraction of timber (divers types of saws, billhooks, axes, barking-knives, chains, grapples, hawsers—all manufactured from high-grade Swedish steels); and the comprehensive displays of the numerous products derived from various species of trees. Nor should I forget such exhibits as a section of the oldest pine tree found in Sweden —only 535 years according to the rings and of smaller girth than many poplars not yet centarians I have seen in England; or the interlocked antlers of two elks which had been fighting and had thus inadvertently become inseparable in death. In the course of being shown round by one of the lecturers I was introduced to a professor of the College who very kindly invited me to join him and his study group of fourth-year students during the next vacation.

So at the end of July I spent a few days at a village in Dalarna as a guest of the Swedish State, though my immediate host was this very charming professor, a man renowned in forestry circles the world over for his important contributions to the science. A couple of the students I had met before in Lapland, where incidentally I had had pointed out to me a forest hut in which one of the younger age-groups lives every year. Partly providing for themselves with their guns, and running the place quite on their own, they form for several months a self-supporting community in the backwoods, though Saturdays take them to the nearest village for some dancing, much to the exasperation of the local lads who resent such invasions. The *skogselever* or forest students are, however, a very popular band in Sweden, and whenever one sees a youth clad in a scarlet waistcoat with bright green lapels one can be sure he is a good fellow. This cheery dress, adapted from a Dalarna folk-costume, is their special pride, and the back generally has conspicuous devices embroidered on it by one's girl friend. From the nature and complications of these patterns there is always much to be learned or guessed about the character of the girl and her relationship with the owner of the garment, though an unfinished device may as often as not imply an incipient romance as a broken one (see Plate 27).

The building in which we lived—the professor, a lecturer and their wives, and about twenty students—was a red and white *herrgård* with detached wings, about a couple of hundred years old and acquired fairly recently by the State. Rising at 6.30 every morning, we breakfasted and went off into the forest all day, returning in time for a late bathe before dinner, which generally included pike, perch or some other freshwater fish. And in the evening the students would get down to their maps and figures, the rest of us sitting in the open with pipes or papers.

Some of the best and most productive forests are found in Svealand (i.e., Central Sweden). The trees, growing less rapidly than those in the South, give better timber for sawing purposes (though for pulpwood these are no advantages), while the density of the woods is much better than in the far North where the trees demand more light and therefore space. In Upper Lapland too it is often extremely difficult to regenerate a wood: the trees instead of seeding every few years, as further south, may do so only every ten, twenty or thirty years, while in parts natural regeneration may occur only once in a century; and even planting (which is costlier) is uncertain. From this, and the fact that a tree may take forty years to reach a height of six feet, the difficulties encountered by a forester in Arctic Scandinavia—in the world's most northerly forests—can perhaps be gauged. Silviculture over most of the country is however moderately simple. As in Finland, the State and companies' forests are managed on what is technically known as the Uniform System, which means that the trees on each stand are of more or less the same age, that there are thinnings from time to time, with a heavy final one to provide enough light for young trees to spring up beneath the remaining selected standards which simultaneously profit from the increased space. This is easier to manage than the Selection System favoured by most farmers which entails the removal of trees here and there, or small groups, from woods whose trees are of all ages. Throughout the country as a whole natural regeneration is favoured as being both better and less expensive than planting.

In Svealand the main obstacles to natural regeneration are caused by domestic and wild animals, though bracken and grass can also be a nuisance. From time immemorial the farmer has had his grazing rights in the forest, from which cows cannot by law be excluded. Fencing off is too expensive, so the animals wander about cropping grass and saplings indiscriminately. The result is the *hagmark* seen round villages—half wood, half grassland. The birches (very tall and straight in Dalarna) and the other hardwoods generally found on such land are certainly charming in appearance, but the forest would benefit greatly from a definite separation of forest from grazing land. The farmers too would probably gain, for in our district for instance there was much less birch than there ought to have been, what with grazing and the fact that so much was removed for charcoal (we were in Bergslagen) during the last century.

Then there is damage, as I was shown, by elk and fallowdeer, who rub off the fur from their antlers on the stems of young trees. But the elk are the worst offenders, especially by eating off the large shoots from the spring right into the autumn. Very numerous indeed in Svealand, where they also feed on oats and rye, clover and potatoes, elk are the curse of forester and farmer alike. So their numbers have to be kept down by hunting. There are said to be about 50,000 animals in the country, and since the stock increases by about 30 per cent. every year there is a considerable margin left for shooting without exposing it to the danger of extinction. Nothing is left to chance; the exact number to be killed in any district is determined each year and special rules of the chase are observed. To my great regret I have not yet witnessed an elk hunt, though I have had described to me the excitement that can be had. With extraordinarily keen senses of smell and hearing, the elk can recognize his pursuers at great distances, and one forester living in Norrland where the stock is comparatively thin told me it was thirty years before he secured his first kill. Not any animal can be killed during the hunting season: a cow with calf is never shot, while a very vigorous dark bull (admirable for breeding) may have to be resisted in favour of a thin grey one which will hardly make an attractive trophy but would make an even worse perpetuator of the race. The method, too, has to be considered: one shot, if a good hit, is the ideal, for the animal then lies down and dies. Other shots or a noise will only send him off in an effort to escape, which means that even if he is found again the flesh will have hardened on his run and eventually turns bad. The more hits there are, the more meat has to be discarded. It is not surprising that elk-hunting, a necessity as well as a sport worthy of kings, is a favourite pastime of King Gustav.

The first day I was shown in one of the State forests we visited some exceptionally fine stands of pine (Plate 28). In the oldest, the clean straight boles, shooting up to about a hundred feet and surmounted by sprig-like crowns rocking gently in a breeze, were an exalting sight for either æsthete or utilitarian (and any really good forester is a combination of both of these). Not far off was a younger stand forming a remarkable contrast with its disease-distorted stems and very resistant side-branches—the result of buying cheap German seed in the past, for up till about 1900 the importance of heredity was not understood. Nowadays seed is obtained only from the best trees during their most fertile period, and the type of site is always indicated. The slightly increased outlay on first-grade seed is repaid many times over by the great improvement in quality and quantity of timber. I was also interested in seeing an area being regenerated by spot-planting (a few seeds are sown in each spot), where two kinds of seed were being tried, some German, some Swedish. It was found that in the case of the former the trees grew up together—

several shoots of equal vigour; whereas with the native there was one dominant tree from the start in each group. (No moral here.)

Various exotics have been tried in Sweden but none are of any economic importance so far. I was surprised to find that the larch, which has been successfully introduced into Finland (one larchwood there is reputed to be the most productive stand in the whole of Europe, with 26,000 cubic feet per acre), grows poorly in Sweden, though *Larix leptolepsis* does rather better than the Siberian larch.

Another day I went out with one of the students who showed me how they were checking up a map made in 1911. Each was allotted an area, and had to make notes on every stand within it, marking in any differences in boundaries (we sketched in a new ditch, for example), average height of trees (judged on this occasion by the eye, but if we failed to agree, we had recourse to a hypsometer—a height-measuring instrument), density of stand and quality (both empirical data), and volume (calculated from yield tables found in the manual that a forester always carries with him, and expressed in cubic metres, though English, Swedish and even Dutch measure is also used on occasion). I noticed how the sites of charring-heaps (the charcoal-burners always keep to given sites which are marked on forest maps) acted as useful checking-points when we were in any doubt of our position. Some of these charring-heaps, now being disused, were overgrown by wild strawberries with fruit so large and prolific that a whole meal could be had in five minutes. Bilberries were almost everywhere very numerous, as the blue-mouthed village children were well aware. Nearly as common in certain parts were the bright-beaded cranberries, not to be eaten raw but when cooked an almost inevitable accompaniment of any dish from dry cereals to venison. In swampier parts among the bog-moss, cloudberries, the choicest of all septentrional fruits, could be recognized as bright pink pearls, each set singly in the middle of a bract-whorl, though the properly ripe berries, limp and dully yellow, had to be searched for among the foliage. I could also enumerate various *champignons* and other edible fungi commonly

Background to Sweden

gathered from July onwards, or describe some of the more interesting plants such as *Monotropa hypopitys* (bird's nest), whose curved, entirely colourless shoots could be seen nosing out of the moss in woods where the pine and spruce grew together; but the botany of the forest floor is a large rambling subject, even up here where undergrowth is far less prolific than, say, in England. I was disappointed in seeing very few wild animals: only one elk, a hare or two (rabbits are a rarity over most of Sweden), several snakes and an occasional vole. Snakes I had certainly not counted on, but they are, I found, rather common on sunny slopes, and the students kept some in a box in the garden. Of the birds I saw, by far the most interesting was the capercailzie, an enormous bird, especially the male, easily recognized in flight by its long craning neck and wedge-shaped tail, and extremely clever at steering though the forest (where it nests and feeds on the wild raspberries). Startled on the nest, it rises with an amazing whirr, causing a violent disturbance in the underwood. The male is famous for its fierce courtship in the spring—a rough-and-tumble affair which sometimes results in one of the couple being killed or at least losing half its feathers.

Why is Sweden such an excellent country for forestry? She has first of all great quantities of valuable, accessible timber, and after Russia is the principal producing country in Europe. Her forests as a whole are comparatively easy to manage: similar conditions prevail over extensive areas; tree species are few; regeneration can generally be secured with comparatively little difficulty; danger from winds, fire and pests is not serious; the necessary labour is obtainable on the spot; rational forestry has already been practised for some time; and the forest, farming, mining and many other industries are all closely interrelated.

For accessibility of timber she has to thank her water-systems which provide unmatchable facilities for log-driving. Finland and Sweden are the world's most watery countries, with respectively a third and nearly a tenth of their land areas not land at all. But the flatness of Finland and the consequent sluggishness of her water-flow are a disadvantage. So also is the ruggedness of Norway, many of whose rivers are too full of falls and rapids to be suitable for timber-floating. The position of Sweden is intermediate: the currents are sufficiently swift to enable loose unrafted logs to be floated to the river-mouths; while the waterfalls, though numerous enough to provide almost as much electrical energy as those of Norway, can generally be circumvented if on floating routes. From the Daläven to the Torne River (which forms the Finnish frontier) is a series of parallel rivers rising in the Kölen Mountains and running through immense forests south-eastwards to the Baltic. With numerous tributaries combing the backwoods, the distance from stump to stream averages only a couple of miles. The orientation of the rivers is also significant: unlike the north-flowing rivers of Russia, Sweden's melt from the mouth upwards, floods are rarely serious, and the water from the higher snowfields reaches the main body of the river just when it can be absorbed, thus providing a constant flow ideal for log-driving throughout the whole summer.

This dependence of the forest on rivers is very one-sided. Despite all the work they do for her, the rivers could get on just as well without the forest. There is nothing to suggest, that, if she were destroyed, wholesale soil-removals and dangerous inundations would ensue as in many parts of the world. This is due to the lie of the land, to the lakes and tarns in catchments areas which act as regulating reservoirs, and to the fact that rain and snow keep the ground damp enough for a protective ground flora to flourish. For the forester the precipitation is in some ways favourable: the snow in winter is excellent for sledging; and there is a relatively dry period early in the year at the height of the sledging season. But the conditions result in numerous bogs and swamps (in Norrland they occupy over 20 per cent. of the land below the timber-line, and in the highlands of Småland they are also very common), while the forest soil is too often covered with a layer of raw humus.

Some of the drainage basins are rather big, that of Lake Väner and the Göta River, for instance, which debouches at

Gothenburg, being 18,600 square miles in extent. South of the great lakes the rivers are small and the snowfall capricious, so that timber is now generally transported by truck and train. The country's floating system of 20,000 miles (twice the length of her railways) is nearly all on the fourteen larger rivers of Norrland, Dalarna and Värmland.

Let us then pay a visit to the longest and busiest of these, the Ångerman, which rises near the Norwegian border in Southern Lapland, and which with its tributaries has a total floating system of over two thousand miles.

I was there in April some twenty miles from its source, on one of a series of lakes which help to regulate the flow in the River's lowest reaches. The ground being still covered with snow, the land-owners (some of them Lapps) had not yet switched over from forestry to farming. About every other male in rural Norrland works in the woods in winter: is both farmer and lumberman; in addition there is a large number of permanent employees in State and company forests, not to mention the numerous workers in the mills. Felling was still in progress and logs were being sledged from the forest to be dumped on the piles that had accumulated by the edge of the lake, in whose surface huge cracks were beginning to appear. The mills on the coast, being able to supply only a part of their material from their own forests, send up their agents to buy from State and private owners, paying, I was told, about 7 *öre* a cubic foot in that district. As nearly everywhere in the world, the primary producer receives but little for his produce. The trees have to be grown, felled, lopped, barked, and extracted to lakeside or riverbank all for seven *öre* a cubic foot. Compared with that for similar material in Western Europe, the price of standing timber in highly forested countries is extremely low. In Sweden only a fifth of the gross income from the forest and its industries is represented by the stumpage value of trees felled; which is perhaps not surprising when one considers the sums spent on wages and salaries, and the various other items including profits.

It may be instructive to follow a log on its long journey to the Baltic. By April floating is already in full swing on the lower reaches; by May it has begun on the upper. The driving is done by a special floating association which is also responsible for keeping the banks in order, for it has to pay up on every cubic foot of timber that is smashed or lost. In the past a great deal of work was done on this, as on other rivers, to improve it for floating purposes: rocks were removed and bends revetted to prevent damage to the logs, flumes and dams were constructed, and so on. As the cost of these has now been paid off and the maintenance expenses for so busy a stream are low, floating is very cheap indeed.

Shoved off with poles into the spring current, the log and its companions will be guided through the lakes by the series of solid guide-stakes which are fixed there for the purpose. Thousands of other logs from forests on the way will join it as it proceeds to the lower end of Lake Malgomäj where a tributary drops in from the left, considerable congestion occurs, and tugs have to push and strain to force the mass under a bridge. Mending its pace it now shoots along, bumping and being bumped, sometimes in a crowd which is broken up from time to time by rapids, sometimes alone. Perhaps it will work its way into an eddy and be arrested by an overhanging bush, where it may lie for days until some woodman gives it a prod releasing it again into the mainstream. On coming to falls that are dangerously steep, it will be sheered off by a boom where several lumberjacks will probably be busy with their poles preventing a jam, for it now has to slither end on down a "flume"—a timber trough supported on beds of stone or logs or even at times by trestles. It will be lucky if on one of the thirty-eight falls it is not tossed into a rock-crevice, or caught between boulders from which it will have to be rescued by some hardy lumberjacks venturing into the midstream rapids in a precariously light boat. Or it may even find itself in a really serious jam where dynamite has to be used to free the lower logs. Between the villages of Åsele and Ådalsliden the great gluegold-brown River, flowing due south, crosses from Lapland into its own province of Ångermanland. With countless logs crowding in from the tributaries and others still being added from the banks, the Ångerman from an aeroplane looks like a gutter into which boxes of matches have been emptied. The valley, now only six hundred feet or so above sea-level, is from here onwards sprinkled with clearings and farms, and in time our log passes under the large railway bridge of Forsmo which carries the main Bothnian line over roadway and River near the Faxälven tributary and the town of Sollefteå. This is a salmon-fishing district, and above the town the River has been elaborately step-dammed to regulate the water-flow without preventing the fish from moving upstream. From Sollefteå our log, occasionally encountering a steamer on water that is now navigable, continues through a well-meadowed valley out of which forested ridges rise to the right; passes Nyland at the head of the estuary (though the Bothnian water, being nearly fresh, can make but little difference to the salinity); and, now that the River is wide and calm, begins to feel itself free. Until, right across its path, it sees an enormous boom.

Sandslån, dealing with eighteen to twenty million logs every year, is the largest sorting-station in the world. Apart from a navigation channel which is kept free, the whole River at this point is divided into a series of booms parallel with the banks. All over these are dotted the sorters, employees of the floating association: those at the top grouping the logs according to ownership, those further down subdividing these groups into saw-logs and pulpwood, those at the lower end binding them into rafts. There may be as many as a hundred different owners, but every log, having been hammer-marked with the owner's brand before leaving the forest, will eventually be separated from all the millions that may be there at a time into its own compartment, unless, that is, it has sunk, been lost or smashed on the way (which is the fate of about one or two per cent.). Groups of rafts, hitched one behind the other like stiff-jointed toy snakes, are then tugged down to their respective mills, most of which lie about the river-mouth though some may even be in Southern Sweden. Kramfors is the largest mill on the Ångerman, and though smaller than Östrand further down the coast (which is actually the biggest in existence) is very impressive with its great clump of buildings with streaming chimneys and neatly aligned stacks of timber drying in the yards along the banks. Presuming that our log is a saw-log, it will probably be hauled out within a month or two, be sawn up in standard sizes, and be taken out to season with others of the same grade and size in one of the well-ventilated roofed-over stacks in the lumberyard. But it is just as likely to be pulpwood, in which case it may lie for over a year in a mill-pond (which in winter will be kept from freezing by the exhaust steam from the boilers). As only about half of every saw-log is lumber, enormous quantities of waste material—trimmings, edges, sawdust and so on—have to be utilized. Much of it feeds the steam engines (power may be either steam or hydro-electric), some is used for sulphate pulp, some for wallboards; and in future fuel oil and sugar may be manufactured from it commercially. Researchers are also trying to devise more profitable uses for the waste in chemical pulpmills, where ethyl alcohol, turpentine and ammonia are among the dozens of important by-products. Having followed our log down river and suggested some of the ways in which it might have been sliced up, ground, boiled in chemicals, burned, or pressed, we can wave it a good-bye as its remains are loaded into a cargo boat, and express the wish that we shall meet it again—perhaps in an Australian window, in the tissue wrapping of a Californian peach, in the silk stockings of an Italian girl friend, or in the very paper on which these words are printed.

All economists who have studied the matter agree that the world demand for timber will continue for a long while to be very great. In regard to supplies they are far less unanimous, some holding that a grave timber famine is in sight, some that the potential growth of softwoods could be tripled or that the great stocks of tropical hardwoods (so far hardly touched) comprising half the world's timber could be drawn on. Although science to-day can find substitutes for almost everything, it certainly behoves a country to look to her timber resources, especially when as in Sweden they mean so much to her national economy.

Background to Sweden

Can the Swedes continue to produce as much timber as ever, or are they living on their capital? Being famous for their scientific achievements, they are not likely to have left so vital a question to mere guesswork. Stock-taking, necessary in every business and not less so in forestry, was the means used for securing the answer. The difficulties of obtaining relatively accurate figures for the forest resources of a whole country are immense. Such a task had never before been attempted, and it was left to a Swede to evolve a practicable method. This was done by the County Forester of Värmland in 1911.

Only in 1923 were the final preparations complete for the National Forest Survey. On maps of each county parallel lines were marked from border to border, cutting across valleys and ridges roughly at right angles. The gang assigned to each area then traversed these, measuring with callipers and recording on paper the diameter of every tree at breast-height within five metres on either side of the line (what the Americans call "cruising"). The strips, then, were thirty-three feet wide and the distance between them from one to twenty kilometres, according to the type of country. Other observations were made simultaneously and over 180,000 sample trees were carefully measured (to provide data for growth rate, volume and age). For six summers this field work continued, supplemented by elaborate clerical work in the winters, till in the end the total length traversed on these line surveys was nearly 32,000 miles.

Of all the figure totals thus laboriously computed one especially had been awaited with much impatience. This was the annual growth of the Swedish forest, which by a comparison with the annual cut (already known approximately) would answer the central question whether the forests were being overcut. Contrary to expectation, it was found that they were not; there might even be a surplus. But no one could be quite certain: the annual cut (the amount of wood removed every year by man and destroyed by natural agencies) cannot be accurately estimated; while the annual growth may change with climatic variations. So, to be on the safe side, the whole forest area will be resurveyed at intervals; and the second census is already under way.*

The problem of cutting, however, is far more complicated than one might suppose. In the forests of Norrland, for instance, where there is an undesirable surplus of old trees, it is suggested that felling for a while should exceed the growth; but in other districts the very reverse may be necessary.

Quality as well as quantity must be considered, despite the probability that pulping (which can absorb poorer timber) will increase at the expense of the sawmill industry. Many movements are afoot to raise both quantity and quality. Boglands are being drained and planted up and existing woods improved by drainage: over 70,000 miles of ditches have been dug in thirty years. In the South a special association which exists for interesting public bodies in buying up waste land for afforestation has been remarkably successful. Research, most of it organized by the Forest Research Institute (located in the grounds of the College of Forestry), is always going on in various fields; while the Society for Tree-Breeding which has recently started work may one day produce results comparable with those already achieved along similar lines in the case of agricultural crops, cattle, or poultry. Of more immediate import are the attempts being made to reduce wastage. Although foreign experts visiting Sweden and Finland always remark on the lack of waste in their woods, the Swedes themselves admit to moderate losses during logging and say they ought to be reduced. How to minimize the far more serious mill wastage is, as we have seen, one of the main problems being worked on at present.

But after all these facts and figures where is the essential Forest? We have seen with what immense difficulty some of the figures were obtained. Yet it is easier to put the Forest into figures than into words, pictures, musical scores. *That*

* Since this was written the second forest census has been completed. It shows that the estimates of the first were wrong and too optimistic. As a result of calculations based on this mistake, more timber has been cut than was replaced by new growth in the period concerned. This over-cutting means that the Swedish timber cut will be limited for several decades below the figure previously thought possible, until the balance between use and growth is restored.

requires a Frost or a Gulbransen, a Lagerlöf or a Sibelius—
some great artist who has lived in it, and to whom its needles
have served for spiritual phlebotomy.

Like the ocean it is slow to acquire and lose its heat: in
spring the snow lies there when outside it has all melted; in
autumn when the first flakes are flying it is still warm. Enter
it during the heat of day and you will keep cool, by night and
you will not grow cold. A shield for man, beast and bird, it
breaks up the lances of storms, shivers the assegais of Arctic
winds. Like the ocean it is dark and deep with mystery; and
like it also is suggestive of infinitude. Every tree like every
wave is the same yet different, turns and yet is still, rises and
falls. All needles, cells, chromosomes are alike, yet no two are
the same. And even as the ocean's systolic rhythms answer
the sun and moon, so also do the Forest's, new tree-rings being
calendared for the years, and sunspot-cycles recorded in the
trunks.

But its rhythms may also have the precision of a machine.
"A vegetable manufactory"—that is how Wordsworth scorn-
fully labelled those coniferous plantations that certain ill-
advised landowners had chosen to establish in the English Lake
District. And for a Northern forest the description is probably
accurate in a way he had not imagined. "A vegetable manufactory": wheels of branches driven by a photosynthetic motor
running alternately on sunlight and oxygen, water and carbon
dioxide; the unseen auxiliary motor of root mycorrhiza; the
exudation and trickling of resin lubricants; the high efficiency
of it all, waste products being converted into fuel by fungi,
insects, microbacteria; the exhaust fumes, now of carbon
dioxide, now of oxygen; the endless mass-production of specialized cells; the continual assemblage into stock-patterns, the
poles becoming longer, wider and cleaner during the process;
the nonchalant ticking off of annual rings at the end of every
shift.

But stop! . . . lest my vegetable love should grow vaster than
empires and more slow.

VI · ISLANDS IN LAKES

EXACTLY HOW MANY lakes Sweden possesses I should not pretend to answer even if I knew when a lake ceases to be a lake and becomes a mere, a tarn, a pond, a pool; or how sluggish, broad and damned-up a river must become before that part of it can rightly be termed a lake. Nor is there an unanimity among authorities, some putting the figure at seventy thousand, others at over a hundred thousand; though all seem agreed that only the vast-flung country of Canada may contain a larger number, and that even Finland made up of one-third water is no rival in this respect. Not that, knowing a friend to be very freckled, the exact number of freckles on her face can prove very enlightening: suffice it that the lacustrine nature of Swedish scenery is more than anything responsible for that contrast and relief without which the landscape would be unbearably gloomy and wearisome. In winter, to be sure, the lakes, frozen across and covered with a pall of snow, so far from being conspicuous features in the scene, might often be overlooked altogether by the casual traveller, were it not for the log-piles on their edges and the men fishing through holes in their surfaces or sawing out blocks of ice for the storage of food during the warm season. But in summer the lakes like many human freckles are once more in evidence: they are the most significant single feature in the landscape, breaking the monotony of the huge coniferous forests, or forming a mirror for the ponderous clumps of granite or the light silveriness of the birches.

1 : *Kållandsö*

HUGE AND SHAPELESS—almost an inland sea—Väner, the largest European lake outside Russia, sprawls over an area equal to that of Norfolk. Unlike the typical Scandinavian lake, it has not been liberally stocked with islands: there are only a few desultory clusters here and there apart from a flat archipelago off the eastern shore. Right in the centre lies the little uninhabited cluster called Lurö, alluring alike in name and situation, and so inaccessible that all my attempts to reach it ended in failure. So, consoling myself with the thought that there is nothing to be seen but the scant ruins of a monastery among dense pinewoods, I set off for Kållandsö. Being separated from the peninsula to the south by a mere yard or two of water, it is about as much of an island as Hayling though infinitely more agreeable and unspoilt. The undulating farmland, with little windmills capping the knolls, drifts rather indeterminately into woods or water, carrying off on either side a series of casual side-roads from the main thoroughfare, which, twisting for some miles northwards, eventually opens on the romantic lakeside Castle of Läckö.

Never in the history of Sweden have the aristocracy enjoyed a more brilliant period than in the half-century following on the death of Gustavus Adolphus. Officers and diplomats, returning from the wars with large fortunes, invested their money in land and commerce, or erected mansions to display the booty they had captured. Without any middle class as a bridge between them, the nobles and the lower classes grew further apart, the former increasing their riches in proportion as the latter (whom they callously exploited) became deeper sunk in poverty. No one (except the Provost-Marshal, Per Brahe) was more magnificent than Magnus de la Gardie, one-time favourite of Christina and Lord High Chancellor at a time when the Swedish Empire, girdling the Baltic, was at its zenith. Läckö, his principal fief, included forty parishes with three hundred estates; the income from his land-holdings alone amounted to half-a-million crowns a year. The old Castle of Läckö, given to his parents by the great Gustavus himself, was charmingly situated overlooking Lake Väner; but of course it would need rebuilding. So he enlarged it out of recognition, employing some of the foremost artists on its decoration, and thus making it a fit seat for the would-be Mazarin of the North.

But the times were changing. Charles XI, now coming of

age and finding the State finances and the services in a deplorable position, threw himself into the task of re-appropriating the vast sums amassed by the Regents and the nobles during his long minority. Poring over figures and "Reduction" decrees sometimes for twenty hours a day, he soon succeeded in enriching his coffers at the expense of the aristocracy. No one was spared, not even his brother-in-law de la Gardie, whose servants it is said had at one time to pawn their belongings in order to feed him. His splendid Castle was confiscated, and since no one could afford to maintain it, its two hundred and eighty rooms have ever since stood empty, gazing glumly across the slaty lustreless waters of the immense Lake.

One old writer, describing the original Castle (which had till the Reformation been the seat of the Bishops of Skara), gives this curious piece of information about the well: It is "cut out of the hard stone above two hundred feet deep", he says:

> "This cutting was not done with iron instruments alone, but by flame which was daily fed with three hundred fattest flitches of bacon successively day by day, fire being put in and taken out. For it is found by experience that nothing will sooner penetrate the hard rock there than lard and hog's grease."

2 : *Visingsö*

IN THAT HUGE necklace of lakes strung across the ample bosom of the Swedish mainland the principal jewel is a vast turquoise pendant dangling from the middle. Though only second in point of size, Vätter admits no competitor whatever in the matter of beauty, being the bluest and shapeliest specimen in all the North countries.

One evening in July I sat on the deck of a lake-steamer spitting cherrystones into the clear crystalline water below. Two becalmed yachts waiting to put in to Jönkoping, the famous match town at the southern extremity of the Lake, and disturbed by our backwash, rocked gently to and fro doing their best to block the view of Huskvarna, a small but modern garden-city tucked in a corner of the dark-green Småland hills, and noted for its hardware, sewing machines, bicycles and the visits of foreign sociologists. Full of importance the captain stood on the bridge training his eyes on the distance as earnestly as if we were rounding Cape Horn in a hurricane.

After an hour or two, the slit on the horizon having swollen into Visingsö, which lies midway between shore and shore about a third of the way up the Lake, we put in at a tiny harbour on the east of the Island.

Much history is dotted over the few square miles of Visingsö. There, in the Middle Ages, died King Magnus Ladulås or "Barnlock", remembered as a just law-maker, protector of the *bönder* against the high-handed nobles who hitherto had been accustomed to travel about with their retinues, stopping where they chose, and demanding food, fodder and lodging of the farmers without making any payment in return. *Bonde* is often and very wrongly translated as "peasant"; nor can it be rendered "bondman"—that is exactly what a *bonde* never was, for when King Magnus removed the last vestiges of slavery towards the end of the thirteenth century there was no ensuing serfdom whatever. The Swedish *bönder* are also unique in history in having been represented in parliament from the first—from the fifteenth century, that is, when even Danish and Norwegian yeomen were still hardly better than thralls. Extremely jealous of their ancient freedom they have always been willing to fight for their rights, and more than any class were forward in supporting the national liberators. Even the poorest country people have always had their own land and cattle, the system of tenant-farming never having existed to any considerable extent in Sweden.

But the name that is inseparably connected with the Island is that of the now extinct family of Brahe. What the visitor first sees on landing are groups of horses and carts (for the Island has only two or three cars) waiting under the ruins of Visingsborg, a castle once owned by Per Brahe (the Provost Marshal referred to above and the richest Swede of his day). As Governor of Finland he had acquired a thousand estates there alone; as a member of the Regency during Charles XI's minority he (like de la Gardie) had had every means of enriching himself; being Lord of Visingsö, he was fond of retiring to his castle on the Island since here only the water set a limit to his domains; but just as a reminder that he also owned over five hundred square miles of Östergötland he erected a huge sumptuous palace on a commanding hill-top just across the Lake.

Since this palace is now a burnt-out shell and Visingsborg is also in ruins, the well-preserved Brahe Church remains the most interesting reminder of the wealthiest man in Sweden's *Stormaktstiden* (or Period of Greatness). Though some of the larger castles like Läckö of course have their own private chapels there is nothing in the country quite like this church built (most of it) by the Brahes. Entering through a medieval porch, I found myself looking down the central nave, a succession of cross-groined arches sprouting on either side, their capitals ornamented with tablets of silvered brass, while above and ahead a series of rich dark blue scroll-paintings executed in the contemporary (seventeenth century) German style flourished exuberantly in the low vaults. Like most old churches it is a sort of museum, with here some fine twelfth-century ironwork on the vestry door (proving that Sweden even then used her chief metal with exceptional skill), and there various objects wrought by certain Finnish, German and Danish artists. But above all there is an exquisite wooden statue from about 1500 of St. Bridget. (The best of the wooden sculptures till that time are all of foreign workmanship. This, Plate 32, is as fine a piece as will be found from the short Swedish period, a time of national awakening, just preceeding the Renaissance; and happily its source of inspiration is the country's greatest and most famous saint, whose parents incidentally were ancestors of the Brahe family.)

Much of the building undertaken by Per Brahe here and on the mainland was carried out by Russian prisoners-of-war. Unlike de la Gardie he was lucky enough to die before the "Reduction" decrees were enacted by Charles XI, so it fell to his nephew to return to the State what I suppose would to-day be the equal of several million pounds—a disappointing start for a young man who had just come into his uncle's fortune.

July is a good month for visiting Visingsö. The heavy shade

of the oakwoods is then welcome to the cartloads of tourists as they are driven through the southern parts of the Island, their legs dangling over the sides; while the drive northwards runs through cherry orchards where the girls have baskets of fruit for sale at the roadside and through fields where harvesting is already in progress. And when eventually the driver draws rein outside the Church of Kumlaby and you climb into the tower for the view, the shapely prow of the island, smooth and yellow with cornfields, points northwards across water that by now has attained its smilingest and most intense turquoise. But never go there to bathe, for even then, even in August, the temperature of this very deep Lake seldom rises to 50°. It was more like five when I tried it.

3 : *Sollerön*

PROBABLY NOT A tithe of the visitors to the Siljan ever set foot on Sollerön in the apex of that exquisite triangular Lake placed so intimately in the centre of Dalarna. Which is curious, for the delight of meeting a body of water when on land is only equal to that of meeting with land when on the water; pleasure compounded of both—that given by islands in lakes or by lakes in islands (as in atolls of the South Seas) ought to prove quite irresistible.

One afternoon some years ago I cycled out with a friend on to the long bridge connecting Sollerön with the western shore, and stopped for an evening bathe at a wooded islet on the way out. Having spent two days traversing almost unrelieved hill-forests, we were pleased to encounter once more signs of civilization as we rode onwards into the middle of the Island where a large white church reminds you that you are supposed to be in a village. While taking a drink nearby we fell in with someone who offered to show us the local sights—a school-master, we found, from a valley to the north-east, from a village called Älvdalen (whose people were probably the last ever to use the runic form of writing).

It appears, then, that Sollerön was the earliest inhabited

place in all these parts. Thither came the early settlers, finding on the island a refuge from the wild beasts of the surrounding forests. The oldest extant monuments are from considerably later times: the schoolmaster took us to a large Viking cemetery on the northern slopes where long barrows of loose stones raised over nameless chieftains lie scattered here and there in the birch-sprinkled fields which sway downwards to the placid pewtery Lake, beyond whose reaches the purple-forested hills stand magnificently at random. Ruric perhaps recruited some of his Varangians from among these lake-dwellers; many at least must have seen service in the Baltic States.

Nearby is a wooden homestead, still inhabited, dating from the fifteenth century—a remarkable feat of endurance for a timber structure. The chimney-pots here and around the Lake with their delicately ornamental tops are unique in design and expressive of the romantic nature of the people.

I hardly know if one can speak of the "inhabitants" of Solleron. For many of them are nomads—nomads with their headquarters on the Island.

Any traveller in the mountainous parts of Sweden becomes acquainted with *fäbodar* (the nearest rendering of which is "shielings"), groups of log seters used as summer dairies and cattlesheds and nowadays not infrequently rented by parties of skiers in the winter. For from time immemorial it has been the custom for certain members of each farm to take the cattle every summer to the nearest hilltops, sometimes as much as thirty miles away, in order to find better pasturage at higher altitudes. Dalarna is to-day the most southerly province in which *fäbodar* are still to be found in any numbers. In nearly all views across forested dale-country clearings sprinkled with a few dark huts can be descried on the hill-tops in the distance. My first visit to one of these mountain dairies was, I remember, made from a village called Skattungsbyn, north of the Siljan. Old Mother Kattra, keeper of the local *vandrarhem*, gave us instructions how to reach there and provided us with a sandwich lunch. Setting out on foot, pushing our bicycles, we tramped for miles and miles through the forests following a line of telephone poles till it eventually came out on a ride. This rough track, fre-

quented at the rate of about two carts a year and in winter when
under snow used for timber extraction, led us for further hours
up a long, long, steepish incline till, just when we were des-
pairing of ever arriving at our destination, we heard the tinkle
of a cow-bell. Presently among the shaggy-lichened spruces we
came to a clearing where two or three unshaven young men
were scything the hay in a small rudely-fenced field. Besides
the cattle-sheds there were several dwelling-huts, one of which
we entered to procure some milk from an old woman stirring
away at a cauldron which hung over an open stone hearth in the
corner. After chatting for a while we left her at her monotonous work of stirring, testing, emptying and filling, in the
process of making cheese and *messmör*. One of the men, talking
slowly and ponderously (for among themselves they speak a
dialect quite unintelligible to the ordinary Swede), showed us
the damage done to one of the sheds which had been broken
into by a bear. But that had been in winter; then it was summer
—a strange green-and-brown summer, flowerless and ascetic in
those remote Northern hill-forests. And the air was charged
with a faint thunder from the nearby Helvetetsfallet, the
Waterfall of Hell.

The people of Sollerön, unlike other farming people, move
no less than four times a year with their cattle, spring and autumn
being spent in *hemfäbodar*, perhaps only a mile or two from the
Lake; summer in *långfäbodar*, cruder and in more inaccessible
places; winter in their homes on the Island.

That evening the schoolmaster who had shown us round the
Island accompanied us to the top of Gesundaberg, a steep
shapely hill on the north-western shore of the Lake and his wife
(who had been singing the whole way up) brought out some of
her home-made raspberry *saft* which we drank on the sward
gazing across the whole Siljan, Sollerön lying arrestingly and
unforgettably in the foreground.

4 : *There Are Others*

MUCH COULD BE written of the islands of the Mälar—of
Björkö, for instance, with its traces of Birka the main trading

centre of Viking Sweden; or of Riddarholmen, oldest and loveliest quarter of the capital, where the Mälar gives way to the
Baltic (technically, at any rate).   But the Mälar is *all* islands;
and I doubt if any system of water-patches which sprawls so
untidily in every direction ought, despite its beauties, to be
described as a lake.   And then there is that island in Lake
Hjälmaren where the great Engelbrekt was murdered; and that
... But enough.

To the connoisseur of islands few countries are as exciting as
Sweden, whose coasts are fringed with archipelagos, and whose
lakes—Archimedes-baffling in number—are well peppered with
islands drenched in history and half-drowned in beauty.

VII · BERGSLAGEN

1 : *Bergslagen: A Cross-section*

THE LAPLAND IRON-MINES are not the only important ones in the country. There are the scattered deposits of Bergslagen, smaller it is true—there is nothing like the Kiruna Mountain, a compact block of 15,000 million tons of ore—but nearly as rich (averaging 53 per cent. of iron, as compared with 60 to 65 in Lapland), and with a much smaller percentage of phosphorus, thus making them the best in the world for the manufacture of steel. Sweden, exporting mostly from the north, very wisely keeps the bulk of the better phosphorus-free ores for her own industries. Possessing over nine-tenths of Europe's high-grade ore, she may well reckon iron next to timber as the mainstay of her economy.

In Bergslagen, which covers a large part of Svealand, mining has been carried on for over two thousand years, and in the centuries before charcoal was superseded for smelting purposes half the world's pig-iron came from here. Even in the Middle Ages there was a distinct class of *bergsmän*, or miners largely exempt from taxation, occupying a position between the *bönder* and the aristocracy. The wealth too—if wealth it may be called—had a fairly wide geographical distribution, though it was mainly centred in the south of Dalarna, which poets still call by her ancient name of Järnbäraland ("Iron-bearing Country"), and in Västmanland to the south. . . . So from early times down to the last century smelting was carried on throughout this extensive district where the forests provided charcoal for the furnaces, the waterfalls and fosses power for the hammers, and the lakes and rivers an easy means of transport. The very common place-name ending in *-hyttan* enables one to locate many of the sites of these forges even to-day, while tiny deserted kilns may still be discovered beside streams in the depths of the forest.

Copper, silver and other metals were also mined in Bergslagen at one time, but to-day little is produced. Since the Great War, however, a new non-ferrous mining district has been opened up in Norrland, thus fulfilling the prophecy made by Paracelsus during his visit to Sweden in 1500 that great mineral wealth would be discovered between latitudes 63 and 65. Boliden is already known for its output of various metals, arsenic and other substances.

By far the greatest of the old mines was Falun in Dalarna. Although its days of importance are over, it is still working and under the same owners, Stora Kopparbergs Aktiebolaget, the oldest company in the world. A purchase deed from 1288 (when the mine was already sixty years old) can be seen in the absorbingly interesting museum at the edge of the open part of the mine. From this cavity and the twelve miles of galleries vast quantities of copper have been removed in past centuries. Arranged in jars on a shelf samples of the mine products surprise with their variety: blue crystals of copper-vitriol, green crystals of iron-vitriol, vinegar and sulphuric acid, gold and silver, talc and red paint. There is a well-known tale by Hoffman, the German romantic, concerning the miner who was entombed at Falun on the day before his wedding and was found fifty years later so perfectly preserved that his fiancée, then an old woman, at once recognized him and died at his side.

After Falun Dannemora (in Uppland) is the biggest name in early mining history in Sweden. Though unimportant to-day, the mines at Dannemora were four centuries ago the best and most productive in the country; and when Gustavus Vasa, seeking to exploit the natural resources of the country, introduced German smelters and smiths into Bergslagen these mines were at once placed under the management of a German. The iron industry seems to have been considerably hampered by the lack of skilled labour. "We have an India in Sweden if only we know how to work the mines rightly", said De Geer, who was the foremost among the Belgian capitalists and industrialists whom Gustavus Adolphus attracted to Sweden. By acquiring large mining areas with access to fuel and water-power, and by bringing in some five hundred families from the mining districts of Belgium, he gave an immense impetus to Swedish industry, and the success of such famous works as Finspång and Lövsta was largely due to his initiative. De Geer acquired the Dannemora group in 1641, and both here and elsewhere in Bergslagen you will still come across Walloon names on shop-fronts and meet people with the darkish skin, diagonal eyes or other characteristic Walloon features which inter-marriage with pure natives has not been able to eradicate. There have been several distinguished Swedes of Walloon origin though none as notable as the De Geers, whose family also produced a prime minister in the last century and a great geologist in this.

Sweden is a country of such exceptional racial homogeneity that even the smallest influx of foreigners is of interest. There have never been any large immigrations of foreigners; nor as in all countries outside Scandinavia have large numbers of alien conquerors swept over the land and settled there: only the closely related Danes during the Scandinavian union of the middle ages inflicted their hated bailliffs and officials on the people. Finns as well as Lapps, as might be expected, are to be found in the North; and other Finno-Ugrian tribes inter-marrying with Nordic aboriginals in the distant past gave rise to various Bothnian types in the northerly provinces; but there was also a Finnish migration about 1600 to Central Sweden, especially to Northern Värmland as place-names bear witness and where a few of the lonelier families are said still to preserve their native language.

Germans have come in at many periods, especially miners to Bergslagen, and merchants to various towns during the Middle Ages; while a good deal of inter-marrying not unnaturally took place in the days when Sweden held territory in what is now the Reich.

A certain number of Scots and Englishmen, as if repaying the calls of the Vikings, have also settled in Sweden, especially Scots during the seventeenth century. Dicksons and Sinclairs, Spaldings, Eliots and Watsons have played and continue to play important parts in the business life of Gothenburg (that most British of Swedish cities), where they were among the earliest citizens; a Keiller founded the machine-shop and foundry which developed into Götaverken, the biggest ship-building concern in the country; a Chalmers established a polytechnic College which has meant so much to the city. Fleetwoods and Carnegies, Halls and Campbells are names you will frequently encounter; Hamilton is actually the commonest name among the nobility; and many Scottish settlers and their descendants came to be people of importance, such as Andrew Boy, Borgmästare of Stockholm during Sweden's Stormaktstiden (or Period of Greatness), George Seton a slum child who became a wealthy banker and was ennobled although he continued to dress like a beggar, or Rutger Maclean the Skåne landowner who was instrumental in having the Land Enclosure Act, long overdue, passed in 1803. In some instances the name has been "Svecified" perhaps only slightly as with Güthries and Rönnow; but who would recognize Eyre as Ihre, or Macpherson as von Fersen? Several von Fersens became important political figures: one of them, a dashing young lover of Marie Antoinette, disguised himself as a coachman and very nearly succeeded in effecting the escape of the French royal family after the outbreak of the Revolution. With their industry and practicalness, their scientific aptitude and democratic outlook, the Scots have many points of resemblance to the Swedes.

Finally there are the Jews, always very few in number, though sometimes (as with the Josephsons of the South) highly distinguished in intellectual and artistic fields. It is quite possible that the influx of Jews and other refugees in recent years will in time have more effect on racial purity than all the little immigrations of the past put together.

2 : *A Cycle Log*

ONE MORNING A few weeks after the end of term two heavily loaded bicycles lumbered out of Upsala in a westerly direction. In the saddle of one was a student from the Gothenburg Nation, on the other the author.

211

Background to Sweden

"Where are you going?" an acquaintance has asked him as we emerged from a shop with a few more oddments to be crammed into our cycle-bags before starting.

"Home", said the Gothenburger, pointing casually as if it were over the other side of the street.

"Why on bicycle?"

"Well, I'm completely broke. Can't afford the train fare"— an answer that would not have been surprising from anyone at the end of the Spring Term, and a sufficiently good excuse for cycling four or five hundred miles.

It was a bright warm day in mid-June with a westerly wind to remind us that we were likely to have headwinds the whole way. Crossing the Västmanland border in the afternoon, we came to Västerås on the Mälaren, the chief town of the province and seat of the *landshövding* or governor of the *län*. There are twenty-five provinces (*landskap*) in Sweden, historical divisions corresponding roughly to the ancient kingdoms of the country and still more or less distinct cultural and topographical entities. But the country is, for administrative purposes, also divided into departments (*län*) whose boundaries very rarely coincide with those of the provinces. Västerås, as its Castle and very Swedish cathedral remind us, was in earlier times of much military importance and a great cultural centre. To-day it is famous as the town of ASEA (Allmanna Svenska Elektriska Aktiebolaget, the Swedish G.E.C.), whose products are known the world over.

A few miles outside the city we found a lakeside *vandrarhem* where we spent our first night. It is remarkable how in such a large and sparsely populated country the tourist can find in almost any district a well-situated and inexpensive rest-house. Through the initiative of STF, the Swedish Touring Club, there are now about three hundred *vandrarhem*, many open throughout the year. In some places they may be the only sort of hotel or pension within thirty miles; in others (towns, for example) they are often located in schools during holidays, and provide a clean plain resort for the cyclist or hiker who wishes to travel cheaply and with a minimum of clothing. They are, if you like, youth hostels; but with this difference: the conditions are better and cleaner than in most countries and the food both liberal and eatable. The prevailing *camaraderie*, which brings one into contact with members of all classes, is especially useful in a country without pubs. I remember in bed one night looking across the room at my two companions of that evening: in the lower berth in green silk pyjamas lay a young count of one of the oldest families in Sweden; in the upper, fully clothed, dirty, and snoring heavily, an elderly retired farm-labourer who spent his summers making cycle tours through every part of the country.

The ideal mode of summer travelling is of course on push-bike. Except in the fells, walking is unsuitable; and motoring, unless you are old or merely going somewhere, is a sacrilege. In any case, the average Swede cannot afford a car. In fact there are fewer cars in Sweden than there are boats. I know of many a family with houses both in town and country, yachts and suchlike who "cannot afford a car". Which means they consider one unnecessary. And not being snobs they would never think of buying one just to avoid public vehicles. I am told that there are places where the car-owner is such a rare phenomenon that he receives a special title: Herr Bilägare (Mr. Car-owner) So-and-So. Knowing the scarcity of cars on most of the roads and the more-than-German passion for titles, I can well believe it. The cyclist, in fact, has usually a monopoly of the road; or, if a stray car should pass by, you receive instead of a scaring hoot a cheerful wave of the hand. As when sailing, no one forgets to wave or to greet you with a *"Hej!"*—other cyclists, haymakers, girls drawing water from a well, workmen putting on the roof of a new house, or old people sunning themselves in their porches.

June of all months, it seemed to us next morning, is the time for cycling—June, the watershed of the seasons, spring on one side, summer on the other; with the linked charms of childhood and adolescence; warm enough for bathing though not too hot for the most strenuous exertions. Every field we passed was blue with cornflowers, embankments and dry patches were covered with the paler but equally true blue of bugloss, and the

Background to Sweden

roses so common on the heavy soils of the lake provinces were at their very best. There were even a few songbirds, but not very many: crows, magpies and water-fowl are the birds of Central Sweden. Magpies are always fresh and smart in appearance, but crows are heavy dowdy birds singularly out of keeping with the spring. And the voice of either is something to avoid. What specially attracts attention is the number of frisky foals which by themselves would make a spring. But lambs there are none—at least one never encounters them, although the Government's attempt to revive sheep-breeding is said to be meeting with success.

Following the Mälar road we eventually came to Arboga, in the extreme south of the province, a very beautiful little town surrounded by avenues of sycamores and prosperous-looking farms. Here in 1435 was held the first Swedish parliament, a meeting convened by Engelbrekt, that greatest of bergsmen, who, by stirring up patriotism and unifying the provinces, prepared the way for Gustavus Vasa. The parliamentary system determined at this *Riksdag* of the Four Estates (of nobles and clergy, burgesses and *bönder*) continued right down to 1866 when it was superseded by the present two-chamber system. Unique in that the peasants from the very first were allowed a say in the management of state affairs, the Swedish parliament has even finer traditions than the older ones of Iceland and England. Simon de Montfort's Westminster assembly in 1265 for all its representativeness failed to include the villeins: England has only become a democracy with the enfranchisement of the workers in recent times, whereas Sweden can claim to be the oldest existing democracy in the world. Many other momentous meetings of the Riksdag, the oldest parliament on the continent of Europe, were held in Arboga in the fifteenth and sixteenth centuries. But although the sights of the town are the ancient buildings—churches and the houses by the river—and Eldh's statue of Engelbrekt, Arboga does not live entirely on memories and tourists: it now manufactures high-grade electrical tools.

Encountering a particularly obstinate headwind in the afternoon, we only just succeeded in reaching some friends in the

north of Närke (or Nerike), in time for a belated *middag*. After
spending the night in a summer cottage on the estate, we were
taken over their large timber *herrgård* of the seventeenth century:
into the spacious kitchen with its splendid display of copper
cooking utensils, into the pantry (on the next floor!), through
innumerable small rooms stuffy through lack of use and
furnished in various styles, and through the bigger dining- and
reception-rooms with their ancestral portraits—this one of a
distinguished *riksråd* or senator in the time of Gustavus Adolphus,
and that of a man who was noted for nothing more than eating
ant-sandwiches. We then saw the outbuildings. First a long
coachhouse stuffed with disused dust-laden harnesses, dozens
of various kinds of carriages and a collection of sleighs for
winter, many being such heavy cumbersome vehicles that you
would think no team of horses would ever pull them up some of
the hills in the neighbourhood. The stables have long been
empty save for a few farm-horses, used for odd jobs in the summer
and for logging in the winter. We were shown into a strange
round building which had served former generations as a
winter riding-house; saw the cowsheds, pigsties and dairies;
and repaired to the conservatories for peaches, a great luxury
in June in these latitudes.

Some centuries ago this place was noted for its sulphur and
through that for its healthiness. Chills, gout or whatever people
suffered from in those days were quite unknown round here; so
that one king, during an outbreak of the plague, escaped here
from Stockholm and eventually returned unscathed. To-day the
old sulphur mine is filled up with water; and a wooden pump,
almost as primitive as a shadoof, raises the water which runs
through troughs to wash iron oxide from the earth. For the
present export is red paint. We crept into the ill-lighted building
where an entrancingly lurid glow was reflected from the
ubiquitous powder, and where several men pounding the dust
and pouring it into paper bags reminded me of Hardy's raddle-
man in *The Return of the Native*. The prevailing colour of the
Swedish cottage, so right and inevitable in its setting, is
determined by economic not by aesthetic factors: red paint
(or more properly, red ochre) is by far the cheapest to produce,

P   215

it is easy to transport in the form of powder, and for use has merely to be mixed with water.

"Cottage" no doubt is a good enough translation of *stuga*, but rather than render *herrgård* as "manor" I prefer to use the Swedish word. "Manor" is misleading because it savours of feudalism, a system that, thanks partly to Engelbrekt, the Swedes would never tolerate. Nor has a *herrgård* the same connection with a village as an English manor usually has; there is often no village at all. The largest and oldest specimens are found in Skåne, the southernmost province, many dating from the sixteenth century when Skåne was still a part of Denmark, and therefore being Danish in character: they are really small castles. Since they are very rare in the northern provinces, it is to Central Sweden we must turn for the typical Swedish *herrgård*. Here they were often built of wood, but large timber specimens close on three hundred years old, like the one we have just seen, are exceedingly scarce to-day. Their lanterned roofs with round Mansard windows, and the formal layout with two (detached) wings flanking a courtyard are reminders that the main building time for these as for more sumptuous mansions was Sweden's *Stormaktstiden* when baroque ideals were spreading northwards; though the style was necessarily modified for the purposes of a quiet country life and achieves something of the same flavour as our Queen Anne style. Columned porches or verandahs were generally added from the eighteenth century onwards, so that the appearance is often that of a colonial home in New England. A *bruks herrgård*, especially common in Bergslagen, is the residence of the manager or owner of some works—mine, pulpmill, factory or suchlike. Though possessing all the charm of an old tradition, the *herrgård* is far from being an anachronism: it is not turned into a hotel, a golf club, or a school, nor is the property chopped up for building purposes.

Leaving in the late afternoon, we cycled northwards and returned to Västmanland. All the fourth day we passed through scenery typical of that province—great hill-forests with here and there the grey dumps and the tall shafts of iron-mines protruding above the trees; and in the lower parts fine agricultural land sloping down to the lakes where the silver shafts of the birches were mirrored in the clear water. There were no longer many roses, but the herbaceous flowers in the open were exquisite. We dismounted to have a good look at one enormous meadow, ostensibly a clover field but really an expanse of marguerites and erect-flowered campanulas with every crevice filled up with pansies and forget-me-nots. "A sight to dream on, not to tell", and probably the source of very bad dreams indeed for the farmer who owned it.

Kopparberg, with its splendid old shingle church and *tingshus* (law courts), is about the most interesting town in the west of this province. From there we turned westwards and the country became wilder; no longer were there any farms by the sides of the lakes, or, if there were, the cottages would have turf roofs, giving them a shock-headed appearance all in keeping with the half-savage atmosphere of the district. Suddenly the road ran down to a large thriving village, and in a few minutes we were enjoying the hospitality of some friends in the *bruks herrgård*.

Our host was kind enough to arrange for two young engineers to take us over the steel works after dinner, thereby giving us the chance of seeing at first hand something of one of the country's largest and most important industrial concerns. Based on Sweden's three main natural resources, iron, timber, and water-power, this company may be taken as a type of the joint concern especially common in Bergslagen. It was founded three hundred years ago, mainly for the production of silver. In the eighteenth century it erected what was then the biggest ironworks in the country. To safeguard the supply of charcoal it acquired extensive tracts of forest (it now owns 470,000 acres), and this in its turn gave rise to the wood industry. All the timber, after conversion in the company's pulp- and saw-mills, is put on trains for exports. (It sometimes returns—in the form of boxes with South African fruit.)

Since it was Midsummer week, there was little activity in the steel works. About half of the annual production of 70,000 tons is rolled steel. It is a fascinating sight to watch the glowing metal pass through the rollers, the bars each time becoming longer, till in the end the flattened strip writhes like a snake, is gripped, stretched and measured. Some fifty kinds of quality steel are manufactured, each for a special purpose: some may be converted into razors in America, be used as ball-bearings for vehicles in Brazil, tools in Europe or valve-springs for motors in Australia. Half of the metal is exported in the form of ingots and even these must be free from flaws: we were fortunate in seeing some of the molten metal being poured into the moulds from one of the newest furnaces (worked off the company's own hydroelectric plant) which heats up to 3,000° centigrade; and elsewhere some ingots were being ground with a deafening hiss as showers of sparks flew out around us.

It is said that as early as the fourth century the Swedes knew how to steel their weapons. But not till eighty or ninety years ago did the steel industry really begin on a large scale. Göransson, by perfecting the Bessemer process, revolutionized steel production throughout the world; and although other processes are now commoner the name of Sandviken (where he established his works) is still intimately connected with high quality steel. More recently electro-steel has been produced; but further technicalities I must resist.

I could not help envying the business man who can live but a few thousand yards from his office, in such wild country and in such an exquisitely furnished house, with its gardens (then full of lilac), tennis courts, and lawns almost English in their smoothness.

After encountering some fine lake scenery on the Värmland border, we continued to Filipstad, a town not very remarkable in appearance but one especially sought out by American tourists, since it is the birthplace of Ericsson whose ironclad *Monitor* played a memorable part in their Civil War. This, together with other inventions (including the screw propeller), secured him so much prestige that on his death the United States decided to convey his remains across the Atlantic in one of her cruisers, an honour never accorded to any other foreign-born benefactor.

Much of Eastern Värmland—about 700,000 acres—is owned

by the giant concern, Uddeholms AB: forests, huge ironworks, immense saw- and pulp-mills, power-stations and even an electric railway, the rather rickety N.Kl.J. which takes you up the valley of the dark Klarälven. In the south-eastern corner of the province, set in delightful surroundings, is the famous Bofors ordnance works of which Nobel acquired control in 1894. Although Nobel is best known as the inventor of dynamite, I have read that his invention of explosive capsules and detonating charges for high explosives is of even greater importance. It is a strange irony that the same man should be one of the most influential pacifists of the modern world: that some £10,000 of the interest on his immense fortune, a fortune largely made from articles of warfare, should annually go towards a Peace Prize!

It was in this ominous direction that we turned from Filipstad, taking a small road, but one familiar to my companion, for it led to his old school, "the Swedish Eton". Lundsberg, founded in 1896 by an Anglo-Swede, William-Ohlsson, is the oldest of the four schools modelled on the English public school system. What purpose, it may be asked, do such schools serve in a country where state education for all is a key element in their democracy? Except for some *folkhögskolor* or people's high schools (attended only by pupils over eighteen), there are no boarding-schools—a fact which accounts for the unchallenged influence of the home on children of all classes. In country districts where distances are great children will often be boarded out during term-time with relations or other families in the nearest town; or where this is impracticable, as with poorer, remoter farming communities, they will perhaps go to school but every other day or even less frequently. These four "English" schools then are a radical departure from the norm. Their main object, one might suppose, is to cater for a select number of snobs. A supposition which happens to be false. They are of course limited by their very nature to the well-do-to; for Lundsberg, although it may at times give financial assistance to the sons of needy Old Boys, offers no real scholarships. But for boys whose parents for some reason or other—perhaps owing to divorces, which are comparatively easy to secure—find it difficult to have them at home through-out the year; for the sons of Swedes living abroad; for those of ardent Anglophiles and suchlike, these schools are found to be especially useful.

Lundsberg began with five pupils. There are now a hundred-and-fifty, including one or two girls, daughters of members of the staff, and the ages range from ten to twenty. Most of the six houses, the largest having thirty boys, seemed to me almost as large as an English house for twice the number. There are two or three boys to each bed-study, a good-sized room with two windows and well furnished; while extra hanging- and locker-space is provided elsewhere. The pictures, I noticed, though including a few English scenes were mainly animal studies by Liljefors, photographs of Gösta Ekman as Charles XII, or at least something national in flavour. The heads of the houses are the only prefects. The fagging system is almost non-existent: the younger boys will perhaps have to rake the gravel outside on Saturday afternoon, but that is about all. The food, distributed from a central kitchen, is good, plainish and ample. The main meals are at about ten and three, with morning chocolate at 7.30 and an evening supper. There is no school uniform.

Among the subjects written and spoken English is specially stressed. And the head master, being a keen musician, himself gives instruction in singing and plays the chapel organ.

The house, the main school buildings and the chapel (in the style of a country church) are all scattered among the birches on a hillside. A bit lower down lie the playing-fields and tennis courts by the edge of the lake where in summer they swim and row, and which in winter is used for bandy, speed-skating and particularly the thrilling sport of sail-skating. There are also, of course, a well-equipped gymnasium (used by all) and a *bastu* or house for Finnish vapour baths.

On the top of the hill, rising above the spruce-tops, is the dome of the school observatory. A long clearing, made for a ski-jump (the platform is just visible to the right in Plate 30) leads the eye downwards and beyond—over a fine panorama of typical Lower Värmland scenery among which this fortunate school is remotely situated. In the short days of winter the boys will sometimes ski out into the forest, and finding some charring-heap, will sit round warming themselves while the charcoal-burner tells them exciting stories of the ghosts and supernatural beings he still believes in. For doesn't the lonely burner, nodding beside his slow-smouldering stack, dozing along the frontiers of dream and reality in the half-light where shapes have bulk and nothing is improbable—doesn't he depend on trolls to rouse him when the pile needs attention? And then when it is quite dark the boys return in procession with flaring torches to a spicy supper well calculated to stimulate the imagination during sleep.

The forest is also a favourite resort in the summer, not infrequently for a bit of mischief. A certain master was once out walking when he came across a collection of rather ill-concealed cigarette-ends. Determined to catch the lads at their clandestine smoking-party, he climbed a tree near the spot the following Sunday afternoon, and waited. Eventually some of the young bloods came along, caught sight of him, but pretended not to notice. Making themselves comfortable on the moss nearby, they spent the whole afternoon talking and doing other harmless things. The master, it is said, was seen to walk rather stiffly for the next day or two.

Having taken leave in the morning of our host (the bursar) and hostess, who had hospitably put us up at their summer cottage by the lakeside, we called on the headmaster who received us in his study lined with books in all languages and with photographs here and there of the sons of the Crown Prince and other Old Boys. Taking refreshments on the lawn, we spoke mostly of schools and he described some interesting educational experiments he had seen abroad. The importance of games and inter-house matches was not, I gathered, one of the features belittled in the process of adapting the English system to Lundsberg. Field athletics as throughout Scandinavia also bulk large: their athletes have actually beaten the pick of some of the leading public schools in England. Of great charm too was the Rektor's Norwegian wife who also spoke English enviably well. I was not the first foreigner to enthuse over the school: a certain Irishman, I am told, was so impressed during his visit that he has secured a Swedish tutor for his sons who will eventually go there.

Waving from the doorstep of their little *herrgård*, they broke into an English song as we mounted our bicycles. After a stop at the tuck-shop to buy provisions we began our sixth day's cycling: southward to Lake Väner and then across flattish open country with extensive yellowing cornfields and occasional dairy farms to Karlstad, the chief town of the province. Every reader of *Gösta Berling* has heard of Karlstad and since that book is translated into 39 languages the name must indeed be famous. It was founded in the late sixteenth century by the father of Gustavus Adolphus, Charles X, who started the mining industry of Värmland. Till then nearly the whole province was a forest as primeval as those of North America, where about the same time other Swedes were also engaged in colonizing (on the Delaware). That there is a strong similarity between the old homesteads hereabouts and those of New England is hardly surprising when one considers the parallel circumstances of their origin: that both were built by Northern Europeans out of similar materials shortly after the pioneering stage when the settlers had begun to accumulate wealth. The climate, the vegetation, even the soil, are also much the same as in Maine or New Hampshire.

I remember visiting the Fryken, Selma Lagerlöf's Löfven, for the first time some years ago, and being astonished to find the landscape so familiar that I could even recognize a few of the places from memory. There was no mistaking Gurlita Cliff, for instance, although it was not marked on my map even by its real name, Tosseberg Klätten. It was a clear day in July, harebells were in full bloom among the horsetails by the roadside, and from time to time we stopped to eat some of the magnificent wild raspberries that were everywhere abundant: but the air was cool, the pure air of the mountains. We cycled right up to the front door of Rotneros Herrgård (for my companion was a friend of the owners) and rang the bell. The maid, possibly because we were wearing blue shorts, took us for Germans; but we were taken in and shown the present Ekeby, a replica of the old building burned down some years ago, as well as the original Cavaliers' Wing which is still intact. I was fortunate in seeing things not shown to the ordinary tripper: to be one of the few out of the thousands of pilgrims from all over the world to receive special attention, although dressed only in cycling shorts! Across the Lake is Mårbacka where Selma Lagerlöf is now living at the age of eighty in her old ancestral home, her birthplace, bought back with Nobel prize-money; while year in and year out the pilgrims come and go, and in the summer the pleasure-steamer named after her moves up and down the lake, never for a day failing to remind her of her fame.*

"Landscapes corroded by literature". There is always this danger for the traveller in Europe: that someone will have got to a given district before him and written a book about it. In a crowded country like England, I often feel an actual resentment at not being allowed to discover a place for myself—that almost every landscape has been sung. (I sometimes wish I were illiterate.) One must always see it through the eyes of a Hardy or a Wordsworth, a Brontë or a Blackmore. At least, one *does*; but then without such an interpreter one might never have come to understand it all: it is the things that the writer has said that we want to say ourselves, possibly because he has taught us what they are. Värmland is the literary province of Sweden: Tegnér, author of *Fritiof's Saga*, and Fröding, two of her greatest poets, were *värmlänningar*, as well as Geijer, the poet-historian who, I remember he tells us, was descended from a German mine-master who settled there in the seventeenth century. It is fortunate that they were not all topographical writers like Lagerlöf: some fine boundary disputes concerning literary territories might otherwise have arisen, and later writers would have had nowhere to stake out their claims. I have, however, discovered an especially intriguing little lake-side town on territory hitherto exploited only by artists (who have formed a colony there); but I won't divulge its name since I intend to live there one day, possibly using its local colour as a literary backdrop.

Fröding: we passed the dingy building in Karlstad where

* This was written just before her death in 1940.

this most popular of Swedish poets worked for awhile on the local newspaper. But Fröding's habits were ill-suited for regular occupations; he did not even take his degree after five years at Upsala. Besides, he went mad—madder, that is than Blake, madder than Cowper, genuinely insane, and certifiable. It comes out in his more cryptic lyrics like a harbinger of surrealism, though how much his better poems owe to touches of insanity it is hard to say. G. K. Chesterton would have found some difficulty in Sweden in maintaining his thesis that it is only extreme rationalists, not artists, who become mad. Look at Fröding—look at Richard Bergh's incomparable portrait of him as The Bard: the great figure sitting up in an immense bed, and the cloudy forehead, the eyes that have ranged over terrible territories, and the huge stormy beard. Look at Josephson, the painter and poet from the south, whose dark hypnotic eyes rolled in as fine a frenzy as ever an artist knew. Look at that curious artist with the un-Swedish name of Hill. And look too at Strindberg, "so *delicately* mad", as Ibsen said, who at one time was unable to work without a portrait of him on his desk.

But we are in Karlstad. It is Midsummer Eve, so we dine at the very best hotel in town, having an elaborate *smörgåsbord* spread out over our table to begin with. This, of course, is a more restful and plutocratic manner of receiving it, though I confess that I would rather go up and help myself at the central communal table found in most restaurants, mainly, I suppose, because there is no limit to the quantity one can take of one's favourite dishes. I am quite ashamed to think of my gluttonous visits to the restaurants at Gothenberg Station, where the sumptuous spread of *Smörgåsbord* puts to shame any of those kingly feasts described in fairy stories. Our meal over, we take a walk down to the park by the side of Lake Väner where innumerable cars and bicycles are parked for the dancing. Everywhere throughout the country there will be dancing to-night. Maypoles have been decorated and erected, platforms have been made, while along the coast and on the islands they will dance on the village jetties. We buy ten-*öre* tickets, choose girls, and whirl round in the excitement of a Swedish waltz. Sometimes we stand out and watch the swift circulation of couples. Lots of the boys are dancing together, not because they are homosexual, not because they cannot find any girls, but just because they are too shy to ask them. Once a Communist, probably a little full of drink and annoyed that someone is dancing with the girl he wants, comes up and asks us what we are doing at his dancing-place. Even at midnight the yellow twilight filters through the pines. At two we return, leaving it to others to promenade in the traditional manner in order to see the sun rise.

On Midsummer Day everyone seemed to be abroad, even more flags than usual were flying, houses were decorated with young birch-trees, girls were dressed out in spotless white, and judging from the heartiness with which greetings were exchanged spirits seemed to be high. The road westwards of Karlstad passes through forests of pure pine on dry sandy soil so straight, dense and uniform that the telegraph poles are completely lost among the living trees. But leaving the Väner plain we found more interesting country and pushed on westwards till we reached an exquisite though rather lifeless riverside village called Nysäter. It also happened to be an interesting one: there were a Viking burial-mound and a complete medieval street of wooden shops which looked as if they had been evacuated several centuries ago. And a mile or two away are some trenches built in 1905, a tangible reminder that feelings on that occasion ran dangerously high. But, as everyone ought to know, there was no war when Norway separated from Sweden to which she had been united for ninety years. It has been called the only example in recent history of an entirely peaceable settlement of a major dispute between two governments. Nor to-day is the wisdom of the separation ever questioned; the relations between the countries are extremely friendly. Yet the Norwegians have never quite forgotten the treatment they received at the hands of Denmark in centuries gone by. How, indeed, did such an unsuitable union manage to persist for so long? Denmark with her simple homely farms behind lilac hedges; Norway with her log seters perched precariously in the wild and stormy fells. I once heard a Norwegian teasing a Dane about Ejer-Bavnehöj, his highest peak, which towers up to just over five hundred feet; and well he might, for isn't Norway all mountains, doesn't she take the eight-and-a-half thousand feet of Guldhoppigen as just another hill? . . . To-day, after over six centuries, Norway again has her own sovereign.

Our eighth day took us to the very south-western corner of Värmland, a part of the province noted for its breeding of farm horses which are sent all over the country, and we passed through Årjäng, a village well-known for its trotting-races. After fighting through torrential rain on steeper, more Norwegian roads, and stopping now and then to empty the water from our shoes, we arrived at the house of some friends who, despite our miserably sodden appearance, welcomed us with open arms.

In the evening we were taken over their pulp-mill which stands at the junction of two lakes. The logs (half of them from their own forests, the other half bought from private owners) are floated down to the end of the upper lake where they must lie in the water a whole year before they can be used. Since the mill is for mechanical pulp, the procedure is simple. The logs are removed from the water, cut into convenient sizes, shot into a drum to be barked by knives, and are then slashed up by revolving grindstones. The resultant fibre-meal is washed, re-washed; sieved, re-sieved; passed through rollers to be squeezed dry and along bands of wool for further drying. The tablets, like thick wallboards, after being pressed for the final drying, are bound in bundles ready for shipment. Small steamers belonging to the mill take them through a series of lakes and canals to Lake Väner; but in winter the bundles accumulate in a large warehouse, awaiting the spring thaw. The mill operates throughout the year, the power being provided from a small waterfall, which also supplies the village with cheap electricity for lighting and cooking.

The director is said to take a great personal interest in his employees, and not infrequently he and his son will be seen joining with them in village football. The comfortable two-storeyed workers' cottages, each with a garden of half-an-acre, would indeed be a thrill for any sociologist.

A late night with some of the lads of the village provided a convenient excuse for our succumbing to Värmland hospitality for even longer than usual. And so we lazed throughout the morning on the verandah of the enchanting lakeside *herrgård*. The spring was here less advanced than it had been a week before in the east: some lilacs were still in flower and the roses were not yet out. Some rhododendrons, very rarely introduced into these latitudes, the pride of the garden, were at their showiest; while the terrace stonework was attractively decorated with the Lapland *Saxifraga cotyledon*, known from its fine sprays of pure white flowers as Bride of the Fells.

> *"And that this place may thoroughly be thought*
> *True Paradise, I have the serpent brought"*—

in the form of bad teeth. For even the children of this district have black teeth, probably the result of a deficiency of calcium in the water; though one would think that, were the cause so simple, the missing element could be introduced into the food, just as Swiss school-children are given specially prepared chocolate.

It was not till four that we started. Turning southward we were very soon in Dalsland, a province which is all lakes and forests (half the place-names seem to end in -*skog* which means forest, or in -*rud* which denotes a clearing). That the landscape is thought to be typically Swedish is perhaps shown from the fact that Hasselbom's well-known picture *Our Country* was painted from a hill-top in Dalsland.

Except in the far south the roads of Sweden are distinctly bad, and owing to the sparsity of the population and the length and nature of the winters, very few are metalled. But the lack of motor traffic and the general absence of fences makes them attractive to the cyclist who in time comes to think of them as his own special thoroughfares. And delightful it is to forget all about cars and motor-cycles, to have the road entirely to one's self, and to rush down the long slopes with the wind thrashing the chest and rippling down the back and an occasional insect bouncing off the nose.

Background to Sweden

The roads of Dalsland appeal only to certain moods. You must imagine you are on a switchback and that you are controlling both speed and direction. If you are driving and meet another car, you must be prepared to go back a mile to the nearest *mötesplats* in order to let it pass. If you are cycling you must expect not only the usual transverse corrugations of the surface but also deep and sudden sand-drifts, especially at the sharpest corners and the bottoms of the steepest hills. "A close contact with the soil": very easy I discovered as, rushing round one curve, I skidded in the sand, headed for some granite jags at the roadside, but threw myself over just in time. "Nature at close range": no more difficult I found when a little further on I narrowly missed charging into some cows (I could almost feel my head in the bovine belly, and hear the resultant leathery thud). Cows on the forest roads are commoner than human beings; and the tinkling from the bell of the leader is often the only sound emphasizing the silence of the great woods. In accordance with ancient rights they are allowed to graze in the forests but finding the best grass in open places generally remain by the roadsides. Even as far south as this the prevailing breed is the hornless black-and-white fell-cow, a hardy smallish animal with an excellent yield for its size.

As half our time was spent walking up hills of improbable steepness we had a chance of noticing the interesting ground flora of the spruce forests. The pink almond-scented *Linnea* was very common and in full bloom. This is the only flower named after Linnaeus, and although small it is by no means a bad choice: it spreads quickly, while its shapely bell-like flowers and rounded leaves, both in neat pairs, are the perfect embodiment of order. Interspersed with that were horsetails, mosses and other primitive plants; while the silvery shoots of *Lycopodium*, the oldest plant on earth (though the particular specimens seemed as virile as ever), squirted over the needle-matted floor in every direction. In the damper spots, among the *Sphagnum* and small arum lilies, were drifts of the resin-scented *Myrica gale* or bog-myrtle; and here and there on the dark forest tarns the white water-lilies were beginning to open.

Having crossed a wild, mountain-girdled lake on a ferry,

consisting of a very crude pontoon pushed by an outboard motor, we stopped for dinner near the Norwegian frontier (for it was our intention to strike the coast at the southernmost point of Norway). Most of the inhabitants thereabouts were Norwegians, or at least spoke the language. One sociable guest at the pension came to talk to us as we ate our *filmjölk* and veal and sipped the home-brewed juniper wine. He told us that he came from Oslo and that even in that city of tall people he had rarely met anyone of his own height. But now, at his age, to find someone *taller* (for so my companion was)—to be beaten by a young lad and at *his* time of life! No, he couldn't get over it. How old did we think he was? For politeness' sake we suggested fifty-four or fifty-two. No! he was seventy. "You wouldn't think it, would you? Seventy years this spring." He certainly *was* exuberant for his age; and we eventually left him waving a very hearty goodbye from the verandah.

We came to the frontier, first the Swedish boom and then one kilometre further the notice "HÖGKÖRNING", where we changed to the right of the road. Sweden and Portugal are now the only continental countries where driving on the left is the rule of the road. It says something both for her Anglophilism and for the essential difference between Norway and Sweden. Another kilometre brought us to the Norwegian boom. The officer wanted our passports. Having left mine in Upsala I was stumped, for even here a frontier is a frontier. Nothing could be done: we had to return.

"I hope the Swedish guard will remember you and let you through again." If he hadn't I should have been compelled to wander to and fro in the neutral area (address: No-man's-land) perhaps for ever. And so we made a very undignified retreat, our heads bowed with shame. Nor were we unnoticed by some small boys who, evidently remembering us, stopped their game of football to have a good laugh at the supposedly black characters who had been turned back at the frontier.

Dalsland again. It was now growing dark. We rode among quiet twilit lakes which duplicated the saffron-tinted clouds. Wonderful to be abroad on such an evening! One almost looks for elves in the light gauze of mist hovering over the water. One also looks for a sweater in one's cycle-bag.

We were damp, chilly and tired when, sometime in the night, we began to take an intense interest in barns. Since this was to be our last night, we had decided to spend it in a barn. Finding a large, apparently wholesome one in the neighbourhood of Ed, we sniffed round the door and took our bicycles inside. Then, having climbed to the top of a pile of straw, we threw ourselves down for a good sleep. Vain hope! For even if we had not periodically slithered bacwards on to the floor, the cold wind, filtering through the widely spaced slats, would have found its way through any thickness of straw. We discovered a larger pile, buried ourselves in it and thought of eiderdowns and sleeping-bags.

A gloomy morning discovered us pulling straws from the hair, shaking our clothes, doing neck exercises, and agreeing that blankets are indispensable for barn-sleeping. We of course had a dip in the nearest lake before finding the lowest eating-haunt in the whole of Ed (a comparatively sophisticated tourist centre).

The road southwards took us to the blunt humps of granite so typical of the Bohuslän landscape. Having taken the wrong route, we found ourselves on the dullest road in the whole province. The fields were poor, the woods stunted, the cattle pinched and mangy, the houses mean and (judging from those we entered in order to buy pommac) the dirtiest in the whole of Scandinavia. Nor were the inhabitants any better. And throughout the length of this depressing and interminable valley wriggled a brown abject stream—in what direction no one would bother to wonder. There was only one cheerful note— the lavish display of useless road-signs, such as a laughable series of finger-posts, all marked "KROKSTAD CHURCH. 5 KM", pointing to the most conspicuous landmark in the whole valley.

In the afternoon it began to rain, fierce torrents being thrashed against us horizontally by a wind sweeping in un- impeded from the North Sea. It was with drooping colours and dripping clothes that we arrived at the head of Saltkälle-fjord, our journey completed. Four hundred and sixty miles in ten days. Not very much in point of mileage. But, recollecting what we had done in six provinces and the headwinds we had met with nearly the whole way, we considered it enough. So ended the first of my three cycle-crossings of Sweden.

VIII · IN THE LANDS OF THE GEATS

1 : *Svear and Geats*

ABOUT FOURTEEN HUNDRED years ago there were two main tribes in Sweden—the Svear who had subdued the surrounding petty states and whose capital was Old Upsala, and the Geats or Gautar separated from them by the great lakes and confined roughly to Väster- and Östergötland. The Svear, who even at that date appear to have had very forcible monarchs, pounced on the Geats, thus starting a series of wars which raged through much of the sixth century and resulted in the ultimate triumph of the Svear and the beginning of the Swedish Kingdom (Sverige, as it is called to-day, being a contraction of *Svea Rike*, kingdom of the Svear). The unification to be sure had not always been achieved in a very gentlemanly fashion: one Svea monarch, for example, who was given a roasted wolf's-heart in his youth to make him more courageous, is reported to have invited all the petty kings around him to a feast, to have made them drunk and then to have burned them to death in the building in order to grab their territories more conveniently. But at least it came about quite early, and the subjects, if we consider all classes at all periods, probably had fewer causes for complaining than those of even the most forward countries in Europe.

In *Beowulf*, our great national epic, which was written down in the tenth century, but deals with events (semi-historical and otherwise) occurring four centuries before that, there are several episodes concerning the wars of Svear and Geats. We are told how Hraedcyn, King of the Geats is slain in battle, and then Ongentheow of the Svear, and how eventually Beowulf himself (who cannot however be identified with anyone in history) becomes King of the Geats.

232

In the Lands of the Geats

"There was strife and struggle twixt Swede and Geat
o'er the width of waters. War arose
hard battle horror, when Hrethel died,
and Ongentheow's offspring grew
strife-keen, bold, nor brooked o'er the seas
pact of peace, but pushed their hosts
to harass in hatred by Hreosnabeorh" —

so runs one passage in the poem; and another:

"The bloody swath of Swedes and Geats
and the storm of their strife were seen afar,
how folk against folk the fight had wakened."

Several Northern writings refer to some of these persons and
episodes: in the Danish history of Saxo Grammaticus (*c.* 1200),
well-known as containing the story of Hamlet, there is a vivid
account of one of the major battles; while Ongentheow appears
by the name of Egil in the *Ynglingasaga*, written in the thirteenth
century by the great Icelandic historian Snorre Sturlason.
(The Ynglings, who it is thought originally came from Väster-
götland, moved to Norway where they founded the great dynasty
whose doings the historian records.) And Snorre, by the way,
tells us somewhere that Gautland (i.e., Götland) was named
after a king called Gaut who had a son called Gautrek the Mild
and a grandson called Algaute and a great granddaughter
called Gauthild (who incidentally married a King of the Svear);
but research suggests that it is really the Göta River that gave
its name to the Gautar, and probably also to the original Goths
who came "as from a hive of races or a womb of nations",
crossed the Baltic to the mouth of the Vistula well before the
fourth century B.C., and swarmed over Europe and down the
sloping civilization of the Mediterranean.

Until three centuries ago the Swedes had but a single direct
outlet to the west—through a narrow wedge of territory on the
banks of the Göta River sandwiched between the Norwegian
province of Bohuslän and the Danish one of Halland. This
being so, one would have expected to find some sort of port

on the River at an early period in history. And so one does: there was Old Lödöse, founded in Viking times, long one of the chief places in the country, and later on protected by the fortress of Älvsborg built in the fourteenth century. And then followed several towns on the site of present-day Gothenburg: New Lödöse, begun by Sten Sture in 1473; another founded by Gustavus Vasa in the next century; and in the early seventeenth century the first Gothenburg, which however was soon attacked by the Danes who burned it to the ground and captured Älvsborg for which they demanded a colossal ransom. The Dutch, at that time the chief traders and bankers in Northern Europe, fortunately came to the rescue by advancing the necessary capital. From the Low Countries also came the chief architects and engineers of the new Gothenburg (founded in 1619 by Gustavus Adolphus) which was laid out with canals and broad straight thoroughfares in the Dutch manner. Came also Louis de Geer and other capitalists who did much for Swedish industry. For a century Holland had more or less a monopoly of the foreign trade of Sweden, and while this was useful for the particular port of Gothenburg the country as a whole was cramped by the selfish attempts of the Dutch to prevent Swedish commerce from expanding, to frustrate her attempts at colonization, and to exploit her resources purely for their own advantages.

In the eighteenth century, when the Dutch monopoly was broken and the country began to recover after all her exhausting wars, Gothenburg became increasingly lively with her trade, now extended to a variety of countries and with an East India Company of her own. Always in touch with British traditions from the time Scots and Englishmen settled there in her earliest days, Gothenburg from now on became the confirmed "Anglovert" she has ever since remained. Her position was especially favourable during Napoleon's blockade of Britain, when she served as a convenient depot for smuggling our goods into the Continent. And throughout the last century she rapidly consolidated her merchantile impregnability, becoming in a while the chief port in Scandinavia with twenty times the population she had in 1800.

In the Lands of the Geats

To-day if the tourist rises early enough he will see one of the most interesting harbours in Europe as his ship steams in through the skerries, then up the Göta River towards the modern city (proclaimed from afar by the sturdy hill-top tower of the Masthuggs Church) now passing the island fort of Älvsborg; now the factories and shipyards on Hisingen; now perhaps a large passenger liner of the Swedish-American line, now a sailing barque from Australia, and with pleasure-craft, coastal freighters and old-fashioned *Skärgård* steamers growing thicker and thicker every minute; till eventually his vessel slows down near Fiskehamnen (where the herring-fleet lies huddled together in its own special little harbour), and tugs come alongside manoeuvring it to its berth under the solid buildings stuck on granite cliff-faces, just opposite the big floating-docks and shipyards of Götaverken and a mere rocket-shot from the centre of the City.

The leisurely or elderly tourist generally accomplishes the journey through Väster- and Östergötland by steamer on the Göta Canal—a trip of about 360 miles, taking two and a half days. Three hundred miles: the distance looks impressive, especially if you remember that the Panama Canal is only forty in length and Suez a hundred and one. But canals are cheats: their dimensions offer no key to their importance or the magnitude of the labour expended in their construction. The Corinth Canal, only four miles long, is cut through solid rock; Suez may be twenty times the length, but many a four-mile section could be marked where no work at all was required or only a bit of dredging. Sweden's are nothing if not poseurs: "The Göta Canal", one reads in tourist brochures, guidebooks, travel agencies, "is three hundred and sixty miles in length"; but to learn that three hundred and six of these miles are natural river, lakes and sea one is reduced to the *Encyclopædia Britannica*; while on the Dalsland Canal—quite well boosted in its way— I doubt if there is more than half-a-mile of artificial work linking up the succession of lakes and rivers from Southern Norway to Lake Väner, about eighty miles in all, which bears the name Canal. I have been by boat through most of the

Background to Sweden

Dalsland water-system, and would wager that however questionable its pretensions to rank as a canal it is scenically the most enchanting in Europe. It is also notable for a rather theatrical convergence of roadway, railway, aqueduct and step-locks at a place called Håverud, where if you are a painter you can get into the same picture a car crossing the roadbridge, beneath which a train crosses the railway bridge, beneath which a steamer crosses the aqueduct, beneath all of which runs a river, not deep enough, it is true for a submarine, but there is always room in the sky for an aeroplane banking above the roadway. No one however should ridicule the Göta Canal which after all has fifty-four miles of artificial work (which is more than the Panama and nearly as much as the Kiel), while no less than fifty-eight locks are responsible for raising steamers three hundred feet above sea-level and then taking them all the way down again. The idea dates from 1516 (only 2,896 years after the first Suez Canal was built!) and Swedenborg among others did a bit of abortive cutting a couple of centuries later before the scheme was finally taken up by a Baron von Platten, who formed a Canal company and brought over a Scot, Thomas Telford, as engineer (1810-32). The Baltic having been linked with the North Sea by a waterway, the first craft made the journey between the two chief towns in Sweden about a century ago.

Being addicted to a more energetic form of travelling than steaming on canals, I decided once more to cross the country on pushbike. Most of my friends were at that time doing their military service, taking a holiday abroad, otherwise occupied, so I set out alone, knowing that I should probably fall in with company now and then, and in any case intending to pay some calls *en route*. Havelock Ellis in one of his essays suggests that the best way of travelling is alone. But while agreeing with him that moving in parties (especially of one's countrymen) is insufferable, I cannot see that "even a single companion is a mistake" if that companion be a native of the country in question. The delight of such journeys, he maintains, is not "the pure joy of travel: the companion is responsible for a large part of it". And why not, if the companion is a native and therefore part of the country? Few lands are without the traces of man, and where there are traces it is as well to understand them: to witness not only the changes man has wrought in his environment, but also the effect that environment has had—and may, at any illuminating moment, still be having—upon some particular native. The increased pleasure and naturalness of having some knowledgeable person to give one at the time one needs it the information that one would either attempt to track down sooner or later or miss altogether; of having someone to answer one's questions, to explain things that might never have been formulated in questions, and to show one how to conform more easily to the habits of the country; the adventitious pleasure of having some companion to share one's joys and hardships (though hardly one's indignities)—all these, which it is unnecessary to enlarge upon, give further support to my argument. And in this I am quite sincere. It is not that I am frightened or bored with my own company; or that I have not long ago outgrown that childish habit, all too easily engendered in English boarding-schools and sometimes never discarded, of keeping in company just for the sake of not appearing lonely or eccentric. It is only that I think it more delightful, more profitable, generally to travel with a native, especially in the wide-spread North where changes in external details are comparatively infrequent. But variety in modes of travelling as in all the arts is desirable: it may well be that to move about now alone, now in company, is the ideal. At any rate I was alone this time, so here goes!

2: *Conversion of Sweden*

HAVING FOLLOWED THE main road northwards to Trollhättan and Vänersborg where Lake Väner funnels into the Göta River, I struck eastwards across what is the chief cereal plain in Middle Sweden. Approaching from this point you pass through the little abrupt clumps of diabase, Hunneberg and Halleberg, which rise sheer from the roadway; out of sight to the east are the larger, more undulating Billingen and

Mösseberg, which rather closely resemble English downland. But northwards the flat grainlands sweep uninterrupted into the Lake of Väner. Or very nearly, for standing alone in the north-west is the charmingly named Kinnekulle whose well-moulded profile I cycled towards one toneless evening in mid-July. All of a sudden I was "leafwhelmed somewhere within the hood of some branchy, bunchy, bushybowered wood"; the road became very steep: I had to dismount and walk up-hill. But turning left on the hill-top at the most northerly point, I saw, remote and improbable, half way up the sky, the vast pewter-like expanse of the Lake. Following this avenue along the ridge, I came eventually to a finely situated hotel and *vandrarhem*, where nothing was lacking in the way of food and pleasant company to cheer an otherwise lugubrious evening.

At that time I hardly realized what attention this distinctive spot has always received from the Swedes. Here, for instance, is a description I have since discovered in an old book:

"Of the Wonderful Garden of the Mountain Kindaberg"

"There is a most high mountain among the Vestrogoths ... commonly called Kindakulle. It is so high that it appears to mariners that are forty Italian miles from it in the Lake like to a black cloud in the air. Wherefore many that are driven by tempests and force of the winds endeavour by all means to come to the foot cf it, where they know there is a most safe harbour. On the top of this mountain there are such pleasant boughs, herbs and fruits of divers kinds (excepting the vine) that come up of themselves, not more rare than sweet, as if they were sowed or planted, that there scarce can be found a more delightsome place in all the northern climates. There is a sweetness that cannot be related, and that is multiplied by the concert of divers birds, except the popinjay. . . ."

But why the exotic references: why "Italian miles" and "the vine"? Well, the author was Olaus Magnus, the Catholic Archbishop of Upsala who at the Reformation was exiled to Italy, where he wrote his long, intriguing account of the Northern nations. (I am quoting from the abridged English translation which was made in the following, the seventeenth, century.) To continue the description:

"That most pleasant place", he says (and now the voice assumes an ecclesiastical tone) "is known to very few, and

> they only old men. Nor is it easily to be discovered to young people, lest being released from more severe discipline, they should cast themselves down to all pleasures, or rather beastliness, and would hardly or never be reclaimed to good manners. For pleasure itself brings on use and custom and constrains men; custom necessity, and necessity despair, without this mountainous place and elsewhere. . . ."

A curious passage, and for the most part not inaccurate to-day. To call a hill of a thousand feet "a most high mountain" is an excusable exaggeration; while Linneaus also likened the place to a garden: the wealth of plant species found on the rich red sandstone and calcareous soils is certainly remarkable. But the "old men"? No! not to-day. Rather is the place a resort specially of the young. And the following day I was asked to accompany one of the many lads at the *vandrarhem*, who happened to be going off in the same direction.

The morning was fresh and finer, and from the hill-top road we had excellent views across the Lake. The features of Kinnekulle are largely determined by the geology: exuberant woods of tall mixed deciduous trees, interspersed with fertile meadows behind low limestone walls; and old limestone churches sheltering beneath enormous ash-trees. By far the most notable of these churches is at Husaby on the very southern extremity, with its grave (outside the porch) of Olof Skötkonung, the first Christian King of Sweden, who was baptized there by an English missionary.

The part played by Englishmen in the Christianization of Scandinavia is a story almost as little known as it is hard to come by. As early as the close of the seventh century an Anglo-Saxon missionary appeared in Denmark—Willibrord, who though well received by the King returned without accomplishing anything. Then Germans and even Franks tried their hands

Background to Sweden

at converting the wild Danes during the next few centuries; and King Harald Bluetooth, baptized by a German in 960, left a runic inscription claiming that it was he "who made the Danes Christian". But Anglo-Saxons and Anglo-Danes really did most of the conversion and left most influence. Canute the Great, especially, brought over many English bishops; it even seemed likely at one time that the Danish Church would come under the see of Canterbury. English saints were very popular in Denmark, St. Thomas among them—as a baptismal font still to be seen in Skåne depicting scenes from his death serves to remind us. The only missionary work undertaken by the Danes themselves outside their own country was the conversion of Esthonia, conquered by them in 1219.

The most striking results of all were achieved in Norway, which (if we ignore a few insignificant local missionary attempts emanating from Germany, Denmark and France) was entirely Christianized from England: the Norwegian Church became the only real daughter of the English; English influence was exclusive till the middle of the thirteenth century and persisted till 1290. What Haakon the Good, fostered at the court of Athelstan, had failed to accomplish in the mid-tenth century Olaf Tryggvason, baptized in Andover, accomplished in the years 995 to 1000: the whole of Norway was converted, as well as the Shetlands, the Faroes, the Orkneys and Iceland. Another king baptized in England, Olaf Haraldson (1016-1030), who during his lifetime proved extremely unpopular and was murdered by rebels and Danes, soon afterwards was proclaimed a saint, and in time became the most popular saint in the North. The fact that he was well-known in England, where fifteen churches were dedicated to him, is a further reminder of the closeness of the two countries at the time. And then Nicholas Breakspear, the only English Pope, established an archbishopric at Nidaros (Trondheim), where Eystein, a friend of our St. Thomas, created a splendid cathedral on English lines.

The conversion of Sweden was both late and prolonged, being spread over three centuries. In 829 came Anskar, a German who had made some unsuccessful attempts in Denmark; converts were made; the Emperor established a special archbishopric for the North with its seat in Hamburg; and Anskar as its first incumbent continued his work in Sweden and even had some success in Denmark. But little more was to come from the South. When, a century and a half later, the first English missionaries arrived, they found the Christian community so insignificant that the country was still really heathen.

The greatest of these, the man who did more than any other individual for the conversion of Sweden, was Sigfrid who had gone to Norway as Olaf Tryggvason's court bishop, and after his death moved to Denmark (where he married) and then to Sweden. It was he who baptized Olof Skötkonung in the year 1008 a few hundred yards from Husaby Church. The spring, whose waters were at one time reputed to have miraculous powers, is there to-day; modern Swedish kings have drunk its waters and carved their names on a rock in the grotto. The Conversion of King Olof was certainly the master-stroke of "The Apostle of Sweden"; it inevitably furthered his prestige and influence, especially when other members of the royal family followed suit. Evidently a man of considerable energy, he succeeded in christianizing both Öster- and Väster-Götland, and in extending his activities to Småland, a more difficult province where three of his nephews were murdered and where he himself died and was buried at a ripe old age somewhere in the 1060's (at Väksjö). It is said that a few days before his death the old man absent-mindedly ordered a bath on a fast day and was reproved by a voice, whereupon he left the bath and confessed his fault.

Eskil, one of his relations, did much to evangelize Södermanland; but, intervening at a pagan sacrifice at Strängnäs, was attacked and stoned to death in the year of Hastings. He became the patron saint of that see, and the trading town of Tuna in the district was renamed Eskilstuna—a place which has now become the Sheffield of Sweden. Neither he nor Sigfrid was formerly canonized, but such an omission was not uncommon in those days.

Another important though less popular saint was David the English Apostle of Västmanland, first bishop of Västerås and founder of probably the first monastery in Sweden (at Munktorp). Not much is known about the lives of these men, but a legend survives concerning David in his old age. His sight having become dim, he one day mistook the nature of a ray of sunshine coming through the window of Munktrop Church and hung his gloves upon it. They remained miraculously suspended, and thereafter David continued to make use of the solar support. But one day they fell. Wondering what sin he had committed, he retraced his steps and discovered that he had trampled on some ears of barley in a field. So he prayed for forgiveness, making an offer of a gold ear of barley, and the ray once again supported his gloves. He lived for a while on an island in the Mälar still called Dåvö (David's Island); and nearby is Botkyrka, perpetuating the name of Botvid, a Swede converted in England who did good work in those parts, but like many an early worker suffered the death of a martyr.

Slowly but fairly steadily the land was christianized. In the late tenth century the great heathen temple of Old Upsala was destroyed. In the twelfth century Upsala became the ecclesiastical centre of the country, with Stephen, an Englishman, as the first bishop. About eight of the early Swedish bishops including Stephen were Englishmen, and nearly all the local saints.

To Henry, another English bishop of Upsala, and to King (afterwards St.) Erik belong the credit of leading the First Crusade to Finland (about 1154), where Henry established a bishopric at Åbo (Turku), was martyred and became the patron saint of that country, and where another Englishman, Thomas, also carried on missionary work. On their Second and Third Crusades (1249 and 1293) the Swedes penetrated further and further through Southern and South-eastern Finland, conquering as they went and eventually coming into conflict with Novgorod. This Russian state, ruled by a Swedish dynasty, dispatched no less than 1,227 priests to Carelia, which became the main battleground for Swedes and Russians till the Peace of Nöteborg split it between them in 1323. It was the Novgorodians who founded the monastery of Valamo in Lake Ladoga in 1251, and who attempted to convert various Finno-

Ugrian tribes scattered over Northern Russia such as the Siryenians of the Pechora region who (thanks to a St. Stephen) had a written language as early as 1375 though not for long.

It is interesting to notice that in both Norway and Finland Christianity was forced on the people at the point of the sword —a method that, very wisely, was not tried on the Swedes with their conservative and independent outlook; or, where it was, one that met with no success. Only in Småland, then the most southerly province, was there any coercion, for which one may thank Sigurd the Jerusalem-Farer of Norway. That forcible conversion was elsewhere abhorrent is shown by the fate of St. Eskil; and witness the cases of a certain King Inge whose abolition of the Upsala sacrifices and attempt to destroy the Temple resulted in a rebellion, his deposition and a heathen reaction; and of Woldred, one of the English missionaries, who having hewn down an idol of Thor was murdered and thrown in a bog.

So, although they were not pioneers, the English were mainly responsible for the conversion of Sweden. As one writer observes: "Under Canute the Great Sweden was closely linked with the other Scandinavian countries and with England, Canute exercising a sort of imperial prerogative over Sweden." In 1152 an English legate from Nicholas Breakspear (the only English Pope) after establishing an archbishopric in Norway went to Sweden to do the same. But the Swedes and the Götar were unable to agree on the site, so Breakspear left matters with the Archbishop of Lund (which town was then in Danish territory), appointing him "Primate of Sweden". From that century Denmark and Sweden, unlike Norway, turned rather to other countries than England, and what English influence there was (on architecture, painting, etc.) probably filtered through from Norway. In Sweden there are no records of English monastic foundations as in Norway and Denmark: it was rather the other way about, for England later on turned out to be one of the countries in which the Swedish Order of St. Bridget became established.

Apart from Husaby there are many other places in Västergötland connected with the early history of the Church. Out on the plains is Skara, site of the first Swedish bishopric which was founded as early as 1013, and can boast in Rikulv and Hervard two English incumbents during the first century of its existence. Its severely plain limestone Cathedral (twelfth-fourteenth centuries) whose twin, gargoyled spires are a landmark for miles around, is one of the Swedish churches in which English influences are said to be discernible. And at Skara also were important houses of the Dominicans and Franciscans.

These two orders and the Cistercians were the dominating ones in Sweden, although Carthusians, Carmelites, Antonines and Knights Hospitallers were established there as well, and the Bridgettines throve at Vadstena for a century and a half before the Reformation. The earliest and greatest of these orders was the Cistercians. Most of their abbeys are now in ruins: Alvastra, the first, founded in the 1140's, where St. Bridget received her training, on a hillside in Östergötland; and Gudhem on the uplands south of Skara. But two are not, Vreta and Varnhem, the latter also near Skara. The great abbey church of Varnhem, thanks to its careful and competent restoration by Professor Sigurd Curman, can be seen in much the same state it was in seven centuries ago—a magnificent structure in Cotswold-coloured limestone, with a black shingle roof, capped by a spire and corner pinnacles and having an astonishing triple tier of buttresses around the apsidal east end.

It was in this direction I continued, leaving behind me the charming and historical hill-garden of Kinnekulle.

3 : *Conscripts*

ON THE ROAD to Skövde, a town some twenty miles east of Skara, I passed by Axvall military camp where Army conscripts in their grey-green field uniform (much like the Italian) and others of the Coastal Artillery (in sailors' dress) were stationed for joint manoeuvres. But on learning that the friend I was looking for was laid up in the military hospital at Skövde (in which town one of the four divisions of the peacetime Army is centred), I proceeded there, found the barracks and was eventually shown into a ward full of outrageously healthy-looking and exuberant youths (most of whom I gathered were merely shamming ill for the sake of a few days' holiday).

Even here in this country which has not been to war for a century-and-a-quarter conscription has long been in force, though the term of military service is shorter than in most continental countries, amounting to one hundred and seventy-five days or for technical units two hundred and twenty. Students (who provide the majority of the reserve officers) generally do about nine months—at two separate periods, if they wish; and the time chosen is often just after an examination, for there are few better ways of combining a complete mental rest with a holiday on pay and a chance of improving one's physique. Since the professional cadres of officers and N.C.O.'s number only 19,000, the importance of the reservists is obvious.*

In summer one's friends, scattered about the country in camps and barracks, are tantalizingly inaccessible. By far the most popular place to be stationed is the island fortress of Vaxholm guarding the entrance to Stockholm, and every summer visitor to the capital must have noticed the hundreds of young men in uniform saying good-bye to their girl friends and crowding into the last *Skärgård* steamers on Sunday evenings. Owing to the fine physique of most young Swedes, the conscripts cut a pretty smart appearance: to me, though I am but a casual observer, they are more impressive than regulars in certain other countries I have visited. I was once told that in their food, which like army food anywhere is poorish if not worse, a certain substance is put which tends to suppress sexual excitement without impairing energy; but what this talismanic anaphrodisiac may be I have never succeeded in discovering.

Another twenty or twenty-five miles south of Skara and Skövde is Falköping. But why, oh why? A nondescript place in a dull open valley between some downs called Mösseberg and Ålleberg, it appeared to have no *raison d'être* whatsoever. And I bear it a special grudge for its not having had a bathing-place

* This was written in 1939.

for a hot July afternoon: apart from Skåne the plain of Väster-götland is about the only district in Sweden where you cannot easily find a lake or river to bathe in just when you wish to. By now quite hardened to finding highly specialized industries in the most unlikely spots—in villages in the middle of forests or by lonely lakes, I was not really surprised to discover that Falköping has the oldest and largest factory in Europe for self-acting blind-rollers used in vehicles. But the location was not purely capricious: the town (it is more like a large village) being a major railway junction on the Gothenberg-Stockholm line can thus secure with ease all the wood and steel necessary for these blind-rollers and distribute the finished products by rail at costs that are not excessive for such comparatively light non-bulky goods. Nor was it out of mere caprice that man decided to inhabit the downs of the Falköping district at an early date, since much of the surrounding country was then part of a series of great lakes which, stretching towards or into one another, very nearly made Southern Sweden the island that at one time the continentals believed her to be. Having no desire to spend the night there, or to investigate at close quarters the ancient mounds and dolmens scattered liberally over the downs (and of a type I already knew), I bought a ticket and a *velocipedbiljett*, followed my bike into a blue, comfortably and modernly upholstered Diesel-engined railbus (made by ASEA in Västerås), and in an hour found myself in the resort of Hjo (pronounced "You") on Lake Vätter, thus avoiding the tedium of cycling across the dead flat plain—cereal country and bogland—which in prehistoric times formed an easterly extension of the Lake.

4 : *Mainly Females*

Gränna is in Småland. Set on the easterly shore of Lake Vätter, amid open fields tilted towards the afternoon and sheltered behind a range of hills, it accumulates heat steadily throughout the day sucking up the sun's rays from the clear skies and off the light blue water. Having landed from the

Visingsö steamer at midday, I began to look round me, amazed at the wealth of flowers to be seen everywhere and the number of garden strawberries and cherries offered for sale. But no sooner had this sunny colourful spot put me in mind of the Mediterranean than I was violently transported to the Arctic.

For just then I chanced on the cottage where Salomon August Andrée first saw the light some eighty years ago. Now a museum, it contains a complete photographic record of Andrée's extraordinary attempt to reach the Pole in a balloon. In 1897 he took off from Spitzbergen with two companions. And that was the last that was seen of them. For two years search-parties were sent out; but nothing happened. Years passed; no one knew where or how they had perished; and they were beginning to be forgotten. Then, in 1930, a Norwegian whaler discovered their remains on White Island off the north-east of Spitzbergen. You can see in these photographs how their skeletons were discovered with their clothes torn about by bears which had evidently been at their bodies, how some of the remains of their camp were embedded in solid ice, and their primus stove still containing oil was found in a perfectly usable condition. All the paraphernalia was removed by a ship specially chartered by a Swedish journalist; the funeral belatedly accorded these long-lost heroes was a national event. Chemists were meanwhile engaged on deciphering the diaries and developing the exposed films which had lain in the open for a third of a century; and the published results were magnificently justified. The wildness of the adventure can be gauged when one learns that Andrée's balloon was not even a dirigible: provided the wind was fairly constant, a cable dragged along the ground and would keep them on a fairly even course, but the possibilities of tacking were severely limited. And what if the drag-line broke away—as it did at the very beginning of their venture? Apparently undeterred, they let themselves be whisked forward, and for over three days they remained at the mercy of the winds, sometimes being blown one way, sometimes another, now rising to a considerable height, now dropping so low that they had to throw overboard as ballast 440 lbs. of provisions and the heavier scientific instruments. But on the

R

fourth day, July 14th, they were bumping over the ice so violently that any hope of getting clear again with their load of necessities was abandoned. A photograph taken by Andrée shows the balloon at 83° N 30° W after it had been forced down on a large ice-floe; another clearly shows him scanning the horizon from the roof of the car. So after a week's preparations they set out by sledge in the direction of Franz Joseph Land, sometimes being forced to ferry from one floe to another in their canvas boat. On August 4th they had progressed only thirty-three miles to S.S.E., and finding that the current would prevent their reaching Franz Joseph Land, they headed for the Seven Islands (North Spitzbergen) which they intended to reach in six or seven weeks. But immense difficulties lay in their way as they moved from floe to floe, with one of the party ill, and at last after a narrow escape when the ice split up just outside their tent they were forced to land on White Island on October 5th. Twelve days later they were still alive, but the last pages of the diary are so badly weathered that only a few pathetically disconnected words can be deciphered. One of the party died and was buried in a cairn; Andrée and the other were probably frozen to death in their sleep.

Continuing northwards along the beautiful Lake road I came into Östergötland, where eventually the land flattened out westwards leaving before me a compact, detached hill called Omberg, rather smaller than Kinnekulle and even more densely wooded. The *vandrarhem* there is one of the best I have found; it was more like a small country house. But the flies were so numerous in the garden that eating out of doors (as we did) was an amazingly difficult achievement. After *middag* I fell in with a few of the guests who were going to climb to the hill-top for the view. We emerged in a clearing in the beechwoods just in time to see a fiery swollen sun heading for the lustrous gash of water, as wide as the Straits of Dover, which divided the landscape to the west, leaving just a narrow band for the opposite shore. Since Omberg juts out towards the middle of the Lake, nearly the whole eighty miles of Vätter lay prostrate before our eyes, from Visingsö (serenest of Lake islands) in the south to a vague ridge on the northern shore where the Poet of

Vätter lives in his old age. What the Fryken was to Selma Lagerlöf, this Lake (or one end of it) is to Verner von Heidenstam—or would be if any one writer could claim it. Within a year of the former's birth at Mårbacka the latter was born at Olshammar—over on the north-western shore, in the Forest of Tiveden celebrated in his poetry. The masterpieces of both were published in the same year; both are members of the Swedish Academy and winners of the Nobel Prize (he received his "in recognition of his importance as representing a new epoch in Swedish literature"). At least I am presuming that *The Carolines (Carolinerna) is* von Heidenstam's masterpiece: it always will be for me—this exquisite prose epic which was one of my early Scandiolatrous enthusiasms. Talking of Charles XII, it happens that my companion that evening told me he had just been visiting a church on the plain to the east to see a grave of a certain ancestor of his who had been taken prisoner at Pultava, and after spending nine years in Siberia returned to his family, who had long given him up as lost, with enough vitality to last him another twenty years.

Then in the morning to see some of the local sights. Two of the party were going down to Ellen Key's house: would I join them? I thought there was no harm in going: there might be a chance of picking up some odd information about this famous feminist so eagerly read by our more enlightened mothers and grandmothers. Plunging down through beechwoods on the steep hillside we eventually came out on a house, not yet reached by the sun, standing at the edge of the Lake. We were shown over the rooms by one who evidently worshipped every relic of her former mistress: here was a small wastepaper-basket that had belonged to Ellen Key as a child, there the candle which had burned at her bedside the day she died; nearby was the dress which . . . but how much more interesting her articles of faith than her articles of clothing! An important influence in modifying the nineteenth century hypocrisy and prudery towards sex, Ellen Key was in some ways working for the same ends as Oscar Wilde or D. H. Lawrence; but how infinitely more spiritual and yet more common-sensible her outlook! As a feminist her healthy idealism was especially stimulating. Woman, she held, must have the opportunity for complete development, both because of herself and because of her mission as mother. The achievement of equal educational, economic and political opportunities for men and women, though a necessary goal, was not her main purpose. She deplored, for example, women's indiscriminate competition in what she considered men's work. But, of course, like Havelock Ellis and Mary Baker Eddy with whom she could be compared in many respects, she found herself frequently misunderstood and misrepresented, and in 1900 decided to give up her life to work out her ideas on paper. Her numerous books, some dealing with education and pacificsm, had a very large sale indeed, especially in America where she lived for a long while. An extremely level-headed feminist she insisted all along that women were fitted primarily for motherhood. Monogamous marriage is, she held, the most desirable type of union, but love without marriage is preferable to marriage without love. When, in time, Ellen Key won her inevitable fame and wealth, she was tempted to remain abroad. But a friend sent her a piece of embroidery (which we were duly shown) depicting the forests of Sweden, and being a woman she was induced to return. This place called Strand which she built within spray-throw of the Lake remained her home till she died in 1926, since when it has been used at her request as a summer home for poor working women—a suitable idea, for it was partly through her influence that the Swedes came to look after the welfare of their old and poor so remarkably well.

It is curious to turn from Ellen Key to one who in some respects was her English counterpart. Mary Woolstonecraft had published her *Vindication of the Rights of Woman* in 1792, and shortly afterwards "accepted the protection" of an American called Imlay. They were never actually married, for she considered the ceremony superfluous, though afterwards she married the philosopher William Godwin in order to safeguard the interests of their children (one of whom lived to be Shelley's wife). The letters she wrote to Imlay during a tour through Scandinavia in 1796 are of definite interest for their opinions and descriptions, although her experience of Sweden was confined to carriage rides through Bohuslän to and from Norway, to the road to Hälsingborg on her way to Denmark, and to a visit to Trollhättan. The condition of women was, as we might expect, of especial interest to her: she remarks that the Swedes are in general attached to their families, despite the ease of obtaining divorces (statements that hold good to-day) and "the total want of chastity in the lower class of women". The ladies, she thought, were lazy both mentally and physically and grew fat at an early age, though they had "mostly fine complexions". Indolence is about one of the last faults one would reproach a Swede for to-day, and even the richest girls are brought up to be useful in the house, to learn cooking and to develop their intelligence without being ashamed of it. But it is still more surprising to read that "in the article of cleanliness the women of all descriptions seem very deficient". It is quite probable that such conditions did prevail at the time if we remember that drunkenness, ever the national vice, was then at about its worst. Mary Woolstonecraft makes numerous references to encounters with drunkards, to revels or to just heavy drinking. Her description of Swedish meals is one of the best I have read:

> "Spices and sugar are put into everything, even into bread; and the only way I can account for their partiality to high-seasoned dishes is the constant use of salted provisions. . . . To which may be added the constant use of spirits. Every day before dinner and supper, even whilst the dishes are cooling on the table, men and women repair to a side-table, and to obtain an appetite eat bread and butter, cheeze, raw salmon, or anchovies, drinking a glass of brandy. Salt fish or meat then immediately follows, to give a further whet to the stomach. As the dinner advances, pardon me for taking up a few minutes to describe what, alas! has detained me two or three hours on the stretch, observing, dish upon dish is changed in endless rotation and handed round with a solemn pace to each guest: but should you happen not to like the first dishes, which was often my case, it is a gross breach of politeness to ask for part of any other till its turn comes. But have patience, and there will be eating enough.—

Allow me to run over the acts of a visiting day, not over-overlooking the interludes.

"Prelude a luncheon . . . then a succession of fish, flesh and fowl for two hours; during which time the dessert (I was sorry for the strawberries and cream) rests on the table to be impregnated with the fumes of the viands. Coffee immediately follows in the drawing-room; but does not preclude punch, ale, tea and cakes, raw salmon, &c. A supper brings up the rear, not forgetting the introductory luncheon, almost equalling in removes the dinner. A day of this kind you would imagine sufficient,—but a to-morrow and a to-morrow.—A never-ending, still-beginning feast may be bearable perhaps when stern winter frowns, shaking with chilly aspect his hoary locks; but during a summer, sweet as fleeting, let me, my kind strangers, escape sometimes into your fir groves, wander on the margin of your beautiful lakes, or climb your rocks to view still others in endless perspective; which piled by more than giant's hand scale the heavens to intercept its rays, or to receive the parting tinge of lingering day—day that scarcely softened into twilight allows the freshening breeze to wake, and the moon to burst forth in all her glory to glide with solemn elegance through the azure expanse."

Thus wrote Shelley's mother-in-law—how differently from one of our diplomats a hundred years beforehand who execrated the Stockholm Skärgård as "the very refuse of nature", or from Evelyn the naturalist who was yet disgusted with the bare rocks at Clifton! She is entertaining also when describing their beds.

"It seemed to me that I was sinking into a grave when I entered them; for, immersed in down placed in a sort of box, I expected to be suffocated before morning. The sleeping between two down beds—they do so even in summer—must be very unwholesome during any season: and I cannot conceive how the people can bear it, especially as the summers are very warm. But warmth they seem not to feel; and, I should think, were afraid of the air, by keeping their windows shut."

The men, she observed, were "distinguished for their common-sense and turn for humour, rather than for wit or sentiment"; she was much struck by the sympathy and frankness in the peasantry and disliked the formal manners of the upper classes (the Francophil Gustavus III, it might be mentioned, had been dead only a few years):

> "The Swedes pique themselves on their politeness; but far from being the polish of a cultivated mind it consists merely of tiresome forms and ceremonies. So far indeed from entering immediately into your character, and making you feel instantly at your ease, like the well-bred French, their over-acted civility is a continual restraint on all your actions. The sort of superiority which a fortune gives when there is no superiority of education, excepting what consists in the observance of gentleness forms, has a contrary effect than what is intended; so that I could not help reckoning the peasantry the politest people of Sweden, who only aiming at pleasing you never think of being admired for their behaviour."

Despite the changes effected by good State education for all, and by other factors, there may still be some truth in that passage, though I am myself inclined to think that in an age of slovenly manners a certain stiffness is for a while attractive rather than otherwise.

Before dropping these Letters I might call attention to one of her remarks which though she calls it an "obvious" one seems to me fairly shrewd:

> "Sweden appeared to me the country in the world most proper to form the botanist and natural historian: every object seemed to remind me of the creation of things, of the first efforts of sportive nature. When a country arrives at a certain state of perfection it looks as if it were made so, and curiosity is not excited."

Then past the ruins of Alvastra, the earliest Cistercian monastery in Sweden, and down a side road to the shallow reedy mere of Tåkern, haunt of innumerable waterfowl and a main stopping place for migratory birds on their passages between Africa and Lapland. There is a tiny white church on the edge of this lake which I was excited to discover (but the guide-books don't give the reason). Little can the Vicar of Väver-sunda have thought in 1779 when he christened Jons Jacob Berzelius under that ancient roof that this child of a poor *bönde* family would grow into one of the world's great scientists. His life follows the main lines of the usual success pattern: the early struggles with poverty, as when in Linköping he was forced to break in after work-hours to gain admission to a laboratory, the years of study (mainly in Upsala) culminating in his recognition and a flow of honours which made him the most eminent scientist of his day. Not that even then he had received all his due: Sir Humphrey Davy, for example, who drew on his research in voltaic electricity, was content to appropriate all the credit himself, without mentioning the Swede. Though a far subtler and more original thinker than Linnaeus, Berzelius is generally considered by all but specialists as having done for chemistry what his compatriot had done for botany and zoology. In other words, he brought system and order to this science: he is remembered mainly for having introduced the present system of chemical nomenclature. Lavoisier, Dalton and others were already seeking a new formulation, and heaven knows it was necessary enough at a time when comparatively simple sub-stances had still to be represented by elaborate signs unwieldy in use and costly to reproduce in books—signs more appropriate to the age of Lucretius or of Paracelsus. Berzelius abandoned the old sign language and introduced a rational system of chemical shorthand. Being a believer in Dalton's atomic theory, he made his new symbols stand for the relative atomic weights of the atoms. Since these symbols stood for definite quantitative measurements, they gave a clue to the chemical composition of the substances. When the Government put him in charge of compiling the new Swedish Pharmacopœia, he thus described the method he intended using:

> "The chemical signs ought to be letters for the greater facility of writing and not to disfigure a printed book. I .

shall therefore take for the chemical sign the initial letter of the Latin name of each element."

A full ten years of his life were spent in determining the atomic weights of fifty elements with an accuracy far surpassing that of other tables compiled for a long while; some of the figures even tally almost exactly with those obtained with the most sensitive apparatus to-day. . . . But it is easy to overrate the temporal achievements of scientists: if Berzelius had not done this sort of work around 1813 others would certainly have come along soon afterwards; it is only a matter of waiting, whereas if a great artist perishes before his works are created, those works are lost forever, and no lapse of time can give them to us.

The most celebrated name in those parts of Östergötland is of course that of St. Bridget or Birgitta. Born about 1302 in Uppland, she was married at the age of fourteen to the owner of Ulvåsa Herrgård in this province, who later became Lagman of Närke. Although a lady-in-waiting to the Queen and the mother of eight children, she was already at this period beginning to live a simple and devout life, and on the death of her husband entered the Monastery at Alvastra. She had always, it appears, had visions, but now she began to record them, dashing them down in Swedish as they came to her, and giving them to her confessor to be translated into Latin. If for instance a dead friend inquired about a relative, or the worldliness of a prelate needed correcting, St. Bridget would have a revelation, and the correct course would be indicated to the person concerned. Sometimes the visions would be of a political nature: the most remarkable of these concerns the means of establishing a perpetual peace between England and France and is followed by a prophecy of the Wars of the Roses. In some of her homelier revelations she shows a typically Swedish concern for hygiene, for it was revealed to her than although Christians ought not to take a bath for the sake of sensual enjoyment they might for reasons of health indulge in one every fortnight or so. And this passage too betrays her Swedish regard for common sense: like Swedenborg she seems to have been a fine blend of practicalness and mysticism:

Background to Sweden

"It is likewise permitted to the friends of God to receive human consolation, to divert themselves with edifying conversation, innocent games, and other amusements, which in no degree wound charity or honesty. By one example you will understand how useful may those innocent recreations be. If you constantly keep one hand closed, it will occasion a contraction of the nerves, or an extreme weakness, which will render its use difficult and painful. It is the same with the operations of the mind. An habitual state of contemplation would cause man to forget his weakness, and infect him with the poison of pride."

But for the most part, I, though a keen reader of good mystical writings, found these Revelations dreadfully boring: there is on the one hand little of St. Theresa's colour and richness of imagery, and on the other none of that polish and formal rational elaboration found in the visions of Elizabeth of Schönau. The book however was very popular in the Middle Ages and was translated into English.

St. Bridget, having spent a good many years of her life in travelling—on pilgrimages to Norway, Rome and the Holy Land, died in Rome at the age of about seventy. Many years beforehand she had founded the Order of the Holy Saviour with the parent convent at Vadstena on Lake Vätter—an Order that spread to thirteen other countries and at one time numbered eighty houses in all. Vadstena, where she and her daughter, St. Catherine, were buried, became for a while one of the foremost literary centres in the North.

In the year 1406 Philippa, daughter of Henry IV of England was married to Erik XIII of Sweden, Denmark and Norway. Several English knights and barons accompanied the Queen on the journey to her new country, and one of these was so impressed with what he saw of the Vadstena Monastery that he determined to establish one like it in England. A couple of years later two Vadstena monks came over, but it was not till 1415 that Henry V laid the foundation stone of Syon House, one of the most interesting houses of the Bridgettine Order and the only body of religious women in England that has preserved

256

its unbroken foundation down to the present day. Beginning with a hundred and twenty years of prosperity, it was at the Reformation the eighth wealthiest monastery in the country. Then followed three centuries on the continent till in 1861 Syon House was re-established in England, where it still exists at South Brent in Devon carrying on a mode of life according to the original Rule of its Swedish foundress. There are, or were quite recently, about seven other houses, some with only a short history, in various continental countries; but the male branch of the Order is no longer extant.

5 : *Kopingar*

I WONDER HOW many English travellers in Sweden and Denmark passing through towns with the suffix -*köping* (Danish, *köbing*) realize that it is the same as Chipping in Chipping Camden or Chipping Norton, means a market town, and is pronounced similarly (except that the vowel resembles the French *eu*). I think I must have visited every *köping* in Sweden: Falköping and Enköping, Lidköping and Linköping, Köping and Nyköping, Norrköping and Söderköping and Malmköping —all in Middle Sweden. Not to mention Grönköping. But *that* you will never find on any map, no matter what the scale may be. And yet for some Swedes it is every bit as real as, say, Lidköping: it may indeed be a good deal more real. For it is the imaginary town of *Grönköpings Veckoblad*, a weekly paper which (N.B.) appears every month. It is the Swedish *Punch*, the Swedish *New Yorker*—a national humorous paper, though its circulation is not very large: you usually read it at the barber's. In point of style I should describe it as a sort of hybrid between Beachcomber and the "This England" column of the *New Statesman*, with a strong dash of Wodehouse. Probably, however, it derives from the Swift-Addison-Steele tradition, than whom no English writers ever exerted a greater influence on Swedish letters; for during a strong wave of Anglophilism (between two long French periods) in the early eighteenth century, *The Swedish Argus*, founded on the model of *The*

Background to Sweden

Spectator and *The Tatler*, was launched by Olof von Dalin, enjoyed an immense popularity, and more or less created modern Swedish prose. Photographs, touched up, faked or of real people so fantastic that pen caricatures would be tame beside them, help to make *Grönkopings Veckoblad* a vivid and friendly piece of satire on Swedish life. In addition to the regularly featured Sophie Liljedotter, the oldest inhabitant of the town and owner of the famous Månsan (an angora cat), and the Mayor, (this week caught by the photographer as he was being rubbed down after a vapour bath), there is a large number of others who make a more fleeting appearance. If, for instance, there are long-distance swimming feats performed in the Baltic and some girl stays in for twenty-nine hours, then an inhabitant of Grönköping is bound to make some sensational record also: "Fröken Sundin's battle with the watery element lasted no less than one hour, forty minutes" is the caption under the photograph of some grotesquely muscular woman (a stuffed male?) posing beside the sea (whose waves betray a discreet caution in approaching so formidable an object). Almost any event will have its counterpart in Grönköping; prose and verse, photographs and drawings, are all masterfully wielded by the single editor who is also all his contributors. Journalese is a favourite butt for his satire. Or sometimes there may be a sort of Laputan thrust at the highbrows. Take for example, *"An Interesting Little Account of Hitler in Philosophy* on the pattern of the well-known textbook by High School Teacher L———",
a seemingly profound and intricate argument concerning Hitler (this was before he became the most popular joke-subject in the world) and the possibility of his being imperial-bearded—an argument starting with one premiss that Hitler has a moustache and another referring to someone's side-whiskers; making the most brilliant havoc of technical terms; and concluding that it was not Hitler who was being discussed after all. Grönköping, delicious city of the imagination, what strange events have happened within your walls to what fantastic people! May your garden suburbs spread out in every direction, your population steadily swell, and men from all quarters pay you a regular health visit!

In the Lands of the Geats

But let us alight in the square of Linköping, right in the centre of Östergötland and capital of the province. Only a small place, you will say (with some 30,000 inhabitants it is about the size of Upsala). I happen to disagree. I contend moreover (and what truths reside in paradoxes!) that Norway and Sweden instead of being countries of small towns and villages are (and how rare that is!) countries of great cities. Great, not big, ones; for the sort of magnitude that counts lies too deep for figures, and to mention that only five Swedish towns have populations exceeding 50,000 is a prosaic irrelevance. As Walt Whitman knew:

"A great city is that which has the greatest men and women,
If it be a few ragged huts it is still the greatest city in the
whole world."

Not that Linköping is "a few ragged huts": on the contrary it is a fresh, neat town built largely of wood, with waters to boat on and waters to float on, trees to walk under and trees to talk under, shops and business enough for the day and garden-cafés for the evening. Is there not a fountain by Carl Milles in the very square we are standing in?—a fountain whose long rectangular troughs, sculptured in relief, are surmounted by the powerful equestion figure of Folke Filbyter, the wealthy yeoman farmer who came from Bjälbo (west of the city) over seven centuries ago and was the first of the Folkungs—the Folkungs who held that Norway and Sweden should be united, that great dynasty which included Birger Jarl the law-maker, reputed founder of Stockholm. And then of course there is the cathedral, begun in 1150 and one of the earliest, being a pleasant blend of Romanesque and Gothic executed in lime-stone. The fine nave with its English influence is said to have served as a model for many a church in Gotland which island was then part of the diocese. Until the Reformation there were only seven sees in Sweden (including one in Finland) and Linköping was one of the more important. Here in 1152 the English papal legate Nicholas Breakspear (afterwards Pope Adrian IV) convened an ecclesiastical meeting at which the

259

Background to Sweden

Swedes agreed to pay the tax known as Peter's Pence as an evidence of their allegiance to Rome; and here for some reason I have not discovered there existed an English colony during the Middle Ages. A charming old city, now partly given over to manufactures, she is yet rich in culture and possesses one of the finest (though least visited) museum-art galleries in the country.

Eastward again, pacing it out for a while with a young Stockholmer who was hitch-hiking through the province on his own. Any car, he told me, would be willing to stop: there was no fear of bandits as in America. He seemed to enjoy walking long distances on the dusty roads; nor did the heat seem to bother him for he was wearing a laughably heavy skiing sweater and a huge frame rucksack. For my part I was glad to be off those open roads where a thick white dust, so difficult to cycle in, is periodically churned up by a car and settles on one's perspiration forming a thin layer of cement. I was glad when I came to a cool avenue on the outskirts of Norrköping and a road properly surfaced. Some factory hands, I noticed, were spending the lunch hour in the Motala River, bathing in the nude only a few hundred yards from the main road. But no one thinks anything of that over here.

Norrköping—with the r's well rolled. The biggest *köping* of all; it is indeed the fourth town in the country. Here, if anywhere, I had expected to encounter the evils of industrialism—slums, polluted air, acres of depressing factories. But a more innocuous hive of industry would be hard to discover anywhere. It is, however, the worst that Sweden can offer; though I am not forgetting the soullessness of Malmö, or a certain dingy quarter of Gothenburg noted for its evil-smelling canal, or Borås (a smaller version of Norrköping). From the rather grimy Motala River rise huge factories and mills with lofty chimneys spitting (like those execrated by Edward Montgomery) in the face of heaven; while here and there will be found streets of unquestionable squalor. But the spittle is so localized and casual that heaven, showing an admirable indifference, remains clean-featured and continues to smile. Earth, too, takes a lenient view of things; nor does nature sweeping between the factories sully her green, flower-embroidered frock; for this town with a population of only 60,000 is smaller than Cambridge or Exeter: is about the size of Swindon or Doncaster.

A happy country, I reflected (floating in the warm water of a Baltic inlet a few miles away); and partly by luck. Since she is without any coal deposits of importance, the industrial revolution came to her comparatively late, more slowly, and in different forms. Only in the last eighty or ninety years has her industrialization (and that localized) been rapid: in that time she has changed from an agricultural country where three-quarters of the inhabitants were on the land to one of nearly twice the population over half of which is now engaged in manufacturing, commerce and transport.

But beginnings were made much earlier. In the seventeenth century, for example, Louis de Geer, the Belgian capitalist who gave such a fillip to the mining and the iron industries, transformed the village of Finspång into the manufacturing centre of the country, and Norrköping to the south-east, till then a small insignificant place, became its port, acquired industries of its own (munitions and glass at that date, if I remember rightly), and steadily rose in size and importance, though its textile and paper mills (now its mainstay) were not established till later.

Then early in the next century that remarkable figure Jonas Allströmer being impressed by the growing wealth of England tried to launch a Swedish industrial revolution before such men as Arkwright and Watt had been born. After beginning life as a clerk to a merchant in London, and travelling on the Continent, he smuggled some looms out of Holland, various foreign tools and materials, even some English skilled workmen; and in 1724 set up a manufacturing establishment in his native Alingsås, near Gothenburg, the enterprise being supported both by the King and the Government. The place became a sort of technical school for the nation, and over a hundred other factories sprang up in other places in a short time. Allströmer also started a sugar refinery; advocated improved methods in shipbuilding, tanning and cutlery; introduced the potato and the tobacco plants; rescued the cattle-breeding industry from a precarious position, importing livestock from various foreign countries; and founded one of the earliest agricultural schools in the world. Despite all this, despite the fact that their great war era then being over, the Swedes were canalizing their energy and spirit of adventure into pacific occupations, especially the sciences—this premature industrial effort tailed off rather diappointingly in the later eighteenth century.

The next awakening dates from about 1809, when an English engineer, Samuel Owen, was brought over to Stockholm to set up some of the newest steam engines on Watt's system which a Swede called Edelcrantz had procured in England. These workshops mark the beginning of the mechanical industry—an industry in which Sweden now plays so significant a part. The same Englishman, it is interesting to notice, also gave the impetus to coastal and inland navigation by building the first steamboat in the country. From this time onwards industrialization became firmly rooted, though its development, aided by a number of brilliant inventors, was not greatly accelerated till later in the century. Still developing rapidly when the first hydro-electric plants were erected in the 1890's, it began to derive much of its power from this source, so that the electrical age has arrived in the Scandinavian peninsula earlier than almost anywhere.

Thanks then mostly to luck, this country, whose manufactured products (famous for their high quality) find export markets in all quarters of the globe, has been less desecrated by industry than was England in the 1750's—an England of which John Dyer could write so blissfully:

> *"the echoing hills repeat*
> *The stroke of axe and hammer; scaffolds rise*
> *And growing edifices; heaps of stone*
> *Beneath the chisel beauteous shapes assume*
> *Of frieze and column. Some with even line*
> *New streets are marking in the neighbouring fields*
> *And sacred domes of worship. Industry,*
> *Which dignifies the artist, lifts the swain*
> *And the straw cottage to a palace turns,*
> *Over the work presides. Such was the scene*

Of hurrying Carthage when the Trojan chief
First viewed her growing turrets. So appear
The increasing walls of busy Manchester,
Sheffield and Birmingham, whose reddening fields
Rise and enlarge their suburbs. . . ."

"Pursue", he exorted his countrymen, "Pursue,
Ye sons of Albion, with unyielding heart
Your hardy labours: let the sounding loom
Mix the melody of every vale."

Exactly a hundred years later Beddoes was writing from
Switzerland:

"Be proud of Manchester,
Pestiferous Liverpool, Ocean-Avernus,
Where bullying blasphemy like a slimy lie
Creeps to the highest church's pinnacle,
And glistening infects the light of heaven.
O flattering likeness on a copper coin!
Sit still upon your slave-raised cotton ball,
With upright toasting fork and toothless cat:
The country clown still holds her for a lion."

Even now it is hard for the sensitive person to feel differently;
and doesn't Pope say, "Our proper bliss depends on what we
blame"? When will a Swede be justified in using such invective
against his country for similar reasons? Never, I prayed,
though perhaps there are Swedish Dyers to-day just as direfully
short-sighted. I, no blind Scandiolater, at least thought
otherwise as I floated in quiet waters a few miles from the
Swedish Manchester, I whose ancestors have scrawled their
name over the industrial hell of Lancashire.

IX · SWEDES AND TURNIPS

1 : *Ichthyopophagi and So Forth*

Gothenburg,
August 9th

NOW, SIX WEEKS after Midsummer, the nights are growing shorter and darker. Climbing up among the trees to the top of a steep hill in the west of the city has been mostly a matter of groping. Once in the open, however, we can use our eyes again: there is enough light from a new moon and the city's glow to enable us to find out a safe and comfortable piece of sward near the edge of the precipice, yet not quite enough to make it embarrassing for some of the party to indulge in a little idle caressing. Viewed from this height, the skeleton of Gothenburg, outlined with light, appears to have ample room to sprawl out at will. The densest cluster of lights, partly hidden behind one of the hills, is towards the river in the middle distance; the others, scattered among numerous parks, might almost be separate villages. To the left the eye follows a road full of traffic over some hills towards the town of Mölndal; while immediately below us is the Liseberg Amusement Park whose buildings (the remains of an exhibition in the twenties) emphasize their outmodishness with illuminations which at closer quarters are distinctly garish.

Suddenly the lights are switched out, and in the midst of the park begins a brilliant display of fireworks, rockets from time to time soaring out of the swirls of catherine wheels and fountains of coloured star-showers to explode in the open, some not so far from our heads. It is a time of revelry—the opening of the crayfish season. In lakes and rivers all over Sweden parties have to-day been catching these heavily bewhiskered crustaceans whose green-black bodies after immersion in boiling water turn to a flaming scarlet. And now many will be eating them: for

264

weeks and weeks this pre-eminently piscivorous people do homage to the blushing *kräfta* which foreigners sometimes consider the national emblem.

A few days later I was invited to one of these parties in the capital. "Black tie?" I queried, thinking that perhaps the Swedes were returning to their dinner jackets which they usually discard for the summer. "No, red". On being shown on to the balcony about nine o'clock I noticed there was not a guest who was without a splash of red, whether in the form of tie, scarf, or blouse. And when, the first snaps having been gulped down, we tucked the corners of the special red napkins in our collars and began to concentrate, the scene was distinctly Rubensian. The rich glow shed by the Japanese lanterns on the piles of crayfish in the midst of the table was especially appropriate, for was it not Rubens who always put red somewhere in his pictures? Using the short sharp knives specially provided for the purpose, we began cutting our way into the feast with such gusto that the fine plates (which happen to have been brought from China in the eighteenth century by the Swedish East India Company) very soon resembled those kitchen middens from the Stone Age that archaeologists so delight in rummaging. Alas for the Swede's politeness! Where are their famous good manners when, two hands to the task, they dig savagely into the innermost recesses of a leg, or press the smashed shells against their lips in order to suck noisily at the juicy innards?

Sitting on my right was a business man who was telling me how the tempo of Stockholm life had been remarkably accelerated in recent years. No longer does a director casually call up the office from his home in the middle of the morning, look in for a mere hour or two or go off in his yacht if there is nothing much to do. The more practical, materially minded, comparatively unimaginative Southern Swedes and perhaps some Gothenburgers may still consider the Stockholmers too slow, but foreigners who have to deal with them are now agreed that there is nothing much wrong with them as business men. Which does not mean to say they are obsessed with business: having the time and the desire to cultivate other interests and keep up

265

hobbies, and not being afraid of taking decent holidays, they remain more balanced and better adjusted than for instance their English or American counterparts.

> *"Business men boast of their skill and cunning*
> *But in philosophy they are like little children,"*

as an old Chinese poet remarks, describing with much truth the type with which we are all too familiar. The Swede, on the other hand, seems to come as close as anyone to Whitehead's ideal business man of the future, a man with foresight and "an unspecialized aptitude for eliciting generalizations from particulars and for seeing the divergent illustration of generalities in diverse circumstances—a reflective power which is essentially a philosophic habit". But perhaps I am romanticizing: Ivar Kreuger was a Swede.

Voltaire, writing of the Swedes at the end of their great military era, was probably right in saying that they had long neglected commerce and were still poor business men. But in earlier times it was far otherwise. Some of the earliest mentions of the Swedes refer to their trade and commerce, in which pursuits they seem to have been as successful as any of the Northmen in Viking times. In their capacity of mercenaries, both in the western raids where they took the lion's share of the tribute money, and in the east (in Russia and Constantinople) they gained enormous gold-hoards. Many of the Viking expeditions are said to have been undertaken for mercantile purposes, for Sweden was an important trading country, exporting horses, furs, hides, salt and amber, and importing such articles as spices, silks, rugs and jewels. Masters of the Baltic and parts of Russia including the Dneiper and the Volga, the Swedes became the middlemen through whom goods from the Orient and the Eastern Roman Empire were exchanged with Western Europe. On Björkö (Birka) in Lake Mälar (not to be confused with another Björkö near Gothenburg or that in Finland) there was a whole colony of foreign merchants, while off the east coast lay the rich island of Gotland (a free community paying tribute to Sweden) with Visby which in the time of the Hansa League became the wealthiest and most magnificent city in the Baltic.

Sweden can no longer boast of the greatest Baltic city—not at least in point of population: Copenhagen is larger and Leningrad almost three times the size of her capital. But Stockholm, possessing as it does nearly all the advantages of a great capital with few of the drawbacks, is unchallenged in its splendour, in its unique contrasts and harmonies in times, tones and textures. And now with its 600,000 it is as large as ever it should be. May it expand no further! For we have long been warned that modern civilization is being dangerously weakened by excessive urbanization. As late as 1850 only one-tenth of the Swedes were town-dwellers, and although the proportion has risen so steeply that it is now fifty per cent., the decentralization of her industries (due to geographical reasons) will probably continue, thus preventing most of her towns from growing very large. Democracy, said Aristotle, could not survive in a city too large for the stentor's voice to be heard throughout it. Perhaps technical progress has not after all rendered the Greek ideal so obsolete; perhaps it will actually prevent its becoming so; the small city (though not necessarily a city state) would still seem to be more suitable for the functioning of democracy than the large. In the great northern democracy of Sweden there are at present only three towns of more than 100,000 inhabitants; while the largest of these, though hardly small, might very well —judging from its appearance—have arisen in the same manner as those Greek cities which are said to have been built to the sound of the lyre.

2 : *Some Observations on Septentrional Sudatoria*

IN SAGA TIMES nearly every farmstead in Scandinavia had its *badstofa* or bathhouse, often in a cellar in the middle of which was a stove made of piled-up stones held together by clay. Steam was produced by pouring water on it, and around the walls were platforms rising in steps to a higher temperature. The bather moved gradually upwards, thrashing himself periodically with branches and afterwards may or may not have taken a roll in the snow before dressing (as the Finns do to-day). Since this custom has survived in Finland (where it probably did not originate), and indeed has been taken as the most typical thing in Finnish culture, the *sauna* baths have come to be known as Finnish vapour-baths. In Sweden there is at present a drive to build in every village a *bastu* on the same model, an ancient example of which can be seen under one of the houses in the Zorn open-air museum at Mora.

In towns the vapour-baths are of a more sophisticated and modern type, and are the regular resort of all classes of the community, the same building housing two grades of *finsk bad* apart from other types such as Turkish. Those in Upsala (which, incidentally are mentioned—but what isn't?—by James Joyce in *Ulysses*) are the ones I know best, for every week or so I would use them to obtain vicariously some of the effects of exercise. Englishmen visiting the country are often shocked at finding the attendants are women (not *always* old ones); at least I have heard of a tourist, who discovering a female in the changing-room, did his best to remove her—pointed to the door and so on. Growing exasperated at her unbudgeableness, he eventually 'phoned for the police.

After a good sweat-down on the wooden platforms among schoolboys, shop-assistants, over-worked students and elderly business men with limp newspapers propped against the domes of their bellies, the streaming patient emerges from the vapour-room, staggers under a shower, and then prostrates himself on a raised slab of marble where the attendant scrubs him with a huge brush from head to foot with the nonchalance of a laundry-woman. Once more a shower, followed by a dip in the cold water of a swimming-pool which restores him to his senses, and probably preludes a further shower before another attendant, waiting in the changing-room, takes him in a vast towel and dries him, giving him in the end a stimulating slap on the soles of the feet to intimate that the operation is over. Whereafter he is left a free agent to dress himself and comb his hair.

3 : *Meditation in a Kallbadhus*

IF THE PROPER study of mankind is man in the nude then

let the investigator set up his laboratory in Sweden. To go North is to go native. For nowhere outside the tropics do men discard their clothing more readily or come to nature with a more passionate nakedness. What are the lukewarm waters of the Mediterranean to the Spaniards or the Italians, who, loath to leave their cities, can be induced to bathe but two or three months in the year? Or who ever found a Frenchman bathing in the nude? I well remember how one summer in the Landes a fellow bather got cramp, and how we all swam out to help him as the current was carrying him away. All excepting the village life-saver who only ran up and down the beach with a life-belt, because (as we learned afterwards) he was unable to swim: he was kept there merely to see that no bathing slips or brassières were too abbreviated. As for the Englishman, everyone knows him as a lover of nature—the sort of lover described by Oscar Wilde: "For each man kills the thing he loves". And where in England to-day can even children just throw off their clothes and bathe at will as Charles Lamb speaks of doing with his school friends? Only in the tarns on the Yorkshire moors. But come to the Scandinavian North, and before the last floes have vanished from the Baltic or the streams have ceased to be swollen with ice- or glacier-water from the fells, there will be limblaving in lake and sea-pool.

How divinely natural to bathe and sunbathe unencumbered by any dress whatever! Just to do it, not to make a cult of it. Long, long ago the nudist colonies of Scandinavia must have reached dominion status—in the time of Tacitus (shall we say?) who marked out the Nordics as intense lovers of nature. (Although they have been noted for their very strong tendency to personify nature, and for their exceptional physical fitness, the human figure, it is curious to notice, plays but a very small part in their art down to the most recent times.) How typical that the mystical St. Bridget, earliest of Swedes to gain European renown, should have been in the habit of escaping from her convent at night-time to go bathing in a stream! I once heard an Englishman on his return from Sweden professing to be outraged at having been made to bathe in a mixed party in the nude; but the party in question must have been either very young or unusually indiscreet: the Swedes unlike the Japanese do not indiscriminately huddle both sexes in the same small pool: they allow them at least two different coves, or where that is impracticable a separate bathing-house each (like the one I am browning myself in at present).

And how can they bear such exposure up by the Arctic Circle? Though the air in summer may be warmer than that in England, the water is definitely, often very definitely, chillier. "Somebody or other", wrote Montaigne, "asked one of our beggars whom he saw in his shirt in the depth of winter, as merry as a grig and feeling the cold as little as many a man who is muffled up to the ears in sable, how he could patiently bear it. 'And you, sir', he replied, 'you have your face uncovered; well, I am all face'." The Swedes are all face; they can, moreover, without offending the aesthete afford to expose their elegant figures in their entirety. Tallest among nations, lithe, perfectly proportioned and developed, these potential artists' models are all obedient to St. Paul's injunction, "Glorify God in your body!" No skin is more exquisitely fresher or takes a more attractive sunburn (and people are more sunburned here than anywhere except by the Mediterranean). Already by Midsummer the hair has been bleached back to the light and luminous yellow it possessed in the small child. The chest and limbs, which we would expect to find protected against the cold by a liberal covering of hair, are on the contrary entirely without it: nature having got thus far was not going to allow any irrelevant hirsute excrescences to mar her masterpiece. As for the head, everyone can recognize the pure Nordic type of the anthropologists. But the cephalic index is not enough; it tells you nothing for instance about the extraordinary grace and distinction of the nape, those incomparable lines beyond the sculptor's curve. Nor does it remind you that these are faces almost unique among Europeans in showing up well at any distance. Englishmen and Frenchmen are best seen at close quarters: their features are insufficiently statuesque to bear the long view. With the Mediterranean peoples it is the reverse: their complexions are disappointing in close-ups, while their hair composed of a series of dark impressionistic strokes demands a

Swedes and Turnips

certain distance to be seen in focus rather than as a series of distractingly discrete bristles. A Swede's head though perhaps less monumental than an Italian's has yet a fineness of complexion and hair that invites close scrutiny, even if it does not illuminate intellectually, for there is nothing of that sensitiveness or suggestiveness found in the lesser lines of the English or especially the French physiognomy. There would also appear to be a completer integration of the personality—an approximation to the whole man, sound within and without. If, as Bacon says, "A healthy body is the soul's guest-chamber; a sick one, its prison", then the soul up here would be ungrateful to complain of its lodging. Absent is the inexcusable evil of undernourishment, and unknown the sick unnatural tempo of large cities; here is a people vigorous, uninhibited and for generations undisturbed by participation in war. Looking round me at these noble Northerners of all ages and classes I cannot but feel that they have achieved the classical ideal: it is as far as we have got.

I have of course to exclude the old and middle-aged—those flabby specimens who must find it hard to fell through all this fleshly dress the bright shoots of everlastingness spoken of by Henry Vaughan; or those who have developed large white central domes even more obstructive than Shelley's many-coloured one which only *stained* the radiance of eternity while these threaten to blot it out altogether.

How different is the world of youth! And what, I wonder, is the dividing age? I had heard so much about "delayed maturity in the North" that the children I imagined were puny weaklings backward in formroom and on the field. Nothing could be more erroneous. Physically they are taller and their development at all ages is better than I have found it anywhere outside semi-tropical countries. Is this (one often asks incredulously) a schoolboy? A future student may, it is true, stay on at school rather later than our youths, but how much older seem the Swedes of a comparable age—huge muscular chaps in their mid-teens already taller than the southerner or westerner will ever be. Nor have I found any inferiority mentally. There is nothing at all backward about the child of sixteen who (and I have met many) can carry on an intelligent conversation with you in a foreign language. The maturity may be delayed, but then there is more that has to be matured.

What a noble piece of work is man! And even in that nobility lies his tragedy—the eternal tragedy of flesh. No sooner does the head approach completion than decay of the body sets in; before ever the last piece of scaffolding has been removed demolition has begun. Well might Emerson consider man " a golden impossibility". Nowhere more golden than here: every circumstance has conspired to make of Northern youth the supreme achievement in the human field, lacking nothing in body (and little in mind) or the peace in which to develop. So what? With a perversity which would be incredible if it were not so typical man has here gone out of his way to discover some means of evading even this bodily perfection. Like a certain hard-up acquaintance of mine who every time he went to London would squander on outrageously long taxi-drives (from which he received only a certain temporary kick) all the money he had been saving up for months, the Swedes by their reckless alcoholic excesses often jeopardize the health and fitness laboriously acquired at other times, till the day arrives when they have to admit as a penalty the hatefulness of a duodenal ulcer. Spirits have destroyed the guest-chamber of the Spirit.

4: *In Dalarna*

CYCLING THROUGH THE lonely south-west of Dalarna, I came one evening to a village in the valley of the Western Dalälven. In one of the three shops was a coffee-room where I inquired for a bed for the night. Now such a request even from a Swede would have caused a considerable stir in that remote and rarelyvisited parish, but coming from an Englishman—and one clad in an exotic-looking yellow oilskin cape—it shook the place up so violently that some time elapsed before I could extract any reply. Meanwhile the storekeeper's family, roused from their several occupations, gravitated towards the room and began to peer round doors and over counters in an effort to examine the strange creature who had suddenly descended upon them like the turbaned Malay on De Quincey's cottage at Grasmere. Eventually I gathered that someone had been dispatched to a neighbouring farmhouse to find out if they could put me up there. The farmer, came the eventual reply, would be ready to receive me in half-an-hour. So I decided to bathe first in the river, to which I was directed by one of a group who had been collecting in the room since my arrival, a friendly young man of almost polished manners who thereafter accompanied me to the farmhouse.

A rough track through fields of barley led up to the house, which was owned, I learned, by the chief farmer in the district. His wife, a cheerful, robust young woman, came out warmly to greet me, and led me into the living-room to which a bed and washstand had been added evidently for my benefit—a light neatly furnished room with its Mora grandfather clock and white cupboard with bunches of fruit and flowers painted on them and its tall columnar stove of white tiles.

The Dalesmen are far from shy and soon Fru Anna was telling me her story. The daughter of another farmer in the parish, she had been brought up to a life in field and dairy. For nine years she had gone every summer to *fäbodar* in the mountains twenty-four miles away to look after the cattle and make cheese. "These", she said, showing me a row of fine cups, "I have won in milking contests." And last year she had married Herr Ohlsson. The husband, who had come in before for a few moments, was a tall quiet man, probably some ten years older. Soon after the wedding a cousin of hers had arrived on a visit from America. She showed me the folk costume she was making for her, a very bright flowered one which would cost about 60 *kronor* for the whole outfit. One of her main ambitions was to live in America, where, she had been assured, the women don't have to work so hard. A village life in Dalarna, Midsommar in the *fäbodar*, even (I suspected) being the wife of the chief farmer of the district, had lost something of their charm. It is the old dream of a land of greater promise across the Atlantic—the dream that led some of her compatriots to found the colony of New Sweden on the Delaware three centuries ago, the dream that resulted in the emigration of over a million Swedes in the last century. I couldn't help remembering a meeting I had had with an old shabbily dressed man whom I had found sitting on a wayside stone near the Silyan. He told me how he had gone with his family to the Middle West in the eighties, what hardships they had encountered, how he had saved up for years in order to return to the land of his childhood, how his entire savings had been lost in a bank crash, and how finally he had scraped together enough for the passage with a little over to keep him alive for his last years—a poor old returned native, a stranger existing in complete obscurity.

Then I in turn had to answer some of her questions. She wanted especially to know about Oxford, and what did I think of the Oxford Group? My pigeon Swedish (for no one in the parish had a word of English) was not a little taxed in making her understand that Oxford as a whole has no desire to own Buchmanism.

In the morning I went out after breakfast to muse on the veranda in the heavy shade of hops and nasturtiums trained up strings as is the custom throughout the country. In front was a large turf yard flanked by the farm buildings and on one side a well with a great wooden lever—a kind of well found in most of the Baltic lands, but nowhere commoner than in Dalarna. My hostess, smiling as usual, came out and suggested we should go to the fox-farm which the farmer had promised to show me. So behind some trees about a mile away we came on an elaborately wired enclosure within which were several hundred foxes—blue ones from Alaska and silver ones from the U.S.A., as well as a few mink. The older animals, like vicious hardened criminals condemned to solitary confinement, are altogether repulsive, and when annoyed they would whine horribly uttering unearthly waaows. But the younger ones, two or three to a cage, could be quite attractive. All the cages were raised above the ground, even the floors being for the most part of wire-netting. The stale sickly stench must be very unpleasant to work with. But the business is profitable. The skins, I was told, are sold mainly to Germany (some surely for re-export?) and a few to England.

Leaving the *rävgård*, we returned to the farmhouse and I prepared to leave. How much would it be? Fru Anna said 2 *kronor*!—for the night and two meals! I saw to it that she received more. As a memento she gave me two samples of her needlework: a crocheted tea-pot-holder, and an embroidered table-mat. I turned round to watch her waving under the trees beside the white homestead. Farewell, Fru Anna, I shall not forget you nor the way you put your best room at my disposal.

No Scandinavians, unless it be the Icelanders, have preserved their ancient traditions and Old Norse folklore more faithfully than the Dalesmen who for centuries formed the real cortex of the nation—a fact they have never forgotten. Always ready to fight for their independence they immediately flocked to the banners of the big national liberators from Engelbrekt to Gustavus III. As every visitor to Mora is reminded, it is among the Dalesmen that Gustavus Vasa found his first supporters for a rising against the oppressive Danes. But it is not always remembered that, once he had become their ruler, it was they who were the first to revolt against him. A paradoxical people, they are at once puritanical and gay, shrewd and ingenuous, stern and kindly, loyal and independent. So distinct is their culture that Dalarna is really a nation within a nation. In no other province are the original customs and dialects (unintelligible to the ordinary Swede) preserved as here. Only in Dalarna will you see the tall maypoles, which are decorated with hoops and crosses and festooned with flowers and greenery, standing in the villages throughout the summer. Only there the raised larders (*härbre*) in the farmyards, the distinct forms of architecture, furnishing and handicrafts, and the folk costumes worn every Sunday. How far is all this a natural selfconscious survival? Isn't Leksand degenerating into a mere tourist centre? Do not many of the parishioners appear in their folk costumes merely to satisfy the American tourists who with their ciné cameras shoot them as they enter and leave the church? Perhaps it would be better for them to dress like any other Swede or Continental or American. But on watching a funeral, the special orange and yellow aprons worn for the occasion seemed so much a part of the ceremony that I became doubtful. And once I was out on the quiet country roads the sight of brilliantly clad girls walking beside the birches and scarlet-berried rowans was so delightful that I completely forgot to question its naturalness. Here for a moment was the Dalarna I had first been thrilled by in Strindberg's folk play, *The Bridal Crown*.

5 : *Cycling in Dalarna*

To come in tired after a long ride,
Throw down your pack and plunge into the lake
Whose sudden waters shock the flesh and make
You want to do big things; and then wind-dried
Return to take a meal on the verandah:
Filmjölk *and fish, new beans and bilberry soup,*
Served up by Mother Kattra to a group
In shirtsleeves, who can scarcely understand her
(She talks in such broad dialect) but laughing
Create a northern camaraderie
Against the pageant of a twilit sky.

6 : *An Incident*

Stockholm

I CALLED THIS morning on a friend of mine who works in one of the publishing houses. I had been struck by some book illustrations I had seen and asked him if he would phone the artist for me in order to arrange a meeting. Having been put through to his studio, he explained that a "Herr Heywood från Oxford" would like to call on him if he could suggest a time. "Tell him I don't believe in God!" said the artist rather snappily, slamming down the receiver! "In God"? It took several moments for me to realize that the artist, hearing the name Oxford, had taken me for a Groupist. We immediately put through a second call and impressed upon him that I was not a Buchmanite. Apologizing profusely, he explained that he and his friends had been much bothered by Groupists. Would I write to him, as he was just going out of town? It all ended happily and the artist has since promised to illustrate a book for me. But I realized that in a remark I had once heard about an Oxford education's being a definite handicap in the modern world there was more truth than the author of it had intended. Oxford, I believe, has been seriously referred to as "the place immortalized by Robert Taylor", and (more wittily) as "the Latin quarter of Cowley". Seldom, however, can it have suffered a greater indignity than for a distinguished foreigner to consider it merely as "the place where Buchmanites come from". But in fairness I ought to add that Buchmanism in Scandinavia is rather different from what it is in England: its followers are said to be far better-mannered and more intelligent and to include some very cultured men. Among them are several notable writers, one of whom produced the most reasonable Buchmanite testament to be found anywhere; though the writings of their post-conversion period are admitted to be below standard. Whether any of these Scandinavians has a sense of humour I have not yet been able to discover.

7 : *Charles's Smile*

ON HEARING THAT Charles XII's tomb was opened over two centuries after his burial, and that his features were found intact and of extreme beauty.

> *Unalterable smile that armies followed*
> *Into the battle's thickest smokiness;*
> *Victorious smile, exultant in the hour,*
> *Whether it told disaster or success!*

> *Smile that the Russians dreaded after Narva*
> *And fled from on the field of Holovzin;*

The fierce triumphant smile which at Poltava,
    In loss, knew only what it was to win.

The smile the dying soldier could decipher
    Among the recollections of his land,
The same the Swedish exiles carried with them
    Into Siberian wastes—a lonely band.

Defeat, nor wound, desertion nor disfavour—
    Nothing could change the King's immortal lips :
The silver bullet missed it; not its flavour
    Could death diminish; nor could time eclipse.

The smile is fresh to-day; it takes its beauty
    From a mistaken love of Sweden's good;
Magnetic smile, as powerful as ever,—
    Imperishable smile, now understood!

8 : *Two Paintings*

Owl by Liljefors

But come to wild Södermanland
Where forests hem you at each hand.
Come in the twilight to the coast:
The owl is stationed at his post
Upon the pine branch every night—
To see him gives you quite a fright,
Whose eyes are fastened on the seas
And mindful of their mysteries.

Perhaps he sits the winter through
As statuesque as ever. You
May go to look. A week in June

Convinced me that he would as soon
Move as the sky would perish. Yes,
The Vikings saw this ghoul, I guess.

Nocturne by Nils Kreuger

An amazing canvas, crowded, crowding out roundrobins
Spun spirally in a swift outrush of rich
Circle-comforting thoughtbirds, feeling's congyrations,—
Bursting birthmarks shocked with douched cartouches
Swivelling on the ringrims of split arcspicules
Airslung, loosened with a lot of lewd volutes
Horizontally eyewhirlwound, burly with a surface-
tension taut-to-be-untightened, lipt with lightning
In a bewitching mad eyescrew sanely incising,
Burrowing with luminous chafenebulae, gliding
With charged catalysts caught from galactic cataclysms
Round-raving in a depraved forcefulness forcepping
Forward, forward on an illimitable lightbore forged
From the porous screwpour never running out of itself
But radiating: the tunnel of a minduranium
Atomsmashed by an actualized, trim, woundup, titillating
Timespring, spindle of cyclical eyefretsawry
Slewed round on a trochilic trolley-laced twiddle
Writhing with lightwhirls, frighteningly frightfully biting
With teeth tidily dithering from guilt-filling;
Drilling and drilling, driven by will's wings,
Skimming and scalpelling, chiselling by a brushblizzard
Right into the exasperated retina, braving eyebrash,
Gouging, a flashlit sightscoop, screwy, throbbing,
Vertiginously dilating, twirling trepidantly, squirming
With the bobbins unbinding and blinding the roundrobins.

What, what is this madlight sanely incising,
Cool but disquieting, calmly exciting, ebullient
With a churned childcharm precise in its violence?

T   279

Background to Sweden

O kudu-light-of-a-unicorn, heart's gimlet,
Skewer of sense, drill for the floppy intellect
And dangerous corkscrew for the imagination's bottle:
See how this Northern flamethrower has cricked passages
For the night's vertical messages,—a paintavenue
For all of it—nature's collectable raterevenue!

X · THIS TOO IS SWEDEN

LIKE A GREAT narrow ship eighty-seven miles from stem to stern Öland lies in the Baltic off the south-east of the Swedish mainland.

It is not like Tahiti one of those islands you are forced to escape to; not like Elba one you simply have to escape *from*. It has never like St. Helena become notorious; nor like Farallon de Pajaros remained buried in an indecent obscurity. It might like Crete, or like Gotland its neighbour, have been ostentatious about its history; or like Mauritius have discreetly forgotten that it has any. It might like Iceland have come out in a series of boils and freezes; or like Stromboli in one enormous ulcer. It might even like Thanet have grown tired of being an island and decided to join up with the mainland; it might conceivably have vanished altogether, either melodramatically like Krakatoa, or like Podalida and other legendary islands of the Atlantic merely by proving that it didn't exist. But Öland has done none of these things. It is a very restrained island; and does not go in for the spectacular. In fact it literally goes flat out with restraint. A long almost interminable plain, it appears utterly level; but continue far enough eastwards and you will find yourself in the water. Not all at once, not suddenly, but eventually. For there is a very subtle and imperceptible gradient, which the eye is too insensitive to record. Nor is there any mark that enables you to say just where the land ends and the sea begins: the plain slides on eastward under the covership of the Baltic; grass tufts and casual boulders protruding from the shallow water, and everywhere along the tideless coast brown leathery bladderwrack and soft sun-bleached seaweed like shredded packing paper straggle onto the fields. Curious, lonely little fields they are too, separated from each other by loose walls of boulders raked off from the surface (the extra stones often forming huge piles at the corners), and some of them enclosing cattle, horses or sheep. But for the most part the fine chestnut horses roam at will over the open stretches of Alvaren (for so the plain is called), their blond manes streaming in the breezes that rush in unchecked from any quarter. For the winds are wild that act on this Baltic stage, their onslaughts incalculable. They sweep the plain clear of impediments, passing over it according to their caprices—passing over it, but never ignoring it. The wild-armed windmills were made for their amusement and the bushes bent into primitive shapes at their bidding; even in the tameness of animals there is a subdued savagery: the cow here has something about it of its ancestor the aurochs (which was last found in one of the states across the Baltic), and the horses are destined for the Swedish cavalry.

But Alvaren is not quite the whole of Öland. Along the west, for instance, it breaks down in a low escarpment called Landborgen to a narrow coastal plain of rich, deeper soil with comfortable-looking farms and scattered hardwood groves which are thus comparatively sheltered from the winds above. The drop of Landborgen being for the most part abrupt, you can see end-on the apparently dead-level layers of the rock, which however have just that slight tilt that makes the land slope from its highest (about fifty metres above the sea) down to the water in the east. Walking on Alvaren you have no sense of the slope: it is the flatness that obtrudes itself: the straight roads and telegraph poles carry the eye into the distance, and on the footpaths linking up cottage and hamlet the inch-deep covering of soil has been worn away leaving bare the pink slab-limestone with its long conical shell-fossils. *Alven*, the sub-soil; Alvaren has been aptly named. And what sort of plants cover this prostrate rock? It is August now, rather late for flowers, but I have found many stretches of sward still blue with speedwell or yellow with rock-roses. It is mainly a downland vegetation: wild strawberries, yarrow, centaureas, sedums, harebells, juniper and saxifrages—all very dwarfed owing to the scarcity of soil. Other patches are purple with heather; or covered by *Potentilla fruiticosa*, the special plant of Alvaren, a low, hairy, silvered-leaved shrub even now full of flowers resembling those of a large rock-rose. Where Alvaren shades off into land with a soil deep enough for agriculture chicory appears to be the most conspicuous flower—in autumn at any rate. But then Öland is capable, wherever there is a sufficiency of soil, of producing almost anything that can be grown in the south of England. With the driest and mildest climate in Sweden her deciduous woods (below Landborgen) are the richest in species—oaks, elms, ashes, hornbeams and so on thriving in profusion; while botanists often make special pilgrimages to see the wild tulips and orchids in flower. It is a great place for naturalists who, like the birds that most of them come to study, collect here in colonies in spring and late autumn. Bengt Berg, the well-known ornithologist, has made his home on Öland; and that fine landscape-painter, Nils Kreuger, lived here for a while making mysterious pictures of cattle abnormally endowed with character and of dark horses at the sea-edge silhouetted against evening skies.

What of the inhabitants, the *ölänningarna*? Are they a people rooted to the soil? In the sense of being a farming community they were, as far as they could be; but an ill-wind of crop-failures and famine descended on them in the last century, uprooting a quarter of the population from the shallow soil and carrying them off to America in the '80's. Some of them, finding conditions more difficult than they had expected, have since returned to their niggard acres. I came across one the other day, a tough old boy of about seventy, who appeared to have kept all the glumness and reticence typical of the islanders, for he was not to be drawn and all I could get out of him was the statement that he had emigrated with his family in his boyhood and that he much preferred the States. At present there are about 27,000 inhabitants, engaged mostly in farming and quarrying and a few in fishing. The stone industry is concerned with exporting to the mainland both large paving-stones and cement, alum, etc. (manufactured at Degerhamn in the south-west). Sugar-beet, as in Skåne, has now become an important agricultural crop. Cereals are grown rather less, and to-day but two or three of the old windmills are still in use. There are over five hundred windmills on Öland, mostly of the all-wooden bow-legged type that can be swung round bodily into the wind, though there are just a few on the solid Dutch model. Many are now tottering in the last stages of disrepair, others have been rebuilt; some are converted into houses, one even into a church. Whether strung out along Landborgen and seen in the wonderful sunsets that turn Kalmar Sound into a river of fire, or dotted about capriciously, now singly, now in groups, to relieve and yet enlarge the landscape, the mills of Öland are picturesque memorials of a time when the wind helped men to grind their flour. Built from the local oakwoods in the form symbolical of the Weather Island, they are also the only tangible examples of a typical native culture; for otherwise—in respect to domestic architecture and furniture, tools and utensils, harnesses, clothes, vehicles—there has been very little peculiar to the Island.

In more distant times, however, it was far otherwise. What Crete, Rhodes, Sicily and some other islands are for the Mediterranean, so (it has been said) are Gotland, Öland and Bornholm (the Danish island south of Skåne) for the Baltic—disseminating centres of ancient cultures, rich in remains, favoured by nature, and links between the northern and the southern shores. As early as the Stone Age Öland was about as advanced culturally as any of the leading districts in the North—such as Skåne, Västergötland, Uppland, Gotland; in the late Bronze Age (about 1000-5000 B.C.) she was again very considerable; but it was not till about the first century that her greatest period opened. Before this the movement seems first to have been southwards—Goths from the mainland, Burgundians from Bornholm; till about the time of Christ the whole development of Northern culture was subjected to a dominating Roman influence, exerted largely via these Baltic islands conveniently situated near the mouths of the Vistula and the Oder along which rivers lay most of the important lines of communication with the South. Nearly all the thousands of Roman coins from the first few centuries A.D. which have been found in Scandinavia were unearthed in these islands, as well as great quantities of gold, silver, bronze, glass and earthenware articles, many richly ornamented, either made in the South or Roman in design. The first five centuries, it seems, was the really prosperous period in Öland.

> "About or immediately before the year A.D. 500 the flow of gold and the development of native types of objects, suddenly ceases. The downfall of Gautic power in the Island must thus have happened at that time; and Gotland and Bornholm follow about fifty years later (though the former enjoyed a golden age right into mediæval times). Immediately after the loss of Öland communication with the South passes over for a short time to Gotland. Bornholm had never been a Gautic island, but it nevertheless shared the fate of the rest of Scandinavia."

The writer, it will be seen, is holding that Öland was part of the kingdom of the Geats or Gautar; but others think differently. It would certainly be interesting to know the truth, for the same writer, a Swedish scholar, who is one of the chief commentators on *Beowulf*, has attempted to identify Öland with the home of the Weder- or Weather-Geats mentioned in the poem, to interpret one passage as actually referring to the Island; and has mentioned that in the parish of Löt is a point called Hvallsnäs where there is a large mound, thereby not altogether rejecting the idea that this might actually be the grave of Beowulf, who directed that his gravemound was to be built on Hronesness ("Whale's Ness"). Exciting thought! And why not here as anywhere else? Beowulf, who performed such fabulous deeds that history is inclined to disown him, might as a compensation be tracked to earth in his gravemound:

> "Then the son of Weohstan, the hero bold in battle, bade orders be given to many of the men who were owners of dwellings, that they, the leaders of bands, should bring from afar wood for the funeral fire to where the valiant man lay: 'Now shall the fire consume—the dark flame shall tower up—the ruler of warriors, him who often endured the iron shower when the storm of arrows, urged with might, darted over the shield-wall, when the shaft did its office; fitted with feathers, it followed the arrow!'

... Little did any of them mourn that they bore out quickly the precious treasures; they also shoved the dragon, the monster, over the cliff [not that there is a cliff]; they let the wave take him, the flood embrace the guardian of the treasure. There was twisted gold beyond measure loaded on the waggon; the chieftain, the grey-haired warrior, was borne to Hronesness.

"Then, the people of the Geats made ready for him a pyre on the ground, hung round with helmets, battle-targes, bright corslets, as he had craved; then the sorrowing men laid in the midst the famous prince, their loved lord. The warriors began to rouse on the barrow the greatest of funeral-fires; the wood-reek mounted up dark above the smoking glow, the crackling flame, mingled with the cry of weeping ... the tumult of the winds ceased ... until it had consumed the body, hot to the heart. Sad in heart, they lamented the sorrow of their souls, the slaying of their lord; likewise the women with bound tresses sang a dirge ... the sky swallowed up the smoke.

"Then the people of the Weders wrought a mound, which was lofty and broad, at the edge of the headland, visible far and wide to sea-farers. ... They were minded to utter their grief, to lament the king, to make a chant and to speak of the man; they exalted his heroic life and praised his valorous deed with all their strength." (Prof. E. V. Gordon's translation).

The most striking memorial from Öland's period of greatness is, if we ignore the gold-hoards and treasures carried off to museums on the mainland, the remains of the fortress of Gråborg right in the centre of the Island, in its day (it was built about A.D.400) the largest in the North of Europe. Little but the outer ramparts remain to-day: entering through a tunnel-way, you find yourself in a roughly circular enclosure, 225 metres in diameter, now a ploughed-up field. I was also shown under Borgholm Castle the walls of a fortress, dating from the same period, which are now being excavated. This site on the edge of Landborgen and above the best harbour in the Island, was the obvious one for a great fortress, and in the stone up there much of Öland's later history can be read

(Plate 33). Built probably in the thirteenth century and the key to the Island, it fell alternately into the hands of Danes and Swedes, till Gustavus Vasa and his sons finally secured possession of it three centuries later. It was stormed in a war in 1677 when Danish and Dutch fleets landed troops in the south, marched northwards burning and plundering on the way, and unsuccessfully attacked it with 3,500 men. But the final blow came in 1809, long after it ceased to have military importance. The resident at the time, who had been given a large State grant for repairing it, embezzled the sum, and when an inspection was about to take place set fire to the old pile which was completely gutted. Rebuilt, enlarged and restored at various times, this renaissance Castle must in its day have been a magnificent place. It is so even to-day, its massive skeleton with numerous large windows standing against the sky and forming a whistling gallery for the ironical winds.

The churches of Öland are of infinitely less interest than those of Gotland. Of the two distinctly mediæval ones, Gärdslösa has some fine carved portals by a Gutnish (which is the adjective from Gotland!) master of the thirteenth century, and Resmo some mural paintings from the same period. But the rest, though pleasant enough as landmarks—the slim spire of Gräsgård's, for instance—are like a thousand other black-and-white Swedish churches, and only sometimes have details of sufficient interest to bring to a standstill the tourist-laden 'buses that do lightning circular runs round the south or the north of the Island.

The extreme south and the extreme north both have their own special atmospheres. The southern tip, neatly sliced off by Charles X's Wall, comprises the Royal park-like estate of Ottenby—Royal, though not occupied by Royalty, for the King when staying in the Island during the summer resides at Solliden, a fine Mediterranean-villa type of palace on the slope of Landborgen near Borgholm. But in the seventeenth century when the kings went over to Öland to hunt the whole estate was nothing but a deer park. While Christina was making arrangements to abdicate, Duke Charles (afterwards Charles X) retired here out of discretion and to show that he

Background to Sweden

was not pressing her to hasten her plans. In the eighteenth there was a stud there for breeding race-horses, and a large sheep farm; to-day there is neither: the only horses are for the cavalry and one or two for pleasure-riding.

"There are still a few stags of the old descent left", says Selma Lagerlöf in *The Wonderful Adventures of Nils*,

> "and burrow-ducks and partridges love to live there, and it offers a resting-place in the spring and autumn for thousands of migrating birds. Above all, it is the swampy eastern shore below the sheepmeadows where the migratory birds delight to rest and feed." Nils, a small boy from Skåne, had been borne off on the back of a wild goose which came down, according to the author, on April the third, resting a few days before it headed for Lapland. He was amazed at the number of birds: "Ducks and geese walked about and fed on the meadow; nearer the water ran snipe and other coastbirds. The loons lay in the sea and fished, but the real life and movement was upon the long seaweed banks along the coast. There the birds stood side by side close together and picked up grub-worms." And then he found the gulls and sea-swallows fishing for stickleback—the special Öland stickleback; while "along the outermost seaweed banks lay a flock of swans. They didn't bother about going on land, but rested themselves by lying and rocking on the water. Now and then they dived down with their necks and brought up food from the sea-bottom. When they had gotten hold of anything very good they indulged in large shouts that sounded like trumpet calls."

And eventually the wild goose joined his companions, taking Nils with him again into another chapter.

Communications between different parts of Öland is maintained not only by roads: there is a railway running through almost the whole length of the Island. Menaced at the crossings by cars, stray cattle and even (I have heard) push-bicycles, the diminutive trains, whistling casually as they go, strut up and down the narrow-gauge track at the rate of about two a day. But the question is not so much whether the railway

288

was intended as a joke as whether it was intended at all. With perfectly good roads and very little to link up, why have a railway? The buses, of course, are a more recent introduction, so the railway has nothing more than an unmentionable age to commend it.

Its rolling stock, unlike the proverbial stone, gathers all the moss that it can, not to mention cobwebs, dirt and rust; but it gathers absolutely no speed whatever. The journey of thirty-four miles from Borgholm, with fourteen stops on the way, to Böda the northern rail-head took me exactly two hours and three minutes. Stepping from the toy-train which by then was quite empty, I found myself in the middle of a pinewood. With difficulty—for it was evening and the trees were dense—I discerned two buildings, one obviously the "station" and the other a little way down a ride bearing the letters HOTELLET. "Hotel", I thought, was a pretentious name for this woodland pension (which had not even electric light, in Sweden something of a negative achievement), but I decided to spend the night there.

In the morning I slipped off for a bathe before breakfast to the sea about a mile eastwards, and was just in time to see two hefty young fishermen land their catch from a rowing-boat. The few cottages and small farms forming the hamlet went by the name of Svartvik. Where, then, was Böda, which I had seen marked on a medium-scale map of Europe as if ranking with Manchester, Essen or Florence? Were two or three cottages and a church (capriciously built a few miles away between a couple of other hamlets) deserving of mention when such places as Northampton and Sheffield had to be omitted because of over-crowding? The modern geographers had, it seemed, tried to reverse the process of those whom Swift described: instead of placing on uninhabitable downs elephants instead of towns, they had in the open-space provided by the Baltic written in the name "Böda", dumping on the Island a circle that would do for a large city.

A few miles west of Böda is a perfectly rounded bay with just a hint of beach below the freakish little *raukar* or weathered cliffs, about six foot high, forming a sort of extension of Land-

borgen, there being a small stretch of Alvaren even up there—
open and flat as elsewhere but running northwards into the pine
forest which caps the Island. Lounging there during the wind-
less morning—in the water and on the beach—I had the whole
place to myself, and began to think about that blue knob of an
islet that lay in the midst of Kalmar Sound and appeared to be
the centre of a circle suggested by the wide arc of the bay.
Now, there is a well in Borgholm Castle in which a virgin sometime in the shadowy past is supposed to have been drowned, and
eventually (the legend goes) she reappeared, emerging from the
water right up the Sound. Seen from the Castle on clear days as
a blue dot on the skyline, she was named Blå Jungfrun, the Blue
Virgin. That is the beginning but by no means the end of the
romantic story of the islet. For some have identified it with
Blåkulla (Blockulla), a name probably arising from a confusion
between the Virgin Blåkulla, a minor sea-goddess in Norse
mythology, and Blocksberg or the Brocken, the great meeting-
place for the witches of Germany. Blåkulla was the Blocksberg
of Sweden. On Maundy Thursday the witches would blow
through the key-hole of the church door to blow away the Holy
Ghost, and after procuring some scrapings of altars and filings
from church clocks would collect in a gravel-pit, put vests over
their heads, anoint themselves with troll-salve, and call out
three times, "Antecessor, come and carry us to Blåkulla!"
Whereupon they would be whisked off on steeds of the Devil's
providing, generally taking children with them. On arriving
at the spot, described as a building "in a large meadow like a
plain sea wherein you can see no end", they were met by the
Evil One who appeared in the shape of a man with a horse's
foot. After listening to stories of their doings he would teach
them worse acts still. Then there would be dancing, ban-
queting and debauchery; and before sunrise they would return
to their homes, making the sticks and straw whirl round in the
air. It once happened that a boy who was up when the witches
came past in the morning threw his jack-knife into the whirl-
wind, where it struck a witch on the leg, making her fall down
into a dungheap. And he refused to help her out until she gave
him one of her garters, which he kept as a proof that he had seen

a witch. The witch trials held in Sweden as in so many other countries during the seventeenth century attracted a good deal of notice in Britain which had long been interested in such things and which had her own Witch-Finder General. That well-known demonologist Joseph Glanvil appended in 1681 "An Account of what Happened in Sweden in the years 1669 and 1670" to *Saducismus Triumphatus*, his work on witchcraft; and in George Sinclair's *Satan's Invisible World Discovered*, published a few years later in Edinburgh, one could read a similar account "Of the Strange Witchcraft discovered in the Village Mohra in Swedeland". Mora, of course, is in Dalarna, in which repository of ancient superstitions and folk-lore most of the persecutions took place. In Mora alone seventy witches, who confessed that they had followed the Evil One to Blåkulla, that " he had carnal knowledge of them, and that the Devil had sons and daughters by them which he did marry together and they did couple and brought forth toads and serpents", were condemned by a royal commission and most of them were executed. "Fifteen children which likewise confessed they were engaged in this witchery died as the rest; six and thirty of them between nine and fifteen years of age who had been less guilty were forced to run the gauntlet", and others were ordered to be whipped: "The number of seduced children was about three hundred". Then the islet was taken over by smugglers, who still lived there less than a century ago—or so I was told the evening before by a student of Lund who had been there and showed me at the pension an article he had published with photographs of some of the smugglers' caves in the oak-hidden granite. Linnaeus, it appears, had been very anxious to visit it, for botanical purposes, but was held up for several days near Böda waiting for suitable weather. It also figures in a poem called "Torsten Fiskare" by Stagnelius (who was born in Gärdslösa parsonage in 1793)—one of the many well-known Swedes who have written about Öland; while a decisive naval battle was also fought nearby in the past. In fact few islands of the size can possess associations as romantic as the little Jungfrun, now uninhabited and but rarely visited.

After some further explorations in the north I stepped again into the train, this time a single-carriage affair run by a Ford engine dangling rather precariously from the left underside. Having it entirely to myself, I lay full length on the seat till, the fussily protracted journey being done, I found myself once more in Borgholm (pop. 2,000), the only town in the Island.

In Borgholm: where the steamers from Kalmar and Stockholm bring little crowds on to the wharves, and a dull yellow *kallbadhus* projects into the bay and on the other side a rather unsightly white *varmbadhus*; and standing back comfortably from the harbour are the gay but very ninetyish timber-and-glass restaurant, one or two large capriciously pinnacled villas from the same period, a new red-tiled Mediterranean villa of the wealthiest burgher (a shopkeeper whose father was a hotel-porter), and an electric power-house in the neo-Hanseatic style; where all the hotels and pensions are full-up for a six-week season, reaching its climax in early August when the King, von Cramm, Kalle Schröder (the Swedish champion and one-time indoor champion of England), Argentinians and Chileans, Jugoslavians and Chinamen come on from Båstad to play in the local tennis tournament; where the men get impatient at the ninth hole on the miniature golf-course; and that distinguished-looking elderly man in sun-glasses coming out of the bookshop in Storgatan talking to his young dark-haired female secretary is the author of *The Story of San Michele*; and the other streets are so crudely cobbled that you have to ride your bicycle on the footwalks, and the old ladies with sun-glasses do their shopping in the market square, and the icecream man does a good trade and the *varmkorv*-vender doesn't; and those who are not going to bathe at Köping Strandviken crowd into the buses at the Turist Byrå for a *Södra-* or *Norra-runt* sight-seeing tour; and the boys, because of the constant winds, wear crocheted hairnets to keep the locks out of their eyes, and the youths have flowered shirts that might have been cut from wallpaper; and the only thoroughbred dog is a very unsociable Skye terrier; and every garden has a well and the water is so bad that the unwary get tummyaches; where in the evening a great flock of jackdaws flies down from the Castle at 7.30 for a circular flight over the town, while families and loving couples walk up through the oak-woods to drink coffee under the ruins and watch the ships passing through the Sound—or else enter the Black Hole of the Island's only cinema; and where in the middle of August when the summer guests have dispersed the rooms are turned out and the mattresses beaten on the lawn and the owners move in again from the shacks they have temporarily been inhabiting at the ends of their gardens; and the main restaurant closes down for the year, and the golf-course is lit up earlier every evening for fewer and fewer players, and the waitresses at the garden-cafés have time for a bit of conversation; and the days grow shorter and hotter; and the plums, pears and apples rapidly mellowing reach down towards the white garden furniture, and the small black grapes ripen against the clapboarding and the fences are studded with the red globes of tomatoes; and the wasps grow drowsier and fiercer; and the asters and marigolds are over and the roses have done with their second flowering; and you pass down the yellowing lime-avenues as Herr Andersson and Herr Eriksson dig up their last crop of potatoes with the help of their children who have special holidays for the purpose; and you hear the sirens of the steamer and begin to hurry and go up the gangway just in time and lean over the rail and thank your friends once more for looking after you so well, and the water is churned up below you and the cables are cast loose and the quay recedes, and the ship passes down the Sound and you pace the deck taking a last look at the conspicuous ruin of the Castle and one or two just discernable windmills up there on Landborgen—on the proscenium of that stage where varied dramas have been acted, on the edge of that Baltic platform where the winds make their significant but interminable speeches.

1: *Northern Baroque*

Kalmar

EATING AN ICE under the awnings of the Stadshotell on a hot day like this I can easily believe myself in Italy. The housewives doing their morning's shopping at the lines of barrows in Market Square linger between their purchases to cool down or suck a juicy plum in the shade of the brightly coloured umbrellas; and the fatter men passing by on the sidewalk from time to time remove their hats to mop the perspiration with their handkerchiefs. But what above all is responsible for this southern atmosphere is the big baroque Cathedral standing solitary in the middle of the Square—a brilliant specimen of borealized Bernini. With its elaborate two-storied façades, treated as non-structural screens unrelated to the interior, its pomp and grandiosity, it is a typical baroque church, though without the usual cupola or dome. Now that I have in some measure got over my astonishment at finding such a building in Scandinavia I am as full of admiration for the architect's reticence as for his daring. Here are no twisted shafts, no inverted columns, no orgiastic excess of ornament, no prodigal and irrelevant curves; the pediments are surmounted not by sculptured figures but by comparatively plain pinnacles, and the sparse niches are empty. The interior is even more restrained, the white rather plain walls (with their pilasters unpanelled, their capitals unlicentious) giving an essentially Northern feeling, refined and made nobler by a superb centre vault. Against such a clean light-coloured background the magnificent marble-and-gilt altar-piece, the elaborate pulpit and the coats of arms hung here and there on the walls stand out with remarkable effectiveness. There is none of that riotous misuse of marble polochromy or that untidy jumbling of tombs, memorials and so forth found all too often in baroque churches. The effusive seicento spirit of the South, chastened by a Northern simplicity, has resulted in a distinct type of baroque well suited to its environment.

A style essentially Latin and Catholic if adopted at all by Teutonic, Protestant communities, is bound to undergo various modifications. In England there are not many buildings unquestionably baroque, although a great number have been strongly influenced by the style; in Holland baroque never became popular; and in Germany it is commoner in the Catholic south than in the north. Sweden, the chief Protestant power in the middle of the seventeenth century, emerged from the Thirty Years' War under a Queen steeped in Latin culture and rapidly heading for Roman Authoricism. From the time Christina drove through an ornate triumphal arch to her coronation till the day some seventy years later when Charles XII was laid to rest in the baroque mortuary chapel of the Riddarholm Church (the funeral procession, however, took place by torchlight to prevent the poverty occasioned by his wars from being too apparent)—in other words, during the Caroline age—all the visual arts in Sweden were dominated by baroque ideals. For the palaces and country seats now required by a proud, booty-laden aristocracy with money and leisure to spare after the successful Thirty Years' War and the wars of Charles X; and for the new palaces, banks, halls, churches, chapels and so forth that had to be created in this period of greatness there were architects like the Tessins who had travelled in France, Italy and Holland, the Frenchmen the de la Vallées, the Dutchman Vingboons, not to mention a whole colony of foreign artists—Dutch, French, Belgian, German, English, Italian—to decorate interiors or paint the portraits of royalty and nobles. In an atmosphere of wealth (I refer to the first two-thirds of this period) and of new-found grandeur, Sweden, turning to the arts of peace, took easily to a style which had originated among ostentatious, pleasure-loving grandees of the South. Her baroque with its great assortment of foreign influences is probably more various than that of

U

any other single country. Spain alone appears to have exerted no influence—not direct at any rate. It is hard to say what element is commonest, but if the French does not at first predominate over the Italian it does so eventually: indeed, as baroque passes into rococo in the eighteenth century, the French more or less gains a monopoly.

The Tessins, father and son, greatest of Sweden's architects at this and probably any period, provide between them an epitome of her baroque architecture. It was Nicodemus Tessin the Elder who planned Kalmar Cathedral about 1660 on the lines of the Jesuit Church in Antwerp; who was mainly responsible for the form of Skokloster, the sumptuous castle commissioned by General Wrangel to set off to advantage the loads of booty he had acquired in Germany; and who designed Drottningholm, that exquisite royal palace near Stockholm, with its Belgian and German sculptures on the spectacular staircase, its pompous ceiling-paintings by the Hamburger Ehrenstrahl, its sham-marble stucco-work executed by Italians, its gobelins and English tapestries, its perfectly preserved theatre, and its French formal gardens featuring a fountain captured from the Wallenstein Palace in Prague (not to mention an English park and a Chinese-rococo pavilion dating from a century later). Tessin the Younger had studied even longer in France and Italy, had conversed with the great Bernini himself, with Le Nôtre the foremost landscape-gardener of his day, and with some of the architects of Versailles. As architect to the Court he continued the work at Drottningholm after the death of his father, built the Gustavianum in Upsala (Plate 14), a palace for himself in the capital, and a country mansion which served as the model for many a *herrgård* during the next century. But his real masterpiece is the Royal Palace in Stockholm.

I can remember how at first sight I condemned it as monotonous and uninteresting. Alas that my eye should have been so untutored! Uninteresting? It is one of the most instructive buildings in the country, and the more I see of it the more I realize how brilliantly the exotic elements have been blended with the indigenous, forming a colossal dignified masterpiece, expressive of national character. Tessin, commissioned to design a new palace after the old one had been burnt down in 1697, not only took care that the building should be worthy of his country's greatness but evidently felt that it should also be national in flavour. The idea of a huge enclosed block may have been taken from Italian palaces; the display of bigness, grandeur, architectonic power may have been due immediately to baroque inspiration and a familiarity with Versailles; but then in the old Swedish castle, cubic in shape, emphasis had always been on weight and solid massiveness. The long heavy almost unrelieved façades are essentially Northern in their puritanical severity; while the baroque treatment of portals, windows, even the triumphal arch in the south, barely does more than systematize an ornamentation which might have derived from that superimposed on the native castles at the the renaissance. The Royal Palace does not invite, it demands, comparison with Marlborough's Palace at Blenheim, different though the sites may be, the former having all the advantages of a conspicuous one sloping down to the water in the middle of the capital—and making use of it to the full. What Blenheim was to the England of Queen Anne this Stockholm edifice was to Caroline Sweden—or would have been if, for lack of funds, it had not taken sixty years in the building. It cost in the end ten and a half million rix-dalers, which I suppose is somewhere near three million pounds, as opposed to the half-a-million which the English Government allowed for Blenheim. Both buildings are remarkable for their bigness, but in the Swedish not everything is sacrificed to sheer megalomania. One cannot help regretting that Vanburgh, Inigo Jones, even Wren, were not professional architects from the first like the Tessins. Genius is not enough; there would probably be much less to excuse in the work of such baroque-influenced Englishmen if only they had had a thorough training and done more travelling.

In looking at this and other examples of Swedish baroque such as the House of the Nobles and a whole host of smaller and larger country seats or *herrgårdar*, I am struck by the Northern reticence characterizing them—a reticence which seems to be analogous with what has been termed the "Barocco-Palladian compromise" in France, except that here the compromise is rather between baroque and native elements however disguised. It is probably for that reason that the Caroline Mortuary Chapel at the Riddarholm Church, designed by the Tessins in a full Italian style heavy with external pillars, vases, florid sculptures, reliefs and so forth, seems to me to be out of place in such latitudes. The aristocracy for all their ostentation were not really as rich or licentious as the haughty nobles of decadent Spain and Venice, the papal families of Rome, the prince-bishops of Austria and Germany, or the Spanish viceroys in Naples and Brussels; most of them had at least done some fighting in the field; although their oppression of the lower classes was unexampled in Swedish history they were without the callousness and depravity of their Southern contemporaries; and their manners though artificial and stiff were not altogether lacking in sincerity. It is not surprising then that their architecture is generally in unquestionable taste; that Swedish baroque never goes further than chimney-pots made in the shape of altars, an occasional loggia with contracted perspective, and decorations composed of grinning heads (which thus put in a belated appearance as if compensating for the rarity of gargoyles on her Gothic churches).

2 : *Tailpiece*

KALMAR—IT IS one of the pivotal names in Scandinavian history. Already in Viking times a place of importance, Kalmar soon grew into one of the main cities of the realm, commercial, but heavily fortified, and for centuries considered the key to Sweden, suffering all too frequently the sieges of Danes and the Hansa League, who attacked it no less than twenty-three times between 1307 and the Kalmar War of 1611-12 when the stout fortress was captured and most of the town laid in ruins. But to-day this most exquisite of Northern Castles, built on a small promontory to repulse the southern invaders, gazes dreamily out to sea like some old picturesque sailor whose days of exertion are over; and the mind turns readily to the early peaceful times of the Kalmar Union, the great might-have-been in Northern annals (Plate 35).

About every three hundred years, some historians have pointed out, there occurs a major resurgence among the Scandinavians, who with the help of brilliant leaders manage to achieve results out of all proportion to their numbers: the Swedish empire of the seventeenth century, the Kalmar Union formed at the end of the fourteenth, the period of Scandinavian world power reaching its climax in the eleventh—these are the nicely spaced historical milestones cited in favour of this cyclical theory. But if much less is for obvious reasons heard about the second than about the first and the third of these resurgences it by no means follows that the Kalmar Union, had it been successful, would not have had results ever more important for mankind.

In the National Museum at Stockholm is a well-known painting depicting the sack of Visby in 1361: King Valdemar Atterdag of Denmark is looking on while the burghers of this wealthy Hanseatic city which had till then paid tribute to Sweden heap their gold and silver at his feet. A brutal utterly unscrupulous man, Valdemar nevertheless had immense energy and succeeded in regaining for Denmark most of the Baltic territory she had lost during a period of decadence and humiliation. Beginning as king of only Northern Jutland, he won back the whole of Denmark; profited from civil war in Sweden by treacherously wresting from her the three southern provinces and Öland; made himself lord of Gotland; and in consequence received from his people the title Atterdag or "Day Again". More remarkable still, and a far nobler character, was his daughter Margaret, married at an early age to King Haakon Magnusson The Younger of Norway. Now King Haakon was a member of the Folkung family which had ruled in Sweden from about 1250; and ever since the Convention of Oslo in 1319 when the kingdoms of Norway and Sweden became united in the person of the three-year-old Magnus Ericsson the Folkungs had looked on the two countries as one, despite the fact that the royal influence had been considerably weakened during the long minority of Magnus who eventually lost both crowns and spent the last years of his life as a commoner. So when both the father and the husband of Margaret had died and a request from the Swedish nobles that she would help them get rid of an oppressive king (Albert of Mecklenburg) had been effectively answered, she found herself regent of the whole of Scandinavia.

Having chosen her grand-nephew, Erik of Pomerania, as king of the three realms, she succeeded in having him elected—even in Norway which was really a hereditary kingdom; and in 1397 representatives of Norway, Sweden and Denmark were invited to Kalmar to witness the coronation and confer on the question of joint rule. A special committee there made out a preliminary draft of an act of union, a sort of constitution, which provides that:

(1) The three countries shall always live in peace with one another under the same king;

(2) On the death of the king one of his sons shall be elected as his successor, but when the king dies without issue then the worthiest man shall be chosen;

(3) If one of the countries should be compelled to wage a defensive war, the other two shall come to its aid;

(4) Each country shall retain its own laws and the king shall rule according to them, not transferring any law or right from one to the other;

(5) Negotiations with foreign powers shall be conducted by the king in consultation with the councillors present wherever he happens to be at the time.

But the document (still in the Royal Archives in Copenhagen) was never completed in the necessary form or received more than ten of the seventeen seals required before it could become legally binding. Only the first provision, that there should be one ruler, really influenced the course of events; while Margaret evidently found a vigorous personal rule far more to her liking than having her hands tied by written agreements. Historians are generally agreed that she, the first great European queen, never had any far-sighted scheme of developing a united Scandinavian nation—that the thought was as remote from her mind as the idea of nationality was foreign to the whole age. They hold that she was merely continuing her father's work, though in a more honourable manner, exploiting her singular advantages and aiming at a Greater Denmark. Denmark at any rate was considered the principal country of the Union, just as she was the most populous, Norway and Sweden being relegated to the position of mere provinces and having swarms of Danish and German bailliffs and ecclesiastics thrust upon them, while no Swede or Norwegian was ever appointed to office in Denmark. The queen herself ruled with both moderation and goodwill, but (as Gjerset explains):

> "she had created a system of administration the pernicious character of which she probably never fully knew or understood, and it is with some justice that the Queen who originated the system should be made directly responsible for its attendant evils which could neither be controlled nor abated."

During her life however things in the two more northerly countries were not intolerable. Norway, having fallen on a period of political apathy and being without any strong patriotic class (her native gentry dying out, were replaced by Danes, who kept the lower classes in the position of thralls), probably suffered more; in Sweden conditions were better than they had been previous to the Union; not only was the North at peace but the power of the nobles which had here grown with unhealthy speed became drastically curtailed, much to the satisfaction of the lower classes, who although they were still taxed heavily paid up with rather more cheerfulness. So much depended on the sovereign, and Margaret with her powerful masculine personality, her energy and practicalness, ruled with considerable success till her death in 1412.

Erik of Pomerania, who had married Philippa, daughter of Henry IV of England, then succeeded to the throne, a charming young man, according to Pope Pius II, with "yellow or golden hair, large eyes, blond complexion and a broad white neck".

Background to Sweden

But in statesmanship an incompetent: not only did he renew the Schleswig-Holstein quarrel (which has continued between Denmark and Germany on and off down to the present day)— a quarrel that Margaret had almost settled; but he also became involved in a war with the powerful Hansa League. The distress caused by these wars, coupled with growing resentment against the foreign officials who now had to levy heavier taxes, only succeeded in fanning the sparks of Swedish independence; and in the 1430's Engelbrekt the Bergsman, having led a revolt against the Danes, got himself elected Regent of Sweden at the Arboga Riksdag. Then followed a period of about ninety years with civil and Danish wars on and off, Sweden now being ruled by Danish kings, now by native regents (notably the Stures), with sometimes the National party triumphant, sometimes the Unionists—a period culminating in that cruel Danish blunder the Stockholm Blood-bath in 1520, and the following year in the final achievement of independence under Gustavus Vasa.

So ended this early attempt at federal union. It failed, but could it ever have succeeded? The time in some respects was propitious: no appreciable difference in language, nationality or commercial interests existed at that date between the three Northern peoples who by combining their strength hitherto dissipated in wars and rivalries might have welded themselves into a major power. But on the other hand there were the physical obstacles: the vastness of an empire (then the largest in Europe) 450,000 square miles in area even without Iceland and other Norwegian colonies; the difficulties of communication; and the fact that Denmark was twice as populous as the other two states combined (the total population of Scandinavia after the Black Death has been estimated at a million-and-a-half). If only Denmark had treated her northerly neighbours as confederates, allowing them a fair say in their own affairs, all may have been well; but from about the year 1450 when, following a Swedish attempt to maintain national rights, she invaded that country without declaring war, plundered, burned and slaughtered in the most barbarous manner, that deplorable hatred between the two related peoples was engendered, and wars hitherto mainly the personal controversies of rulers were from this time forth for nearly four centuries marked by an intense national rancour permeating all sections of the populace. Equally regrettable is the fact that the Norwegians all that while were held under the Danish heel and forced against their inclinations to become enemies of the Swedes.

In Blekinge

It was quite dark at eight o'clock when, after a rather slow journey across the Möre coastal plain of Småland, I jumped out at the siding of Brömsebro and had my bike handed down from the luggage-van by a stationmaster who if not actually startled certainly appeared to need reassuring. For no guidebook advertises the attractions or the interests of Brömsebro, nor does any tourist bureau advocate your visiting this small village on the Småland-Blekinge border. For a native to stop here would be unusual; for a foreigner it was downrightly eccentric. But I received a certain amount of intellectual satisfaction from visiting this historical spot even if the only tangible reminder of its history is a stone by the roadside commemorating the Treaty of Brömsebro in 1645. In those days this was the southermost point on the Swedish frontier with Denmark and its position on the road from Kalmar evidently made it a convenient meeting-place for representatives of the two kingdoms. A not unimportant agreement had been signed there in previous times, but this was a major treaty decisive in the history of both countries alike, as gratifying for one as it was humiliating for the other. For Denmark, although she hardly knew it and still hoped to repair her losses, it was a climb-down: in returning the once-Swedish islands of Gotland and Ösel (off Esthonia) she acknowledged her adversary as master of the Baltic; the cession of Jämtland and Härjedalen finally secured Sweden's control of all Norrland; while that of Halland for twenty-five years proved to be the first act in the incorporation of the three southernmost provinces of the peninsula. The final act (though by no means the final war with Denmark) was staged thirteen years later when Charles X, after a campaign which left the map of Poland almost scribbled out with his marches, pounced on Denmark which had just frivolously declared war, occupied

Jutland, transported his whole army across the ice of the Belts in one of the most daring military operations ever attempted, took Zealand by surprise and forced on the Danes the most humiliating peace in their history. Sweden acquired by this Treaty of Roskilde not only Skåne, Halland, Blekinge (which provinces now contain a quarter of the population) and Bohuslän, but also the island of Bornholm and Trondjem's Län in Norway (both lost again later), complete exemption from tolls in the Sound and the Belts, and a considerable body of cavalry and infantry, not to mention a guarantee from Denmark that she would abrogate all anti-Swedish alliances and co-operate with her in keeping hostile warships out of the Baltic. "Would that I did not know how to write!" sighed one of the Danes who had to affix his signature to the Treaty. It was only by a narrow margin that Denmark escaped being wolfed altogether (which would indeed have been a Kalmar Union with a vengeance), and the extortionate Charles regretting what he considered undue clemency attempted after it was too late to obtain even more.

Then on towards Karlskrona, passing on the way a place called Christianopel where the young Gustavus Adolphus won his spurs by capturing an important new Danish fortress in the Kalmar War in 1611, a few months before his accession.

Karlskrona, now the principal naval station in the country and Karlshamn, the largest town in Blekinge, were built only after the province finally came into the hands of Sweden. Both these places figured in the national defence plans of Erik Dahlberg, the great engineer who had made possible the passage of the frozen Belts by Charles X, during the reign of whose successor Charles XI (1660-99) numerous fortresses were being built or strengthened. Elfsnabben near Stockholm had hitherto been the naval base, but its distance from the Swedish trans-Baltic provinces acquired at the Treaty of Westphalia in 1648 (which with those of Brömsebro and Roskilde was her third great peace treaty of the century) proved a serious disadvantage, especially as the ice in winter hampered the movements of ships in the Stockholm Skärgård. An excellently situated deep-water harbour was chosen down here: the town docks and arsenal were established just off the mainland on Trossö, one of the inner islands of an archipelago.

From the days of the Vikings till the end of the thirteenth century the navies of the Norsemen had been their main source of strength in peacetime as in war. Then when sail began to give way to oars the Hansa League were not slow to get in on the ground-floor, while Norway, her longships (propelled partly by oars, partly by a single sail) hopelessly outmoded, turned too late to the new two-mast type of vessel to regain her power.

For over two centuries the Hansa dominated the North Sea and the Baltic, except for a short period in the fourteenth century when Denmark under the Valdemars gained the upper hand in the latter sea. What is amazing is that Margaret at the head of the three Scandinavian Kingdoms made no attempt to strengthen her fleet or her coastal defences either against the Hansa or the strong bands of pirates then doing much damage along the seaboards; although, it is true, the political if not the commercial power of the Hansa was appreciably weakened during the Kalmar Union. It was left to the Danish King Hans to hire Dutch shipbuilders about a century later (when the Union was merely nominal) and to build a fleet so strong that about 1510 Denmark, once more a great power, was able to make herself mistress of the Baltic waters.

The foundations of Sweden were shortly afterwards being laid firmly by Gustavus Vasa, among whose wise actions was the complete reorganization of the army (hitherto mainly dependent on mercenaries) and the creation of a fleet. About the same time the Hanseatic cities were beginning to go their own separate ways: two of those most concerned with preventing a united Scandinavia (Lübeck and Danzig) had just helped him in his war of independence, and early in his reign the former of these joined with Sweden and Denmark in routing their common enemies the notorious and elusive pirates Norrby and Klement. But the first real test of the young Swedish navy was in 1535 when eleven of her ships formed the mainstay of a Swedo-Danish-Prussian fleet in its destruction of two separate fleets of Lübeck (which by then had become an enemy). At the

305

time of Gustavus Vasa's death in 1560 the Swedes had six large, nineteen medium-sized and twenty-eight small war vessels in commission.

It was during the Northern Seven Years' War (1563-70) that Sweden first emerged as a naval power, and indeed had far more success on sea than on land. Every year a squadron would be left in the Gulf of Finland while the main fleet would put out to sea for a cruise. Although there were no decisive victories after the first year when Admiral Jacob Bagge beat the Danes off Bornholm; the Swedes, in nearly every encounter whether against Danes, Poles, Lübeckers or all three combined, gained more than they lost; with the result that forty-three warships and numerous merchantmen were taken as prizes and only seventeen lost (in action, storms and so forth). Much of the credit for giving Sweden naval supremacy in the Baltic (and incidentally enabling food supplies to be brought from Germany) belongs to Admiral Klas Horn who at first had been commander of the army in Småland.

In wars against Russia during the latter part of the sixteenth century the Swedish fleet performed no noteworthy actions: it maintained communications and blockaded ports—that is about all. It was moreover becoming too old, and when in the 1590's Sigismund, the Catholic king of Poland, tried to enforce his rights of succession to the Swedish throne, Klas Fleming, the Governor of Finland, placed his division of the fleet at the service of Sigismund, thereby seriously hampering the supporters of the Protestant Duke Charles, who succeeded in gaining the crown only after civil war and a good deal of fighting on land and sea.

Denmark-Norway had meanwhile been enjoying a comparatively long period of peace. That energetic monarch Christian IV (brother-in-law of James VI of Scotland), on finding his fleet old and leaking, decided to build a new one and imported a number of Scottish ship-builders for the purpose. So in the next war with Sweden (the Kalmar War of 1611-12) his superiority at sea was probably the decisive factor.

We hear little about the Swedish fleet during the Thirty Years' War or during the Polish and Russian ones previous to

Sweden's entry into the main war. Its rôle was mainly perfunc-
tory, and although it was handsomely augmented by the
capture of fourteen vessels of the new imperial navy at the fall
of Wismar in 1631 all the important fighting took place on land.

Needless to say the old Baltic rivals were at each other's
throats again before very long: the outcome of the second of the
five Dano-Swedish wars (1643-45) during the century was
mainly decided on the seas. In 1644 the very fierce naval
Battle of Kolberge Heide, fought between two evenly matched
fleets, ended in a draw. The Danes then lost a unique opportunity by allowing the Swedish fleet which they had bottled up
in Kiel Bay to escape. Through the good offices of Louis de
Geer the Swedes had already chartered a Dutch fleet to
strengthen their own; and now Holland, hoping to shake off
the Sound dues which her thousands of merchantmen had to
pay on entering the Baltic, allied herself with Sweden. The
decisive action was fought in the autumn of 1644 when a
Danish fleet was almost annihilated by a much superior
Swedish-Dutch combination under Wrangel. Result: the
Treaty of Brömsebro.

In the fifties and the sixties of the century there was desultory fighting on and off, the Swedes sometimes having as
many as six enemies on their hands at a time and no ally except
the not-very-dependable one England. There was at one time
a very strong English fleet in the Baltic, while a Dutch one (for
a while under the redoubtable Ruyter) was constantly assisting
the Danes; but for various reasons they scarcely came to blows
at all. Except for a couple of notable exceptions, naval wars in
the Baltic have been rather exclusive affairs fought out by
Baltic countries among themselves without much positive
influence on the rest of Europe.

Unlike England and Holland who at various times in their
history have made the mistake of depending too much on their
navies and neglecting the army, Sweden did (at this time) the
very opposite. It was not that her navy had grown dangerously
small: it was rather that it had been allowed to lapse into a
state of grotesque inefficiency. In 1675, for instance, at the
opening of the Skåne War with Denmark, Admiral Stenbock

put to sea with sixty-six ships mounting in all 2,222 guns, but what with collisions involving about six vessels and other mishaps such as the dragging and loss of anchors and the disappearance of Stenbock's flagship owing to other blunders, the fleet thought it better to return to its base, three ships being left "to fish up the anchors the fleet had lost"! Lorenz Creutz, commander in the following year, was also incompetent in naval affairs, though a good soldier and a man of great bravery. His defeat at the Battle of Öland by the Dutch and the Danes (under the famous Tromp), who took advantage of their enemy's mistakes in manoeuvring and the confusion caused by the capsizal and burning of the flagship, definitely lost Sweden control of the Baltic. It was fortunate that her armies had been operating more successfully, for another major disaster occurred at Kjöge Bay in 1677, when the Danes crippled a larger Swedish fleet commanded, *mirabile dictu*, by a soldier Gustaf Horn who had had no previous naval experience whatever.

One of the main concerns of that constructive monarch Charles XI after this Danish war was to overhaul the country's defence system. Having established a sort of military land-tenure, enlarged the standing army, and stationed garrisons in the conquered trans-Baltic provinces, he founded Karlskrona (named after him) in 1680, where a strong new fleet manned by 11,000 well-trained men was constructed under the super-vision of Hans Wachtmeister, the first distinguished member of what was to become one of the main naval families in Sweden. This was the fleet ready for Charles XII at the opening of the Great Northern War (1700-21). The Sound, even now that Sweden owned territory on one side, was still easily closed by Denmark; and Wachtmeister, now an old man, had the satis-faction of affecting a junction with an Anglo-Dutch fleet waiting for him in Skaggerrak by one of those foolhardy ven-tures only justified when they succeed: he decided to take his fleet through a shallow channel called Flintrännen which had been left unguarded for no one had ever before thought of navigating it. But now arose a new naval power in the Baltic: in 1703, Peter the Great, having gained control of Lake Ladoga and the Neva, founded St. Petersburg (complete with naval dockyards) and fortified the island of Kronstadt so strongly that Swedish attempts to take it were foiled with heavy losses to the attackers. In the various minor engagements that took place at sea the Swedes were from now onwards generally the losers whether against the Russians or the Danes (who had in Sehested a very able admiral). But all the important fighting was done on land—until a late period in the War (1616-18) when the daring Tordenskiöld harassed the West Coast and the shipping of his exhausted neighbour, helping to frustrate Charles's plans to invade Norway and achieving considerable successes though nothing equal to his victory at Dynekilen (see pages 24-26). Tordenskiöld was by no means the only Norwegian sailor to distinguish himself in the Danish service: a good deal of the glory of Denmark's navy (and it won far more than her army did) during the centuries of union between the two countries can be put down to the Norwegian officers and ratings in whom the finest Viking traditions were perpetuated. To complete the woeful tale of Swedish decline, it was against the Swedes that the new deep-water fleet of Peter the Great gained its first successes during the last years of this emaciating war (1719-21); while the Russians also raided the Swedish coast, even attempting an attack on Stockholm, and ended up in possession of all the East Baltic seaboard from Viborg to Riga.

A new chapter in Baltic naval warfare opens with the reign of Gustavus III (1772-92), who was determined to break the Russian stranglehold on his country and once more raise Sweden to the rank of a great power. In order to achieve his aim the king realized that a strong fleet was essential, and its building was entrusted to Henrik av Trolle and Frederik Henrik av Chapman (the latter an admiral of English extraction), who submitted the necessary designs. The Admiralty for convenience' sake was now moved from Karlskrona to Stockholm, but the new docks built in the former port about 1786 were the largest at that time in the world. Well might the Empress Catherine, when Gustavus haughtily declared war two years later, regret tremblingly that Peter had built his capital so near Sweden. Although Russia had by this time fifty-four battleships, her fleet was divided into three, two squadrons being in the Black Sea and at Archangel, while of the remaining Baltic vessels many were at first unfit for service. Gustavus possessed twenty-eight admirable ships of the line, most of them straight from the stocks, twelve frigates, and over 350 smaller vessels. A special feature of this and the next Swedo-Russian war (1808-15) was the important part played by the small vessels of the Galley Fleet, Coast Flotillas or Archipelago Fleet as *Skärgård Flottan* is variously rendered. Galleys and small flat-bottomed sailing-boats called prams had already been employed previously but now a great variety of small craft (both Swedish and Russian) specially adapted for use in shallow and confined waters were in commission from gunyawls, 40 feet in length to vessels like hemmemas and turumas up to 140 feet, and mounting perhaps forty guns. Since the plan of Gustavus was to smash through to St. Petersburg both by land and sea, he left with his army for Finland in a galley fleet, which afterwards joined the Finnish flotillas already there, forming quite a formidable array of small vessels under the command of Ehrensvärd, with Svensksund (between Helsingfors and Viborg) as their base. But the main fleet commanded by Duke Charles, a competent though over-cautious admiral, proved extremely slow in coming to grips with the Russians: two actions at Högland and Öland were hardly more than indecisive skirmishes, though the fault in the second instance rests with a Captain Liljehorn whose unaccountable remissness alone ruined a splendid chance of victory. This was the more regrettable since the Russians were noted neither for courage nor seamanship, while their guns were so bad that sometimes more damage was done to their own men than to the enemy. In 1790 Gustavus, directing operations himself, was determined to press forward to the Russian capital; but on the way rather foolishly allowed his two fleets to be bottled up in Viborg Bay. It was only with the greatest courage and difficulty that they succeeded in fighting their way out through far stronger Russian concentrations and falling back on Svensksund for reinforcements. This Russian victory (for a quarter of the Swedish ships had been lost) was just being celebrated in Petersburg when news arrived of a crushing defeat which had cost Catherine a third of her fleet and 7,000 men. The Battle of Svensksund, so brilliantly won through the courage and daring of the king, was the last major achievement of Swedish arms and her biggest naval victory at any period.* It also enabled her to sign the only peace treaty in that century which did not deprive her of territory. But the War as a whole had cost her dearly—far more than what it had cost the Russians, whose fleet henceforth remained the strongest in the Baltic till the comparatively recent rise of German naval power some sixty or seventy years ago. Denmark has never again counted in naval matters since the Napoleonic Wars when what remained of her fleet after the Battle of Copenhagen in 1801 was captured by England six years later, thanks to the bombardment of the city by Sir Arthur Wellesley. Sweden, though slow to rearm, has during this century collected the most powerful fleet of any small nation, one out-matching the Russian Baltic fleet and in certain classes equal or superior to the German. If ever it should be needed, will its men remember some of the old admirals like Klas Horn and the Wachtmeisters, not to mention the Russian flags captured at Svensksund which they have seen hanging in the Riddarholm's Church, burial-place of her toughest warriors?

Not that I myself ever saw much of Karlskrona whose name alone has been enough to launch me on the above sketch of Baltic naval warfare. For I had spent the night a few miles outside the town at a place called Lyckeby. The next morning as I was walking down the street before breakfast in glorious autumn sunshine to buy a paper I halted abruptly before a shop-window where an *extrablad* of the local daily, *Blekinge Läns Tidning*, was stuck headed by the glaring letters "KRIG!" Poland had been invaded. It was Friday, August 31st. Even in my confusion I happened to notice in my pocket-diary the supremely ironic information under that date: "Partridge shooting begins".

The chief naval base of a country almost within gunshot of belligerent powers was no place for a foreigner to visit for

---

* Captain (afterwards the famous Sir) Sidney Smith served with considerable distinction in both this and the Battle of Viborg.

Background to Sweden

casual sightseeing. The local policeman who turned up after breakfast also thought the same: his boss ordered him by phone to accompany me to Karlskrona station, where after some delay during which the film in my camera was developed (showing that I had not photographed Karlskrona at all), I settled myself in a train for Gothenburg. I have memories of an exquisite town, probably the most colourful anywhere in Sweden outside Bohuslän, spread over several hilly islands; of dispatch riders dashing to and fro and a station full of troops; of the unreal heartiness of a batch of conscripts who more or less monopolized the restaurant-car on my train; of the relief of conversations with several rather sociable fellow-travellers on the longish journey through Småland's forests dotted with their nostalgically peaceful lakes—country I knew I should not see again for all too long, and even when (and if) I did, with what different eyes it would be. Unmanly though the feeling was, I wanted nothing more than to burst out at some siding and go over to a lonely lake and forget about it all.

I have little desire to relive the following, my last, day in Sweden: the abortive attempts to get hold of my various Gothenburg friends all of whom were away or had just been called up; the hurried round of shops to buy a few presents— genuinely Swedish articles, of course (such as the leather goods I found on returning home were marked "Made in Czecho-slovakia"); the forced cheerfulness of a final meal by myself at the Trägårdsföreningens Restaurant; the long wait at the docks not knowing if the ship would sail that evening or even at all; the constant swarms of passengers, largely Jewish refugees, families from Poland and the small Baltic states, fussing over their luggage, jabbering among themselves or asking questions of the officers, who themselves were just as vague about sailing orders; the group of gesticulating people sitting on a huge pile of cork on the quay and communicating with a deaf-and-dumb party on board; the endless swivelling of cranes dumping trunks, mailbags and packing-cases in the hold and motor-cars on the decks; the sight of one's bicycle being swung just in front of one, prompting the remark to a chap one had just been conversing with, "See that bike which I bought in Upsala? It doesn't

312

look as if it had carried me well over 2,000 miles, does it? Fine material, you know. And it has a back pedal instead of brakes"; and simultaneously prompting the reflection that one had after all been very lucky to travel before the eruption of war, to woo this unspoilt country while one is not too old to enjoy her physically and yet old enough to understand something of her intellectually. . . . At daybreak next morning we steamed out of Gothenburg, and after cautiously hugging the coast of Southern Norway, crossed over the North Sea and once more found ourselves in the old Scandinavian island of Britain.

INDEX

Åav, Edvard, 83
Abo: see Turku
L'Académie française, 50
Academy of Science, 43
Academy, Swedish, of Arts and
Sciences, 50, 118, 249
Account of the Life of Görtz, 115
Account of Sweden, 115
Ådalsliden, 193
Adam, 42
Addison, Joseph, 257
aderton, 50
Adils, 38, 39
Adrian IV: see Nicholas Breakspear
Athils, 39
Africa, North, 43; South, 163, 217,
254
Åland, 97
Alaska, 133, 161-62, 274
Albert of Mecklenberg, 300
Albertus Pictor, 87
Alday, James, 139
Alexander the Great, 114
Alfheimr, 1
Alfred, King, 104, 137, 157
Alfvén, Dr. Hugo, 76
Algaute, 233
Alingsås, 261
Ålleberg, 245
Allströmer, Jonas, 261-62
Alps, 129, 146, 163, 165
Alsace, 169
Alvastra, 244, 253, 255
Alvdalen, 204
Alvaren, 282-83, 290
alven, 282
Ålvsborg, 234-35
America, 36, 43-45, 80, 83, 104,
145, 162, 172, 177, 196, 218,
222, 250, 260, 266, 273-75, 283;
South, 7, 16
Andersson, Dan, 65; Gösta, 151
Andes, 163
Andover, 240
Andrée, Saloman August, 247-48
Ångermanland, 133, 155, 193
Ångerman River, 144, 192-95
Angevin, 104
Anglia, East, 71, 103

Anglophilism, 220, 229, 234, 257
Anglo-Saxon, 39, 82, 155, 239-40
Anne, Queen, 119, 216, 297
Annunciation Day, 52
anorak, 123, 136
Antonines, 244
Antwerp, 88, 296
Anskar, 240-41
Apostle of Sweden, 241
Arabia, 83
Arboga, 214, 302
Archangel, 310
Archimedes, 27, 207
Arctic Circle, 133, 142, 270;
Ocean, 167, 247
Arden, 168
Åre, 133
Areskutan, 134
Argentine, 292
Aristotle, 267
Årjäng, 226
Arkwright, 261
Armed Neutrality, 120
Armenia, 84
Arnica montana, 20
Arnold, Matthew, 63
Åsarna, 124
ASEA, 212, 246
Åsele, 193
Asia, 53, 83, 92, 157, 161, 163, 165,
266
Asmund, 82
Asplund, 66
Astronomy, 44
Athelstan, 240
Athens, 57
Atland, 41
Atlantic, 167, 273, 281
Atlas Mountains, 163
Auden, W. H., 144
Aun, 38
Aurora, 41, 148-49
Australia, 163, 218, 235
Austria, 162, 298
Av Chapman, F. H., 309
Av Trolle, H., 309

Bacon, Francis, 271
badstofa, 267

315

Karlshamn, 304
Karskrona, 120, 304-05, 308, 311-12
Karlstad, 222-25
kåta, 140, 146
Katrina Belfry, 69
Keats, John, 96
Keillers, 211
Kerilli: *see* Carelians
Key, Ellen, 249-50
Kiel, 236, 307
Kindaberg, Kindakulle, 238
King, Henry, 112
Kiruna, 142, 208
Kjöge bay, 308
Klarälven, 219
Klement, 305
klister, 146
Knights Hospitallers, 244
Knights of the Sword, 107
Knut: *see* Canute
Kola Peninsula, 147
Kolberg Heide, 307
Kölen, 145, 191
Konghelle, 2
Koön, 4
köping, 257, 260
Köping, 257
Kopparberg, 217
Korlaks, 154
Koster Islands, 32
kräfta, 264-65
Krain, 162
Krakatoa, 281
Kramfors, 194
Kreuger, Ivar, 266
Kreuger, Nils, 279, 283
Krokstad, 230
krona, kronor, 273, 275
Kronojägare, 183
Kronstadt, 309
Kumlaby, 204
kummel, 3
Kungälv, 2
Kunstforschung, 72
Kvikkjokk, 151
Kvistrum Bro, 23

Lachesis Lapponica, 42, 123
Läckö, 200-01
Ladoga Lake, 242, 308

Lagerheim, 180
Lagerkvist, Per, 51, 65
Lagerlöf, Selma, 198, 222-23, 249, 288
Laing, Samuel, 133
Lamb, Charles, 269
län, 182, 212
Lancashire, 263
Landborgen, 282-84, 286, 289-90, 293
Land Enclosure Act, 211
Landes, 269
Landor, Walter Savage, 63
landshövding, 212
landskap, 212
langlauf, 128, 150-51
Lappläger, 129-30, 146
Lapland, 21, 42-43, 51, 53, 71, 113, 118, 128-29, 137-52, 155-59, 168, 175, 183-86, 192-93, 208, 227, 254, 288; Pl. 35, 36, 43
Lapps, 128-32, 146-48, 210
Lapponia, see History of Lapland
Larix leptolepsis, 189
Lasse-Maja, 3, 12, 13
Last of April, 67-70
Latin, 66, 78, 80, 107, 117, 140, 255, 277
Lavoisier, 254
Lawrence, D. H., 66, 249
Leach, Dr. Henry Goddard, 104-05
Leche, Roger, 139
Legend of Montrose, 111
Leksand, 275
Lektor, -er, 36
Leningrad, 267
Le Nôtre, 296
Leonardo Da Vinci, 45
Leustadius, 141
Lid, Prof. Nils, 157
Lidköping, 257
Liefland, *see* Livonia
Lifsten, 82
Liljedotter, Sophie, 258
Liljefors, Bruno, 72, 99, 220, 278
Liljehorn, Capt., 310
Lindahl, Erik, 133
Lindholm, 99
Ling, Henrik, 48
Linköping, 105, 254, 257, 259
Linnea, 228

323